Rum, a Tailor's Goose and a Soap Box

Three Murderous Affairs
in the History of Hanover, Massachusetts

John F. Gallagher

John F. Gallagher

PublishAmerica
Baltimore

First printing

Hardcover 978-1-4560-2305-8
Softcover 978-1-4560-2304-1
PUBLISHED BY PUBLISHAMERICA, LLLP
www.publishamerica.com
Baltimore

Printed in the United States of America

To my wife and children, with love.

Acknowledgements

The author thanks the following organizations and individuals for their assistance:

Abington Historical Society, Dyer Memorial Library, Abington, MA; Ancestry.com; Archdiocese of Boston, Chancery Archives, Braintree, MA; Autumn Haag, Research Archivist, Massachusetts Archives, Boston, MA; Shelley B. Barber, Library/Archives Assistant, Boston College, John J. Burns Library; Boston Public Library, Microtext Department, Boston, MA; Braintree Historical Society, James Fahey, Director of Gilbert Bean Museum and Research Center, Braintree, MA; Carol Franzosa, Hanover Historical Society, Hanover, MA; Chinese Historical Society of New England, Boston, MA; Dedham Historical Society, Dedham, MA; Barbara Barker-Kemp, Judith Grecco, Friends of the Stetson House, Hanover, MA; Google.com; Hanover Central Cemetery staff, Hanover, MA; Hanover Historical Society, Hanover, MA; John Curtis Free Library, Hanover, MA; Linda Beeler, Head of Reference, Thomas Crane Public Library, Quincy, MA; Massachusetts Bureau of Vital Records and Statistics, Boston, MA; Massachusetts Historical Society, Boston, MA; Jennifer Fauxsmith, Research Archivist, Massachusetts Archives, Boston, MA; Mount Hope Cemetery staff, Boston, MA; Patrick and Heather Driscoll; Plymouth County Probate Court, Plymouth, MA; Plymouth County Registry of Deeds, Plymouth, MA; Plymouth Public Library, Plymouth, MA; Tom Chin, University of Massachusetts-Boston, Boston, MA; Weymouth Public Library, Weymouth, MA; Wikipedia, The Free Encyclopedia; Wing-kai To, Ph.D., Professor of History, Bridgewater State University; Margaret Johnson, PhD., Professor of Psychology, Bridgewater State University.

The author especially thanks Lorraine McNally, Natick, MA for her assistance in editing this book.

Introduction

A sepia-toned photograph lies in the collection of the Hanover Historical Society in Hanover, Massachusetts. Taken at the turn of the twentieth century, the picture shows a modest, cape-style house, nestled among trees of oak and pine and a row of neatly trimmed shrubs. Just outside the dwelling's front door, a sun-splashed rhododendron welcomes visitors with an imposing display of blossoms. Several well-kept outbuildings stand behind the house and a solitary cedar tree grows in a small field abutting the property. A stone wall in front borders a quiet, unpaved roadway dappled in shade. But the pastoral beauty and tranquility the illustration strives to capture is tainted by a disturbing message scrawled across its surface – "Three Irishmen Shot Here by Seth Perry in 1845."

In 1844, the Old Colony Railroad began construction of a rail line between Boston and Plymouth. By 1845, work had reached the village of Hanson. On March 17, two brothers and a friend, all Irishmen and laborers on the project, decided to lay down their tools for the day to celebrate the feast of their patron saint, Saint Patrick, at a grog shop in Hanover. An alcohol-fueled disagreement between the Irishmen, the grog shop's keeper and a local man ended in tragedy when violence erupted and two men were fatally shot and a third was severely disfigured. The bloodshed aroused the passions of temperance proponents and law-abiding Hanover citizens who decried the violence and the immoral and abhorrent effects of intoxicating liquors.

Nearly thirty years later, and less than ten years after the devastation and sorrow of the Civil War, the body of a woman employed at Hanover's Howard House Hotel was found at the bottom of the Monatiquot River in Braintree with a bullet wound in her head. State constables began an immediate investigation into the crime, focusing their attention on the Howard House's manager, a cunning and ambitious Canadian immigrant who believed he had planned and executed the perfect crime. Information and testimony offered by Hanover's residents helped police bring the victim's murderer to justice.

Three decades later, in 1904, Hanoverians were shocked and dismayed by the murder of an innocent, well-liked Chinese businessman who operated a laundry in the town's Four Corners neighborhood. The slightly built, feisty laundryman fought off a robbery attempt and died in the struggle. His attacker, a recently arrived immigrant from Prince Edward Island, tried to escape but was quickly apprehended after townspeople notified police of their suspicions.

Journey back in history as the author chronicles the circumstances surrounding each of these nineteenth and early twentieth century crimes in rural Hanover. Contemporary newspaper accounts, civil and criminal records, town histories, census returns, vital records, church records, immigration files, archival manuscripts, prison records and other documentary evidence are among the sources used to support a factual reconstruction of all three incidents.

Get a glimpse into Hanover's history and development and the challenges its residents faced as the town expanded and prospered. Gain insight into the facts and circumstances under which each victim, all immigrants, came to America, filled with dreams and aspirations they would never realize. See how the same social issues confronting society today – immigration, racial and religious bigotry and capital punishment – impacted the lives of the victims and their attackers. Follow detectives as they develop leads, question witnesses and suspects, and identify, collect and analyze physical evidence without the benefit of forensic techniques available to police in a modern era.

Weigh the eyewitness and expert testimony offered during trial. Decide whether jurors rendered a proper verdict and if the court exacted an appropriate sentence in each case. Was justice served or was justice denied?

Rum

"I challenge any man who understands the nature of ardent spirit, and yet for the sake of gain continues to be engaged in the traffic, to show that he is not involved in the guilt of murder."

Lyman Beecher, 1845

The discharge reverberated through the stillness of the chilly March air.[1] The first victim clutched his chest, stumbled a few feet and fell dead. Enraged, his brother rushed at the wild-eyed killer and met the same fate. A third man, horrified at what he had witnessed, fled, but was shot in the jaw, a wound that nearly took his life.

It was Monday, March 17, 1845, St. Patrick's Day. The Stapleton brothers, Patrick and James, and a friend named Dowlan, were Irish immigrants and laborers on the Old Colony Railroad. To celebrate the feast of their patron saint, the three men and some co-workers visited several drinking establishments in Hanson and Hanover that day. A stop at a "groggery" on Broadway near Centre Street in South Hanover fulfilled an ominous admonition by its keeper that "he expected some day or other to see his yard stained with blood..."[2]

Perry House on Broadway (Courtesy of Hanover Historical Society)

15

≈

About 1649, the first inhabitants of present day Hanover, Massachusetts, settled along the North River. At that time, the area was part of the town of Scituate. Over the next seventy-five years, the original inhabitants were followed by others who settled beyond the river and into the eastern region of the town of Abington. In 1727, the three hundred persons who resided in those parts of Scituate and Abington petitioned the state legislature to set off eleven thousand acres (fifteen and a half square miles) of land and incorporate the area as the town of Hanover. On June 14, 1727, the governor approved the petition and Hanover was "set off and constituted as a separate township."[3]

It was, in the beginning, principally a farming community, but the town soon expanded and prospered with other industries. Bound by the North River, shipbuilding became profitable as did the manufacture of cannons, cannon balls and anchors, especially during the American Revolution. This industry declined, however, in the 1840s. A demand for larger ships left North River shipbuilders at a disadvantage, as the river's depth could only accommodate vessels of a limited size. Shipwrights were forced to seek employment in the yards of East Boston, Medford, Chelsea and South Boston or adapt their skills to other trades.[4]

Men of commerce built saw mills, grist mills, shingle mills, box board mills and forges along the town's other rivers and streams and used the water to power the machinery for processing grain and producing lumber, tacks, nails, iron bars, wagon axles and locomotive cranks. Carriage makers, harness makers, wheelwrights and plough makers honed the skills of their trades as villages sprang up and business flourished. More than two hundred of Hanover's residents sustained a living as shoemakers.[5]

Hanover's pioneers were people of deep religious conviction. They gathered and prayed in meeting houses in Scituate and Abington until establishing their own places of worship within their growing Hanover community. The First Congregational Church built its first meeting house and was formally organized in 1728. As the town grew and communicants of different faiths multiplied, parishioners erected two other churches, St. Andrew's Episcopal Church in the Four Corners neighborhood in 1811 and the First Baptist Church in North Hanover in 1812.[6]

Hanoverians, recognizing the importance of education, established schools throughout various districts in the town. In 1807, Rev. Calvin Chaddock founded the Hanover Academy and educated students from Plymouth and Norfolk Counties in the arts, languages, "higher mathematics," navigation and surveying.[7]

Although churches, schools, mills and forges were evident during the early industrial period, farms still dominated the landscape along existing roads. Farmers cultivated crops, raised cattle, sheep, pigs and poultry and produced butter, milk and cheese. Many of them supplemented their income by making and repairing shoes.

By 1850, 1592 people lived in the town and two hundred-seventy dwelling houses existed. The homes in which Hanoverians lived at the time were modest cape-style cottages with both end and center chimneys, although a few hip-roofed two-story homes and Georgian and Greek Revival-style homes also appeared.[8]

≈

The Hanover community, like so many other communities throughout the Commonwealth and the country during this era, embraced the precepts of temperance, recognizing that unless its citizens abstained from the intoxicating evils of spiritual liquors, disorder and lawlessness would prevail. A united front swept the nation as temperance societies assailed the evil of drink and its attending consequences of greed, violence and sloth.

In his "Historical Sketch of Hanover," published in 1853, John Stetson Barry acknowledged "…that until within a comparatively recent period, spirituous liquors were a common beverage of all classes in the community, and were freely sold and freely used in every town in this State." He also noted efforts of those dedicated to the temperance cause have "attained but a measurable triumph" within the past twenty or thirty years to "check the tide which threatened to overwhelm."[9]

Barry pointed out some of the positive changes that had evolved within the Hanover community and elsewhere, citing "the thriftiness of our villages; the decrease of native pauperism; the general sobriety of the people; the absence of loungers at the bar-room of the tavern, or at the grocery on rainy days..." He stressed that the efforts to promote sobriety must continue, so "all who are made in the image of God, shall stand erect in their manhood, not victims of passion, or slaves of appetite; but walking the earth in the exercise of those nobler qualities, which distinguish us from the brutes, and which ally us to the angels."[10]

On May 3, 1830, the town of Hanover voted to restrict the sale and consumption of spirituous liquors. The people's mandate dictated "that the selectmen be requested not to license any retailer or inn holder, who shall, between this and August, permit spirituous liquors to be sold and drank in and about their premises, and engage not to sell after that time to be drank in like manner."[11]

On November 4, 1835, the state legislature enacted Chapter 47 of the Revised Statutes of Massachusetts pertaining to the regulation of licensed houses. Sections 1 and 2 specified the punishment for the unlawful sale of liquor without a license as follows:

No person shall presume to be an inn holder, common victualler, or seller of wine, brandy, rum or any other spirituous liquor to be used in or about his house, or other buildings, unless he is first licensed as an inn holder or common victualler, according to the provisions of this chapter, on pain of forfeiting one hundred dollars. If any person shall sell any wine or spirituous liquor, or any mixed liquor, part of which is spirituous, to be used in or about his house or other buildings, without being duly licensed as an inn holder or common victualler, he shall forfeit for each offence twenty dollars. No person shall presume to be a retailer or seller of wine, brandy, rum, or other spirituous liquors, in a less quantity than twenty-eight gallons, and that delivered and carried away all at one time, unless he is [at] first licensed as a retailer of wine and spirits, as is provided in this chapter, on pain of forfeiting twenty dollars for each offence.[12]

Despite the efforts of lawmakers, town officials and local constables to limit the illicit sale and use of intoxicating liquors, offenders persisted in dispensing alcohol without a license.

≈

Seth Perry was born in Hanover in 1793, a descendant of early Hanover settlers.[13]   He was one of twelve children born to Samuel Baker Perry and Anne Bates, who married in Pembroke, Massachusetts in 1786.[14] The Perrys raised their children in a cape-style home in South Hanover on Broadway near Cross Street, where the house still stands.[15]

Seth married Melinda F. Cox of Hanson in 1828.[16] The couple had three children, John Haveland, born in 1831,[17] Caroline Howard, born in 1832[18] and Julia Ann, born in 1836.[19] All of the children were born in South Hanover.

About 1835, a dispute erupted between Perry and Hanover selectmen. Perry had hired a nurse to care for his wife before she gave birth to their third child. The nurse, who was also pregnant, gave birth to her own child while living under Perry's roof. The woman was unmarried and destitute, leaving Perry to support her. No almshouse existed in Hanover during this time, but the town did provide support for the poor and, given the circumstances, the town's selectmen agreed to pay Perry reasonable compensation to care for the woman and child for a suitable period. Later, during a town meeting, Perry presented his expenses to the town and selectmen objected to the cost. Perry insisted upon full recompense and, in a fit of temper, threatened the officials stating, "if the bill were not paid, that the town should suffer the consequences." At this, the selectmen voted not to pay Perry's bill and "stand the consequences."

Perry sued the town, but was unable to follow through on the suit because he could not afford the legal fees. Perry then went to town officials and claimed that his uncompensated support for the nurse and her child had left him unable to support his own family. He demanded assistance from the town and selectmen, by law, were obligated to comply. Officials stipulated that Perry must continue to contribute toward the support of his family as long as the town subsidized him.

The town sent him on work assignments, but he refused to perform the tasks. On his own, he was able to raise sufficient funds to repay the town and when he had paid his debt in full, he vowed that "he would make up the balance of his losses by selling rum."[20]

On two occasions in 1842, Hanover town officials brought Seth Perry before the court in Plymouth for violating the liquor laws. On June 1, 1842, and again on December 1, 1842, Perry unlawfully sold a quantity of liquor to Daniel Willis. The court found Perry guilty and ordered him, on each count, to pay a fine of $20.00 and court costs within five days. If he did not pay the fine and costs within that time, he faced twenty days imprisonment in the common jail in Plymouth.[21] Constables had prosecuted Perry on several other occasions for violating the liquor laws, but Perry, after paying his fine or serving a term of imprisonment, continued his illicit activities, much to the dismay of Hanover officials, who found him incorrigible.[22]

≈

Within days of the St. Patrick's Day murders, word of the bloodshed reached communities throughout the region. Newspapers drew attention to the sorrowful events with headlines such as, "Deadly Affray at Hanover," "Rum and Murder" and "Shocking Outrages." God-fearing people and temperance advocates decried the alcohol fueled violence, denouncing the immoral influence of intoxicating liquor and the evil it perpetuated.

The *Quincy Aurora*, a weekly newspaper, published the first account of the tragedy on Thursday, March 20, 1845. The *Aurora* reported that on March 17, three Irishmen, two of them brothers, went to what was described as a small grocery store in Hanover where liquor was illicitly sold. The community had assailed Perry on more than one occasion for "keeping such a vile place of resort." Perry responded to their disapproval by threatening residents who sought to curtail his activities. According to the paper, Perry had been heard to say "that he expected some day or other to see his yard stained with blood, and he kept about a dozen guns loaded in a back apartment."[23] He refused to be intimidated, scoffed at the law and carried on his illegal activities with scorn and indifference.

The *Aurora* continued its story, relating that the three Irishmen had been in Perry's store less than fifteen minutes when a Hanover resident named Enos Bates, a burly blacksmith, "boasting of his strength," challenged them to a fight. They stepped outside the store and the two brothers, Patrick and James Stapleton, quickly pinned Bates to the ground. Seth Perry then exited the store, brandishing a double-barreled gun, and fired at James Stapleton, striking him in the heart. Almost immediately after, he fired again, this time striking Patrick Stapleton in the chest. Perry then went back into the store and retrieved a musket. He fired at the third Irishman, Dowlan, who was fleeing from the scene, and struck him in the lower jaw. [24]

A slightly different version of events in the *Old Colony Memorial* on Friday, March 22, 1845, recounted how a dozen Irishmen, including the Stapletons and Dowlan, went to Seth Perry's grog shop on St. Patrick's Day. Reporting on their sobriety, the newspaper noted, "Being assembled there they were soon able by a pretty free appliance of strong drink to get themselves a good deal excited, and became somewhat noisy and turbulent, still demanding more rum." According to the article, Perry refused to provide any more liquor and ordered them from his premises. Contrary to the assertion made in the *Aurora* about Bates' challenge to fight, the *Memorial* alleged Bates had become involved in the confrontation only after he took it upon himself to assist Perry in removing the Irishmen from the premises.

The *Memorial's* article also commented on Perry's illegal activities and referred to Perry's shop as "a noted groggery" and added that Seth Perry "had been more than once convicted of being engaged in the demoralizing traffic of selling ardent spirits."[25] Perry, and others like him, faced the wrath of temperance advocates who exhorted moderation or complete abstinence from intoxicating liquors, and the scrupulous attention of local officials sworn to preserve peace and maintain public order.

A third account of the murder appeared in the *Quincy Patriot* on March 22, 1845. The *Patriot's* edition reported the Irishmen had been at Seth Perry's grog shop during the day and "indulged rather freely in intoxicating liquors." The group left at some point and returned in the evening. It was then that Perry, the Stapletons, Dowlan and Enos Bates exchanged words and a scuffle ensued between them.

The *Patriot* alleged that Perry became enraged as the Irishmen started to leave and retrieved several guns from within the shop. He discharged a round at James Stapleton, then Patrick Stapleton, killing them both. "Not satisfied with the death of these two individuals, he seized another musket and fired at the third Irishman, Pierce Dolan (sic), while he was running from the house, shattering his jaw bone in a shocking manner."[26]

On March 29, 1845, Charles Dyer of Hanover, the owner of a tack manufacturing concern in Hanover, wrote a letter to the editor of the *Old Colony Memorial* newspaper, citing an article in the *Boston Courier* that referenced the *Old Colony's* March 22 account. (Dyer later became a Selectman and State Representative from Hanover.) Dyer took umbrage with the account, stating he had been part of the inquest into the incident and that the *Old Colony* article was not factual.

Dyer wrote that Patrick Stapleton and Pierce Dowlan had been at Seth Perry's most of the day with Enos Bates. All were intoxicated. Dyer refuted Perry's claim that he had refused drink to persons at the groggery, stating it was his understanding that Perry poured freely. At about 4:30 p.m., a number of Irishmen, including James Stapleton, stopped into Perry's groggery. Some of these men were looking for a drink, but others were temperance men and did not imbibe. As they approached Perry's, the men found Patrick Stapleton and Pierce Dowlan arguing with Enos Bates.

Everyone stayed inside for about fifteen minutes, when Perry ordered all of them out. Dowlan, Bates and the two Stapletons continued to argue while the rest of the men left the shop and went out into the roadway. The argument between the four remaining men escalated and a scuffle ensued between Patrick Stapleton and Enos Bates just outside the door to Perry's shop.

Just as the men who had left reached the road, they heard a shot, and as they turned in its direction, saw Patrick Stapleton, not James Stapleton, as reported in news accounts, run about thirty feet from the shop and fall. At this, all of the men in the roadway fled. They heard a second shot, then a third, but could not see what was happening because they had reached a turn in the road that prevented a view.

Dyer considered the witnesses at the inquest credible, stating, "In justice to the witnesses in this affair, I must say I never saw men appear better, and manifest a more commendable temper, and desire to tell the facts just as they occurred." He characterized them as "sober men, pledged teetotalers." [27]

≈

The day following the tragedy and after completion of the coroner's inquest, local constables arrested Seth Perry. During the inquest, jurors examined Enos Bates and after deliberation of his account and the testimony of other witnesses, found him not responsible and discharged him. Just as they had when they reported on the murders, newspapers gave varied accounts concerning the circumstances of Perry's arrest. One paper reported an immediate arrest; another related that a coroner's inquest had resulted in the issuance of a warrant against Perry at midnight on the day of the slaying for willful murder and officials arrested him shortly thereafter. A third newspaper reported that Perry had tried to escape, but was arrested by constables before he could do so. A fourth account described Perry's arrest by constables as he sought a warrant against the Irishmen for their assault upon him.

After his arrest, Perry appeared at the Plymouth Town House for a hearing where proceedings attracted an overflow crowd. When the hearing concluded, court officials remanded him to the "gaol" (the British variant for jail) in Plymouth to await trial. According to the *Boston Post*, Perry "has uniformly pretended, since his arrest, to have no recollection of having shot anybody." The only thing he did remember was that he had been badly beaten.[28]

Outraged Hanover residents, estimated at about 1000 persons by newspaper correspondents, gathered at Perry's house the same evening and threatened to demolish his home. According to the *Old Colony Memorial*, the crowd removed five barrels of liquor from inside and poured it into the ground.[29]

On March 20, 1845, an anonymous citizen wrote the editor of the *Massachusetts Temperance Standard* and described the scene at

Perry's house. The writer stated authorities searched Perry's house and "...found seven muskets, all of which were loaded, except the two discharged at the men. There was also a most plentiful supply of spirits, essences, etc., barrels and bottles and runlets of rum, brandy, wine, etc. The multitude gathered to witness the spectacle could hardly be repressed from burning the house, and were only restrained by having the barrels and bottles put out, which they broke to pieces as fast as they came in reach."[30]

The Hanover murder brought renewed pledges by temperance proponents in Boston to decry the immorality of intoxicating drink and the negative consequences of its sale and consumption. An article in the *Boston Courier* on March 22, 1845, reported the murder in Hanover "has caused a deep sensation among the friends of humanity and temperance in this city. That intoxication produced the quarrel which ended thus fatally, is a fact too palpable to be doubted."

Temperance advocates held a meeting at Fanueil Hall in Boston on Thursday evening, March 20, to discuss the "melancholy events of murder, on Monday last, by liquor." The group denounced the murder of the two men in Hanover "by a keeper of a grog-shop or rum-shanty, named Perry," asserting the event had afforded "another most melancholy proof of the effects of the liquor business, as causing crime, murder, pauperism, and great evils to the community." In support of their disdain for the sale of intoxicating drinks, the attendees, in unanimous resolutions, "once more enter our solemn protest against liquor-selling, as an immorality that ought not to continue." Further, "that we will 'cry aloud and spare not,' till the people compel the grog-shop, saloon, and all places selling strong drinks, to change their business."[31]

≈

On Monday, April 14, 1845, a grand jury held in Plymouth at the Court of Common Pleas indicted Perry on two counts of murder and one count of assault with intent to kill. Perry presented himself before Justice Luther Stearns Cushing to enter a not guilty plea on the indictment. The court scheduled an arraignment at the Supreme Judicial Court on Tuesday, May 13, 1845. On that date, Perry, accompanied by counsel, entered a not guilty plea and the court set Tuesday, June 17, 1845, as a trial date.[32]

Perry needed funds to pay for legal representation and so, on June 2, 1845, he filed notice, through counsel, in Plymouth Probate Court of his intent to grant power of attorney to his brother, Perez Perry of Hanover. The court approved Perry's petition and authorized Perez Perry, on behalf of his brother, to "take, keep, sell and convey or trade any part or all of the personal estate whereof I (Seth Perry) am the owner…that may be necessary to apply to the payment of the necessary fees, costs and expenses of the indictments now pending against me and the balance thereof to hold for the order and benefit of first, me, the constituent, and second, of my heirs and assigns…"[33]

≈

After Hanover Coroner Levi Curtis performed autopsies on the bodies of James and Patrick Stapleton and concluded his inquest on March 18, Hanover officials delivered the bodies to Quincy for a funeral at St. Mary's Catholic Church. The brothers were buried in unmarked "pauper's graves" in the church graveyard.[34]

During the autopsies, Curtis inspected their clothing and found one of the Stapleton brothers in possession of more than one hundred dollars. Curtis and other Hanover officials could not identify or locate relatives of the Stapletons for proper disposition of the property. It's likely that officials questioned the brothers' co-workers and railroad administrators to ascertain next-of-kin, but their queries disclosed no useful information. Since the Stapletons were Old Colony employees, left no kin, and died intestate, the railroad assumed responsibility for their legal affairs and appointed staff counsel to petition the probate court for adminstration of their estates.

On March 19, 1845, Joseph S. Beal, an attorney and public administrator from Kingston, and an auditor for the railroad, filed an application and a bond with sureties with Judge Aaron Hobart in the Plymouth County Probate Court, Middleboro, for appointment as administrator for the estates of James and Patrick Stapleton. The petitions for James and Patrick specified both men had resided in Abington as aliens, died intestate and left no heir or kindred in

Massachusetts to inherit their goods and estates under the laws of the Commonwealth.[35]

On April 5,[36] April 12,[37] and April 19, 1845,[38] notices appeared in the *Old Colony Memorial* newspaper in Plymouth, publicly announcing the Probate Court's intention to appoint Joseph S. Beal as administrator of the estates of James and Patrick Stapleton. The notices directed any and all persons interested in the estates of the two men who had an objection to the appointment of Joseph S. Beal to appear at the Probate Court on May 6, 1845, to show cause.

On May 6, 1845, with no objections being filed, Judge Hobart appointed Beal as administrator of the goods and estates of James and Patrick Stapleton. The court ordered him to make and return a "true inventory of all the real estate and all the goods, chattels, rights and credits of the deceased" within three months. The court further ordered Beal "render upon oath, a true account of his administration" within one year.[39]

On August 11, 1845, Beal filed an inventory with the Probate Court that summarized the personal estate of James Stapleton as $57.20 in cash and the personal estate of Patrick Stapleton as $57.00 in cash. Beal listed no other property, real or personal.[40] He divided the total sum of $114.20 found on one of the brothers between both. Railroad laborers during the 1840s were typically paid $.50 a day, the equivalent of $14.69 in today's dollars. The sum of $114.20 represents about 228 days of labor and $3,354.38 in present day figures.[41]

On February 15, 1847, Beal presented an account of the Stapleton's estates to Judge Hobart. He sought allowance for sums he paid to Levi Curtis, E. Gilmore, the *Old Colony Memorial* newspaper and Middleboro Probate Court. He allowed himself $11.73 for services rendered on behalf of Patrick Stapleton's estate, and $11.43 for services rendered as administrator to James Stapleton's estate. Payment of these debts depleted the $114.20 in assets of the two men. Judge Hobart allowed the account and entered it into the records of the Probate Court after sworn testimony by Beal.[42]

Every attempt to confirm the existence of Stapleton kin in America or abroad for proper settlement of their property had failed. Social conditions in Ireland had left many people homeless, displaced, or dead. Patrick and James Stapleton were among the thousands of immigrants during the 1840s who fled the impoverishment and political and religious persecution prevalent in Ireland to seek freedom and prosperity in America. Whether their family had survived in Ireland or had emigrated to America or other parts of the world remains unknown.

≈

As early as the 12th century, the English monarchy required every landholder and tenant in Ireland to pay a tithe to support the Established Church of Ireland, regardless of their religious affiliation. This created much resentment among Roman Catholics whose loyalty remained with the Church of Rome. The Irish paid the tax with one-tenth of their agricultural produce. In 1823, the British government enacted the Tithe Composition Act to allow payment of the tithe in money, rather than in kind. The Act authorized a survey of landholders in Ireland to determine the amount of tax payable. The Tithe Applotment Survey enumerated each landholder in a county parish and recorded his size of holding, land-quality and types of crops. The amount of tithe payable by each landholder was based on all of these factors and calculated by a formula using the average price of wheat and oats from 1816-1823.[43]

In 1835, the British government conducted a survey to assess the extent of poverty throughout Ireland. It became evident that 75 percent of Irish laborers were without any regular work and that begging was very common.[44] To offset the proliferation of poverty, Parliament passed the Poor Law Act in 1838 and established workhouses to provide labor, housing and sustenance for the impoverished population. Many Irish rejected the opportunities offered in the workhouse system, fearing a loss of dignity and freedom.

The British government passed the Tenement Act in 1842, a law that mandated another survey of the land and property in Ireland to determine local taxation. The government appointed Richard Griffith, a Dublin geologist, Commissioner of Valuation. Griffith conducted the survey between 1848 and 1864. The survey, called *The General Valuation of Rateable Property in Ireland*, or more commonly,

"Griffith's Valuation," included the names of lessees and lessors, the amount of land or property owned or leased, and the value and quality of the property.

Nearly all Irish census records for 1831, 1841 and 1851 were destroyed by fire during the 1922 Easter uprising in Dublin. Griffith's Valuation survived the destruction, and is an important census substitute for the 1831-1851 period. The Valuation's surname index points to the adjoining counties of Tipperary and Kilkenny in Ireland's southeast as the likely origin of Patrick and James Stapleton as the Stapleton surname is prevalent exclusively in these two areas.[45]

From 1815 to 1845, nearly a million Irish left their homeland to seek relief and promise in America. Another million left Ireland during the Great Irish Famine between 1845 and 1852. Their arrival was not always welcomed. In Boston, the undernourished and unemployed Irish poured into the confines of the city, some finding shelter in overcrowded tenements, some existing in "shanties." They needed food, housing, clothing, and health care – expensive commodities – the cost of which was suddenly thrust upon a resentful, established society.

An ugly atmosphere of anti-Irish and anti-Catholic sentiment enveloped Boston. As Irish numbers multiplied, fear and hatred rose among the American populace, who viewed them as "idle, thriftless, poor, intemperate, and barbarian," little more than "wild bison" ready to leap over the fences that usually restrained the "civilized domestic cattle."[46]

Attacks upon the doctrines of Roman Catholicism by Anglo-Saxon Protestants began in the 1820s and 1830s. In 1834, an angry mob burned a Catholic convent in Charlestown. The crusade against Rome continued into the 1840s, 1850s and beyond as "so-called native Americans denounced the 'blasphemy' of Roman Catholic doctrine, the 'immorality' of the Roman religion, the 'idolatry' of the sacraments, the 'cruelty' of the priests and the 'subversive' nature of papal authority."[47]

In *The American Irish, A Political and Social Portrait*, author William V. Shannon viewed anti-Catholic and, by extension, anti-Irish animosity by the native population as "an available, respectable pretext..." What natives, especially in the lower-middle and working class, truly resented was the Irish threat to jobs. According to Shannon, "The Irish workingman in the next block and not the Pope in Rome was the real enemy."[48]

Despite this climate of opposition, Patrick and James Stapleton arrived at an auspicious time in America's history. The country was in the midst of an industrial expansion that demanded significant labor resources. To entice Irish laborers, recruiting centers in Ireland and Boston offered "meat three times a day, plenty of bread and vegetables, with a reasonable allowance of liquor, and eight, ten, or twelve dollars a month for wages."[49] Penniless and without skills, Irish immigrants seized on the opportunity and provided "the backbreaking labor needed to build canals, roads and railways in the rapidly expanding country."[50]

≈

During the 1830s and 1840s, railroad development flourished on the East Coast. In Boston, the Old Colony Railroad, incorporated on March 16, 1844, began construction on a rail line that extended from Boston to Plymouth. Although "track construction work was among the least prestigious, most dangerous, and most demanding unskilled work of the nineteenth century,"[51] the Stapleton brothers, Pierce Dowlan, and many other Irish men hired on with the Old Colony. They cleared the right of way, laid the gravel for the rail bed, lugged the cross ties and rails into place, and hammered the spikes into the tie plates to secure the rails to the bed.

The work was oppressive and exhausting. Conditions were so harsh "that a common expression heard among the workers was that 'there's an Irishman buried under every railroad tie.'"[52] In 1843, about a thousand Irish laborers and their families arrived in Concord to build the Boston to Fitchburg rail line. "The men were paid fifty cents a day for their labor, 'dark to dark' – up to sixteen hours straight, to the horror of liberal-minded Concordians."[53]

A song about the Irishman's plight working on the railroad appeared in the 1850s. Entitled "Poor Paddy Works on the Railway," the author of the song has never been identified.[54] The first few stanzas of the song likely capture the essence of Patrick and James Stapleton's journey from Ireland to America and their experience as railroad workers building the Old Colony Railroad in 1845.

In eighteen hundred and forty-one
My corduroy breeches I put on
My corduroy breeches I put on
To work upon the railway, the railway
I'm weary of the railway
Poor paddy works on the railway

Oh in eighteen hundred and forty-two
I didn't know what I should do
I didn't know what I should do
To work upon the railway, the railway
I'm weary of the railway
Oh poor Paddy works on the railway

Oh in eighteen hundred and forty-three
I sailed away across the sea
I sailed away across the sea
To work upon the railway, the railway
I'm weary of the railway
Oh, poor Paddy works on the railway

≈

Seth Perry stood trial for the murder of Patrick Stapleton on June 17, 1845, at the Supreme Judicial Court in Plymouth (In 1891, the Massachusetts legislature transferred jurisdiction of all capital cases from the Supreme Judicial Court to the Superior Courts in the respective counties of the Commonwealth). Constitutional safeguards protected Perry's liberty and afforded him every opportunity to establish his innocence. Article 12 of the Massachusetts Declaration of Rights guaranteed that a defendant in a capital trial had a right to a full explanation of the charges against him, a prohibition against self-incrimination, a right to confront witnesses against him, a right to legal counsel and a right to a trial by jury.[55] The court routinely appointed one senior and one junior counsel to represent capital defendants during trial and at appeal. The court guaranteed that the jury was randomly chosen and impartial by allowing the defendant an unlimited number of peremptory challenges aimed at potential jurors.[56] The court prohibited the use of peremptory challenges by prosecutors, but did allow challenges for cause. In 1869, legislation changed this rule and allowed the prosecution peremptory challenges and challenges for cause.[57]

Chief Justice Lemuel Shaw, Justice Charles A. Dewey and Justice Samuel Hubbard presided over the proceedings. Attorneys Timothy G. Coffin and Perez Simmons represented Perry and District Attorney John H. Clifford represented the Commonwealth.

Chief Justice Shaw was born in Barnstable, Massachusetts in 1781. He graduated from Harvard in 1800. After studying law in the office of Attorney David Everett in Boston, he was admitted to the bar in 1804. He was appointed as Chief Justice of the Massachusetts Supreme Judicial Court in 1830. He received the degree of Doctor of Laws from Harvard in 1831 and Brown University in 1850.[58]

Justice Charles A. Dewey, born in 1793, was a Williamstown, Massachusetts native and graduated at Williams College in 1811. He was District Attorney in Hampshire County from 1830 until 1837, when he was appointed to the Supreme Judicial Court.[59]

Justice Samuel Hubbard was in born Boston in 1785 and graduated from Yale in 1802. The governor of Massachusetts appointed him to the bench of the Supreme Judicial Court in 1842.[60]

In his *"History of the Judiciary of Massachusetts,"* published in 1900, William Thomas Davis reflected on the integrity of all three jurists. Davis was a lawyer with more than fifty years of experience in the Massachusetts court system who believed that "no more learned and incorruptible court ever sat in Massachusetts or elsewhere." He expressed his esteem for Chief Justice Shaw whom he described as "the incarnation of law and justice, and it was impossible to imagine him swayed by prejudice or popular clamor. He was obedient only to the dictates of an unerring judicial mind."[61]

Defense attorney Timothy Gardner Coffin, a respected Bristol County lawyer, was born in 1788 in Nantucket of Quaker parentage. He attended Brown University and was admitted to the bar in 1811. His practice was located at 40 North Water Street, New Bedford. He was a short, thick-set man known for his wit and anecdotes.[62] In *"The History of New Bedford and vicinity, 1602-1892,"* Coffin was described as having "…the faculty of grasping every point in a case, on both his opponent's and client's side, and made use of them to the advantage of his cause. His arguments were full of force and he propounded questions and cross-questions with such rapidity and such variety that to evade his keen-witted perception was almost an impossibility."[63]

Perez Simmons was born in Hanover, Massachusetts on January 2, 1811. His ancestors arrived in America from England aboard the "Fortune," in the spring of 1621. Simmons attended Hanover district schools and Hanover Academy. Upon his graduation from Brown University in 1833 and after study under Providence attorney Charles F. Tillinghast, Simmons was admitted to the bar in Rhode Island. He practiced law in Providence until 1843, when he returned to Hanover to continue his profession as a member of the Massachusetts bar. Simmons was held in the highest regard by his colleagues and "by his forgetfulness of self and indefatigable efforts on behalf of his clients, he marked himself as a faithful counselor and trustworthy lawyer."[64] Simmons later held various political offices in Hanover, including selectman, state representative and state senator.

John Henry Clifford, the prosecutor in the case, studied law under Timothy Coffin's tutelage, and became a partner in Coffin's law office. Clifford was born in Providence, Rhode Island, in 1809. He graduated from Brown University in 1827 and was admitted to the Bristol County bar in 1830.[65] In 1849 he was appointed as Attorney General of Massachusetts. He was elected governor in 1852 and served a one year term.[66] It was later said that Clifford, when he was a prosecutor, presented a closing argument at an infamous Massachusetts trial that "…cannot be excelled in close and conclusive reasoning, conveyed in a language equally elegant and forcible. Its effect, as a demonstration of the guilt of the accused, is fearful."[67]

Before the trial began, defense counsel Coffin and Simmons gathered facts, interviewed their client and questioned witnesses to determine the appropriate strategy for Perry's defense. The lawyers knew it would be impossible to deny that Perry had shot the men, given the number of witnesses to the incident. From the outset, Perry had made it known among friends and neighbors that he remembered being beaten, but did not recall shooting anybody.[68]

Coffin and Simmons considered a number of different strategies, but focused on two – self-defense and legal irresponsibility due to "temporary insanity." They contended that the beating Perry had sustained from the Irishmen placed him in fear of his life. They also asserted the blows Perry received may have "produced a temporary insanity."[69]

To prove temporary insanity, Coffin and Simmons needed expert testimony from a respected psychiatrist. They consulted Dr. Samuel B. Woodward, superintendent of the Massachusetts State Lunatic Hospital in Worcester, Massachusetts. Woodward was considered a 19th century pioneer in American psychiatric care, and his hospital, the first public one in America for the care of criminal and "pauper" insane, was "a phenomenal success in the recovery of patients once considered incurable."[70] Woodward had testified in other cases on the validity of a "temporary insanity" condition as a defense. The defense hoped to elicit testimony from Woodward that showed Perry's mental capacity was diminished due to Patrick Stapleton's sudden provocation and attack. They wanted to establish that because Perry was under such mental stress or tension he could not differentiate between right and wrong and, therefore, was not responsible for his actions.

To prove first degree murder under common law, DA Clifford needed to show that Seth Perry killed with "malice aforethought." Attorneys Coffin and Simmons had to convince the jury that Perry had acted without malice, in self-defense, in the "heat of passion," brought about by incitement, or involuntarily, due to a state of temporary insanity.

Sir William Blackstone, an 18th century judge, jurist and professor, established himself as the leading authority on common law and its principles. Blackstone's *"Commentaries on the Laws of England,"* published in four volumes between 1765 and 1769, provided the common law definition of murder as "when a person, of sound memory and discretion, unlawfully killeth any reasonable creature in being and under the king's peace, with malice aforethought, either express or implied."[71] Blackstone recognized that "all homicide is malicious, and of course amounts to murder," except in three situations – when homicide is justified by law; excused in cases of accident or self-defense; or, "alleviated into manslaughter, by being either the involuntary consequence of some act, not strictly lawful, or if voluntary, occasioned by some sudden and sufficiently violent provocation."[72] Blackstone defined manslaughter as "the unlawful killing of another without malice, express or implied; which may be either voluntarily, upon a sudden heat, or involuntarily, but in the commission of some unlawful act."[73]

≈

Newspaper coverage of the trial was very much like it was for the murders. Correspondents for three of the leading papers of the time, the *Boston Courier,* the *Quincy Patriot* and the *Boston Post*, each gave differing accounts of the testimony offered during the course of the trial and in some instances, injected their personal opinions about the final verdict.

On June 20, 1845, the *Boston Courier* reported that during the first day of trial, witnesses had testified that a group of Irishmen, Old Colony Railroad laborers, went to Seth Perry's grog-shop in Hanover to drink. A dispute and scuffle ensued between the Irishmen and Enos Bates, "an American." Perry ordered the men out of the shop at about 5:00 p.m. All of the men left, but continued scuffling with Bates in front of the shop. Perry shot the two Stapletons dead with a double barrel gun and then, with another gun, shot Dowlan. [74]

As the *Courier's* correspondent listened to the sworn statements of eyewitnesses, he found it difficult to determine the facts of the case, "as those who were present during most of the time, were too drunk to remember accurately." He also maintained that no evidence had been introduced to indicate Perry had been assaulted, "although after the firing he was found somewhat bruised, and his face bloody."[75] This contradictory statement suggests that the reporter assumed Perry had received the bruises under some other circumstances and that his face was stained with the Stapletons' blood and not his own.

A more thorough account of the trial appeared in the *Boston Post*. The editor of the paper recognized the importance of providing complete trial coverage, as in his opinion, "...the accounts which were published of this tragical affair immediately after its occurrence were materially incorrect in some essential particulars, (so) it strikes me that it is worth while to give a pretty full report of the trial in the *Post* from day to day."[76]

According to the *Post*, the trial, which was scheduled to begin at 9:00 a.m. on June 17, was delayed due to the late arrival of Justices Shaw, Dewey and Hubbard. The courthouse was crammed with spectators and included a small gallery that was reserved for the ladies, "about one hundred and fifty of whom, young and beautiful, seemed cheerfully to pay the penalty of curiosity, by submitting to the squeezing necessarily attendant upon their contracted accommodations."[77]

At about 2:00 p.m., Perry was led into the court room and the three justices ascended to the bench. The *Post* reporter covering the trial described Perry's physical appearance as one of "a sickly hue, but it is also marked with deep and broad lines, which indicate the past indulgence of the fiercest passions which war against the soul."[78]

As soon as the court was brought to order, DA Clifford moved for trial. Both Clifford and defense attorney Coffin requested that the court try Perry for the murders of Patrick and James Stapleton together, as in their opinion, the facts surrounding their deaths were the same. The court considered the request, but denied it, stating that "it would be safer, in a case of life and death, not to depart from the usual course of trying but one such indictment at a time," and instructed both attorneys to proceed with the indictment against Perry for the murder of Patrick Stapleton.[79]

The process of jury empanelment began and after eighteen peremptory challenges by the defense, twelve jurors were selected. The jurors included Samuel Thompson, farmer, Middleboro; Israel Briggs, farmer, Wareham; Benjamin Brown, Jr., ship caulker, Scituate; Peleg Bryant, yeoman, Kingston; Isaac C. Curtis, shoemaker, Pembroke; Thomas M. Hatch, carpenter, Abington; Newton Mitchell, farmer, Bridgewater; Joseph Northey, farmer, Scituate; Sydney Packard, shoe cutter, East Bridgewater; Seth Shurtleff, nail maker, Middleboro; Rotheas Washburn, cotton ginwright, Bridgewater; and Nathan Whitman, farmer, East Bridgewater. Interestingly, none of the jurors represented Hanover. It's likely that Perry's attorneys made every effort to avoid the empanelment of a Hanover resident for fear that he knew Perry's reputation in the community and harbored animosity against Perry for his lawlessness.

After the jury had been seated, the court clerk read the indictment against Perry for killing Patrick Stapleton and DA Clifford presented his opening statement. Clifford told the court and the jury that in the afternoon of March 17, 1845, Patrick Stapleton, along with several of his friends, visited the illicit rum shop of Seth Perry in Hanover. In the afternoon, a dispute and struggle between Stapleton and Enos Bates, "an assistant to Perry in the business of his establishment," led to the murder of Stapleton by Perry outside the shop. According to Clifford, Perry took deliberate aim at Patrick and killed him, then turned his gun on Patrick's brother, James, and killed him. Perry also fired at Pierce Dowlan, a friend of the Stapletons, and wounded him. Clifford told the jury that Perry always kept a number of loaded guns on hand inside his shop and that after the shootings, Perry "expressed neither surprise nor resentment; but coolly locked up his shanty and went to a magistrate with the pretended complaint against the companions of the deceased making a disturbance at his place."[80]

DA Clifford had conducted his interviews of potential witnesses well before trial and had prepared his prosecutorial strategy. On the first day of trial, Clifford intended to prove the death of Patrick Stapleton through the testimony of Dr. Joseph Fobes. He would call two witnesses, local residents Joshua Smith and Melzar Sprague, to testify about their observations of the crime scene and wounds they had observed on the victims. His final witnesses on the first day would include Jeremiah McCarty and Dennis Lynch, both Irish laborers for the Old Colony Railroad, who were present at the scene during the shootings. Clifford hoped to elicit testimony from both men about the events that preceded the shootings and whether they had seen who had fired the shots. He also intended to have Pierce Dowlan, who was still recovering from the effects of his wound, testify about his recollections of what had transpired at Perry's rum shop.

DA Clifford called his first witness, Dr. Joseph Bassett Fobes. Fobes had been a resident physician in Hanover since 1838. He was described as being of medium height and burly build and "his visits were always very bustling and business-like."[81] He was born in Bridgewater, Massachusetts in 1814 and graduated from Harvard College in 1839.[82] Fobes testified that he had examined the wound upon Patrick Stapleton's body and determined that it was the cause of his death. Fobes conjectured that the deceased must have been in a stooping or bent posture and at the left of the person who fired the shot at him. The musket ball entered near Stapleton's collar bone on the left side, traversed through his lungs and came out on the right side of his back.

Joshua Smith of Hanson, a fifty-two year old farmer and surveyor, was called by Clifford to verify the accuracy of a sketch of the murder scene Smith had prepared. After the sketch was marked as evidence, Smith referred to it to explain how he had documented the positions of the bodies in relation to Perry's shop. According to Smith, James Stapleton was shot eight feet from the door of the shop, Patrick, thirty feet, and Dowlan, one hundred and ninety feet. Smith indicated that Perry's shop was set back about twenty-six feet from the Broadway road.

Clifford next called Melzar Sprague, a fifty year-old machinist from Hanson, who lived about half a mile from Perry's shop. Sprague told the court that he went over to Perry's shop after the shootings and saw the bodies lying on the ground. He said that James Stapleton was lying on his back about ten feet from the shop with his feet pointing toward the shop door. Patrick Stapleton was on his face, about thirty-two feet from the door. A group of men carried the bodies to Benjamin White's house, which was a short distance away across Teague's Bridge in Hanson. Sprague told the court that besides the wound he saw on the body of James Stapleton, he also noted the print of a rifle muzzle on Stapleton's breast bone, a little above the hole made by the ball.

Sprague saw Dowlan holding on to his face in a wagon in front of Albert White's house on Center Street. (Albert was Enos Bates' brother-in-law. He married Enos' sister, Lydia, in 1836. White's property abutted the land behind Perry's shop.) Dowlan was taken in the wagon to Benjamin White's (Albert's cousin) house where doctors were examining the Stapleton bodies.

Sprague then related how he had gone back to Perry's shop and inspected the interior. He found a double barreled gun inside that had recently been fired. The room was in disarray and there were spots of blood on some birch wood kept by the fireplace. There were barrels, kegs and bottles of new rum and cherry rum inside the shop as well as several other guns. Sprague identified two guns shown to him by DA Clifford as weapons he had seen inside Perry's shop.

DA Clifford summoned Jeremiah McCarty, one of the Old Colony Railroad laborers who had visited Perry's rum shop on March 17. McCarty testified that he and others left their work at South Abington and went with a friend named Welsh to Perry's shop in the afternoon where he found Dowlan, Patrick Stapleton, and Irishmen Shea, Cummings, Kelly, Crane and Connor, as well as "Mr. Bates" and Seth Perry inside. As McCarty entered, he saw Dowlan and Patrick Stapleton asleep in chairs. Welsh and another woke both men up with a splash of water. McCarty told the court that Perry had offered him a drink, which he refused, as he was a teetotaler, and did not partake of intoxicating liquor.

McCarty said that at some point, James Stapleton arrived at the shop. Shortly thereafter, James and Enos Bates began to argue. This led to a fight in which Bates pinned James to the floor. James called to his brother Patrick to help him and Patrick pushed Bates off of his brother. McCarty then walked out of the shop and was followed by several others. He started back to South Abington and as he did, he heard the sound of gunshots, but could not see who was firing.

Dennis Lynch took the witness stand after McCarty and told the court that he had arrived at Perry's shop in the afternoon with McCarty, James Stapleton, and others. This statement contradicted the previous testimony of McCarty, who said that James Stapleton arrived after he had entered the shop.

Inside the shop Lynch found Pierce Dowlan, Patrick Stapleton, Shea, Dorrety, Kelly and other Irishmen, as well as Bates and Perry. Lynch took a drink from Perry and had a conversation with Enos Bates. James Stapleton joined the conversation and an argument ensued between him and Bates. Bates and Stapleton soon began to wrestle and Perry ordered everyone outside. Lynch was the last to leave and passed Perry just before he exited the doorway. The others who had left before him were congregating outside Perry's front door and on the roadway. Lynch took two or three steps past Perry when a shot passed his ear. He saw Patrick Stapleton, "make a jump," and fall on his face. Lynch ran and was jumping over a fence surrounding the property when he heard a second and third shot. He said that he did not see who fired the shots.

On cross-examination, Lynch admitted he had "drank some that day." He said he did not see Patrick Stapleton fight with Bates and insisted that it was James who had been involved in the fracas. He told the court that he was the last, except Perry, who left the shop, because he was lighting his pipe at the fireplace when Perry ordered everyone from the premises.

Defense counsel questioned Lynch about his observations as he entered the shop. Lynch said that he saw Patrick Stapleton, sitting in a chair with his head down, as if asleep. He never saw Patrick Stapleton assault anybody inside the shop. He was asked if he had seen "Connor," one of the other Irishmen present, choke Seth Perry and he responded that he had not.

(The *Post* reporter, as an aside, commented on Lynch's testimony and the difficulty he had understanding what Lynch had to say. He wrote that Lynch's enunciation "was so hurried and indistinct that it was impossible to understand what he intended to say, until he had repeated it over and over again."[83] It is likely that the thick brogues of the Irish witnesses posed communication problems throughout the trial, or that some witnesses, perhaps, were somewhat intoxicated.)

Lynch was excused from the stand and the state called Pierce Dowlan to testify. Dowlan had recovered from his wounds, but still had difficulty recalling details about the day in question. Dowlan remembered he had gone to Perry's shop with Cummings, Callaghan and others, but wasn't sure if it was in the morning or afternoon. After having several drinks at Perry's, he passed his bottle to Patrick Stapleton and fell asleep in front of the fireplace inside the shop. A noise woke him and he saw some scuffling. He said he didn't remember what happened next until he went out into the yard and saw Patrick Stapleton fall. When he saw another man fall, he ran across the road into a field and looked back, only to see Perry, who was wearing a green jacket, with a gun in his hand. He turned to run and was struck by a ball just under his right cheek bone. The next thing he recalled was getting out of a wagon. He was taken into the house where James and Patrick Stapleton were laid out and doctors extracted the ball from his left cheek, where the ball had come to rest.

On cross-examination, Dowlan admitted that he was intoxicated at the time of the incident, but couldn't remember how much he had drunk. He had difficulty recalling what happened inside the shop and couldn't remember who was there, except to say that at some point, his friend Callaghan had taken hold of two guns and Perry told him they were loaded.

After Dowlan completed his testimony, the *Post* reporter noted, "it now being too dark to write, the Court adjourned." The trial would continue the following morning.

≈

On Friday morning, June 18, the prosecution resumed its examination of witnesses. On this second day of trial, Clifford planned to recall Dr. Fobes to elicit details of his examination of James Stapleton and Pierce Dowlan. He also planned to call Enos Bates as a prosecution witness. Clifford had interviewed Bates at length about his involvement on the day in question. After hearing what Bates had to say, Clifford was of the opinion that Seth Perry was not being assaulted, nor was he being threatened, when he fired at the Stapletons and Dowlan. Bates' testimony would help the prosecution prove that Perry's actions had been unjustifiable.

Clifford would call another Irish railroad laborer, John Connors, to the stand to describe the scene of the murders and identify Seth Perry as the man who had shot the Stapletons and Dowlan. Clifford's next witness, Haviland Torrey, a Hanover merchant, would testify about Perry's actions after the crime. Clifford intended to call Benjamin Bowker, a local resident, to the stand to recall the events of Perry's arrest.

The district attorney next wanted to show the jury that Perry had a propensity for violence and he planned to question three witnesses, William Winslow, Thomas Damon and Charles Dyer, all Hanover residents, about their interactions with Seth Perry and their knowledge of his familiarity with weapons and about threatening statements Perry had made in their presence. These last three witnesses would conclude the prosecution's case against Perry.

DA Clifford recalled Dr. Fobes and asked him to describe the wounds found on James Stapleton and Pierce Dowlan. Fobes explained that a ball entered James Stapleton's left breast and passed directly through and out his back. Another ball shattered both of Pierce Dowlan's lower jaws and rested in the fleshy part of his left cheek. Dr. Fobes removed the ball, which was flattened on both sides, from the cheek. DA Clifford exhibited the ball to the jury.

There being no cross-examination of the doctor, DA Clifford called Enos Bates to the stand. Enos was born in Hanover in 1810, the son of Enos Bates, Sr. and Lydia Tilden.[84] His ancestors arrived in Hingham, Massachusetts from Hertfordshire, England in 1635.[85]

None of the newspapers that covered the original incident and the trial mentioned a familial relationship between Seth Perry and Enos Bates. Perry and Bates were first cousins. Seth's mother, Anne (Bates) Perry, and Enos' father, Enos Bates, were brother and sister.[86]

The *Post* reporter described Bates as a very stout man who testified that he had gone to Perry's shop at about 11:00 a.m. on the day in question. When he arrived, Patrick Stapleton, Pierce Dowlan and five others were there. He remained at the shop until the shooting occurred. When DA Clifford asked why he was there, he said that he went there for no particular reason and that he hadn't been inside the shop for three weeks. He told Clifford he had never tended the shop for Perry until that day.

Bates recalled that the Irishmen had been in and out of the shop all day. It was his opinion that they had drunk too much. He admitted he had also taken several drinks.

Bates said that Patrick Stapleton began to sing and cause a disturbance in the shop and that Perry told him to stop. Stapleton ignored Perry's command and continued to sing. Perry, and then Bates himself, told him several more times to stop, that he was causing a disturbance. Stapleton then rose and "clenched me, or scrabbled at me, or something to that amount, and took hold of Perry." DA Clifford asked him what he meant by, "took hold of Perry." Bates responded, "I mean twitching hold, and throwing him down, and jamming him, or something to that amount." Bates denied that Perry "clenched" Stapleton. Bates' testimony was guarded and vague. He couldn't seem to find the proper words to describe what happened. He couldn't say who threw the other or whether they were on the floor, "or at least, I don't known which got the other down on the floor." He insisted no blows were struck. He said that before Patrick Stapleton had fought with him, Pierce Dowlan assaulted him. He turned back to his scuffle with Patrick Stapleton and told the court that he and Patrick had "a scrimmage together, or a skirmish" and that he, the two Stapletons and Dowlan eventually went outside the place. They continued to fight about thirty feet outside the door when he heard the first shot. He saw Patrick Stapleton get up from the fight when he was shot. When Bates looked up, he saw Perry standing in his door with a gun in his hand. Bates began to run towards his home on Center Street and when he was about 30 yards away, he heard a second shot. Clifford asked him what position he was in when the first shot was fired, but Bates said he did not know. He said that he, the Stapletons and Dowlan were clenched together when Perry fired into the heap. Clifford asked him if the Irishmen were angry and Bates told him that he couldn't be sure. He told Clifford that, "as to myself, I don't know that I was much mad."[87]

Defense counsel cross-examined Bates and asked him his opinion of the Irishmen's sobriety. He said that the Irishmen had drunk enough. As he was asked to repeat his version of the fight inside the shop, Bates added that he believed James Stapleton had thrown him upon a heap of brush in the corner of the room. He said Patrick came to James' assistance and remembered that there were blows between them. He didn't recall Dowlan striking him, but said that Dowlan was part of the melee and was engaged with him as they went outside the shop. Defense counsel tried to elicit testimony from Bates that would paint a picture of self-defense and asked him what the Irishmen were saying to him as they were assaulting him. He was asked if he considered the attack upon him as serious. Bates said he did consider the attack serious, but couldn't recall what they were saying to him. He denied seeing either of the Stapletons choking Perry and said that he never noticed that Perry had been bruised. He also denied seeing any of the combatants in possession of a club.

Defense counsel asked Bates about Perry's guns. Bates told the court that Perry was in the habit of keeping loaded guns in his entryway. He said Perry routinely shot at geese flying over during the spring and fall. When asked if he had seen any of the Stapletons fall, he stated that he had not. He recalled that one or two minutes had expired between the first and second shots. He said that James Stapleton went towards the door where Perry was standing after the first shot and that he didn't know which way Dowlan fled.

Chief Justice Shaw asked Bates where Perry lived. Bates told the judge that Perry generally lodged with his sister, who lived next door, but that Perry sometimes cooked his meals in the shanty. The shanty served as a home for Perry and his wife, until she died. He said the shanty consisted of a room and an attached shed. (It appears that Chief Justice Shaw needed clarification as to whether Perry actually lived in the shanty. At that time, under English common law, a man had a right to protect his home from attack – "a man's home is considered his castle." If a man is attacked inside his home by someone who is illegally there, he has a right to defend himself. If he killed the person or persons who had attacked him inside his home, the law considered the killing justifiable homicide. This law, also known as the Castle Doctrine, is still in effect in most states throughout America today.)

DA Clifford took exception to Bates' testimony and informed the court of his surprise at what Bates had said. Clifford told the court that Bates' testimony differed from the statements he had made during the coroner's inquest after the shootings and he wished to impeach the witness's credibility. The justices took Clifford's request under advisement. Later that afternoon, Chief Justice Shaw assented to Clifford's request to introduce evidence that would show Bates had not adhered to his original statement and had testified differently. DA Clifford called David Oldham to the stand to testify about Bates' statements during the inquest, but, "his testimony would not fall within the limits prescribed by the court," so Clifford was unable to question him. Clifford didn't pursue the matter any further.

John Connors was the next witness for the state and he testified that he had been at Perry's rum shop with Michael Kelly and John Crahan between 4:00 p.m. and 5:00 p.m. on the day in question. He said that others were inside, including the Stapletons, Lynch, Cummings, McCarty, Shea, Dowlan, Welsh, Barrett, Bates and Perry. He saw an argument between James Stapleton and Enos Bates, each bragging that he was a better man than the other. He heard Bates say "there wasn't any man good enough for him in the country," and he could, "handle any man, Irish or Yankee."[88]

Connors took a drink at the shop, but found it distasteful and threw it on the floor. He left after two or three minutes with Kelly and Crahan. A few minutes later, he saw the two Stapletons and Bates rushing out the door of the shop. The three men scuffled outside and as they did so, Connors saw Seth Perry, dressed in a green jacket and brown pants, coming down a ladder from a loft inside the house with a musket in his hand. As soon as Perry reached the floor, Connors saw him aim the musket and fire it. He saw Patrick Stapleton staggering, holding his right hand up to his chest. He walked about fifteen feet and fell face down. Connors fled from the yard and after a brief interval, heard a second shot. By the time he heard the third shot, he had lost sight of the house.

When he was cross-examined, Connors revealed some important information for the defense. Connors was asked to describe in more detail the scuffle he had seen outside Perry's door. Connors told the court that Patrick Stapleton was bending down by Bates and that James Stapleton was also over Bates, who was striking at both men. He did not know if Patrick Stapleton was striking or holding Bates. He said that Cummings, one of the other Irishmen at the shop that day, was involved in the scuffle at first. Connors stated that he saw Cummings strike Bates with a stick of birch wood before the first shot was fired. This testimony was crucial to the defense counsel's self-defense theory and strategy. No other mention had been made by any other witnesses that this other man, Cummings, armed with a club, had assaulted Bates. Coffin and Simmons needed to convince the jury that the situation faced by Bates and Perry was one of life and death and that Perry's only recourse in preventing the murder of Bates was to inflict deadly force upon his attackers.

DA Clifford next called Haviland Torrey, a merchant with a store in Hanover Four Corners, to testify about Perry's actions after the shootings. Torrey told the court that Perry appeared at his store at "about candle-light" and asked for Mr. Wood, his partner. Alexander Wood was a justice of the peace for Plymouth County. Perry told Torrey he wanted a warrant for the arrest of five Irishmen who had assaulted him. Torrey told Perry that Wood was ill and unable to assist him with his request for the warrants. Perry told Torrey that the Irishmen had come to his place early in the day and wanted rum and that he had told them he had no rum for them. He told Torrey that they left, but returned in the afternoon with reinforcements, again demanding rum, as it was St. Patrick's Day. Perry refused them once more and they turned against him, forcing him outdoors and pounding him against the house. He never told Torrey he had shot three of the men. Torrey didn't hear about the murders until half an hour after Perry left.

Whether DA Clifford questioned Torrey about Perry's physical appearance is not known as the *Post* reporter never mentioned it in his column. Nor did he report any cross-examination by the defense, which is not surprising, since questioning Torrey any further was likely to elicit even more damaging testimony.

Benjamin Bowker testified that he assisted in the arrest of Perry at about 10:00 p.m. on the night of the shooting. He said that Perry was at the home of Judson Bates, about a mile from Perry's shop, and at the time of his arrest, he was wearing a green jacket.

On cross-examination, Bowker explained that when he told Perry he wanted him to accompany him to Squire White's (magistrate), Perry told him he wanted to see White, too. Bowker noted that Perry was bruised and had a blackened left eye with a cut over it. He was covered with blood.

Defense counsel also questioned Bowker about an incident during the coroner's inquest at Perry's shop. Bowker told the court that Dowlan, although shot in the face, was present and when he saw Enos Bates, who was in temporary and informal custody of two citizens, he rushed him. Dowlan incoherently stated to Bowker that "he wished they had finished him." During an inspection of the shop, Bowker found six guns. He noted drops of blood on a double-barreled gun and a brass gun. He identified the guns in court. He also stated that he saw birch sticks scattered over the floor.

DA Clifford hoped to offer additional evidence of Perry's propensity for violence with his next witness. William Winslow testified that during the first week of March last, while on his way from Scituate to South Bridgewater, he encountered Seth Perry as he was passing his shop. Perry asked for a ride to Thomas Hobart's. Perry got on board and a conversation ensued between the two men. Perry told Winslow that he had "a good many enemies in Hanover." Perry said that Melzar Hatch was one of them and that he suspected Hatch of leading the efforts to prosecute him for his illicit rum selling. He told Winslow Hatch had better beware, as Perry kept "hounds." Perry then showed

Winslow a pistol and said that Hatch "…might hear them (the pistols) growl; that he had given them their breakfast that morning."[89]

Clifford called another witness to verify Perry's familiarity with firearms. Thomas Damon testified that he visited Perry a week before the shootings and Perry offered to sell him a gun. Damon inspected a double-barreled gun and a brass gun, similar to the guns in evidence. Perry boasted about his proficiency with the weapons and showed Damon a board he and his brother had used as a target and how he had beaten his brother in a match.

On cross, Damon explained that he went to Perry's shop the day after the murders and noted blood in the entryway. He also saw blood on brush and wood inside the shop, as well as two or three drops on a cleaver. He found evidence of blood on the rear of the building, as if a wounded person had leaned against it.

The defense asked Damon about his observations of Bates' physical condition. Damon told the court that he had seen Bates on March 16, the day before the tragedy, and saw a cut on his lip. Damon added that when he formally arrested Enos Bates two days later, on March 18, he observed that Bates had sustained further injury to his mouth.

Charles Dyer, the tack manufacturer who had written a letter to the *Old Colony Memorial* denouncing the paper's accuracy in reporting the St. Patrick's Day events, testified next and related a conversation he had with Seth Perry about a year before. Perry wanted to know why he and other townspeople, particularly Hatch, objected to his rum-selling. Dyer told Perry he only objected to his selling rum to his brother-in-law, who used it to detrimental effect, and asked Perry not to sell him any more. Perry told him he'd sell to whomever he pleased. Perry asked him if he knew that he possessed loaded "growlers." Dyer told him he had heard that Perry carried them but that he was not afraid of him, "as I had never injured him – had always treated him kindly, and was still ready to treat him so."[90] Upon completion of Dyer's testimony, DA Clifford informed the court that the prosecution had presented all of its evidence.

≈

Defense attorney Perez Simmons rose and offered his opening statement. Before he informed the jury of his theory of what happened on the day in question, Simmons remarked upon the actions of those who had ransacked Perry's shanty while he was in jail. Simmons told the jury that among those who had destroyed Perry's property were the men who had been the principals in prosecuting Perry for his rum-selling. Simmons related that on last Thursday, June 12, temperance advocates held a convention at Perry's shanty, complete with speeches and bands that paraded around the property playing a death march. The presence of the "unexampled crowds of spectators" at the courthouse was evidence of the excitement caused by these events, suggesting public opinion was against his client and that Perry may not receive a fair trial because of it.

Simmons then turned his attention to the state's case against his client. He found it absurd that the state would try to convince the jury that Perry, unprovoked by threats or assault, had arbitrarily shot dead two of his customers and wounded a third. How could a jury, he asked, familiar with human nature, possibly believe that such a thing had occurred? Simmons told the jury that the defense intended to prove that Perry never fired his weapons until after he and Bates had nearly been beaten to death by the Stapletons and their companions. The fight outside Perry's shop was a continuation of the fight inside with Bates, Perry's assistant, who was being set upon by "ten intoxicated and exasperated Irishmen." Perry, in defense of Bates and his house and home, did what any man would do under the circumstances and did so justifiably and without malice. Simmons also commented on the testimony given by the prosecution's witnesses, stating that their versions in court differed significantly from what they had been heard to say in conversation before trial.

The defense first wanted to establish that Perry, had in fact, been severely beaten. Simmons would call Perez Perry, William Reed, Benjamin Hall, Joshua Mann, Andrew Bates, Martin Prince and Ethan Perry, all local residents, to testify about their observations of Perry's physical condition on the day of the shootings. The defense also intended to call Dr. Samuel Woodward to the stand to testify about Perry's mental state during the affray.

The first witness for the defense was Perez E. Perry, Seth's nephew, who lived about twenty yards from Seth's shanty. Perez testified that he heard two shots on the day of the incident and looked out his bedroom window where he saw ten or twelve men running from his uncle's place. About four or five minutes later, he saw his uncle running toward his house, blood streaming from his face, a cut on his forehead and his eye bruised. After his uncle washed his face, he left the house and went towards Albert White's place, then to Mr. Hall's and other places, returning back at the house soon thereafter.

William Reed, the next witness for the defense, told the court he saw Seth Perry at Albert White's at about 5:00 p.m. with blood on his clothes, his forehead cut and his eye half closed and blackened. Attorney Simmons asked Reed if he had been at the scene of the shooting on the day in question. Reed responded that he had, and had seen the bodies of the Stapletons lying near Perry's shop. About a month later, Reed testified, he returned to Perry's shop and saw dry blood on the floor at the entryway and on the woodwork inside the shop.

Simmons asked Reed about Perry's use of firearms and Reed told the court that Perry kept guns for sale and barter and that he occasionally participated in target shooting with neighbors. Simmons asked Reed a question to help prove Perry was defending house and home on the day of the tragedy. Reed told the court he knew Perry to use his shop as his dwelling house. In another question to refute the testimony of Dowlan, Simmons asked Reed if he had any conversation with Dowlan after the shooting. Reed said that he spoke with Dowlan the same night and Dowlan told him he did not know who shot him and didn't know where he was when he was shot.

On cross-examination, Reed told the court that when he was near Perry's shop the night of the killings, he spoke with Perry. While talking with him, both saw Enos Bates walking toward them. Perry shouted to Bates, but Bates kept walking. Perry said to him, "Bates, you know all about this thing – come up to the house and tell them." Bates, according to Reed, replied, "I know nothing about it," and left.

Benjamin Hall, who lived in the same house with Reed, testified to Perry's physical appearance after the shooting. He also told the court how he had seen blood stains in the entryway to Perry's shop and elsewhere. He said that Perry was excited the night of the shooting when he saw him, but did not appear to be intoxicated.

Attorney Simmons called Joshua Mann to the witness stand and asked him to explain where he was and what he observed on the day in question. Mann told the court he saw Perry in the road near his shop but could barely recognize him because of the bruised and bloody condition he was in. Perry was "agitated and in a tremor." He said he went into Perry's shop the same night with a lantern and saw that the interior was in disarray. Mann also testified that he was at Benjamin White's house and had seen Dowlan there. Enos Bates was nearby and when Dowlan saw him, Dowlan said, "Keep him out of my sight," then kicked his leg at Bates and started at him, but was stopped when two men stepped in between them.

Andrew Bates testified about his observations of Perry's condition on the night of the shootings. He also told the court that Perry was a gun dealer and that he and Perry sometimes went "gunning" together.

Martin Prince, a forty-five year-old black laborer from Hanson, testified that he gave Seth Perry a ride in his wagon to Hanover Four Corners sometime after the shooting on March 17. They stopped at Oren Josselyn's store where the witness helped Perry clean up and "washed his head in spirits." When Prince was excused from the witness stand, Oren Josselyn was sworn and verified Prince's account.

Ethan Perry, a 43 year-old farmer who had known Seth Perry for more than thirty years, also testified as to Perry's physical appearance on the night of the shooting. The morning after the tragedy, the witness went to Perry's shanty and inspected the inside. He saw bloodstains on the wood pile near the fireplace and on the floor. He found what he described as two "very heavy bludgeons." A crack in one contained a tuft of hair.

Attorney Simmons, preparing for the imminent testimony of Dr. Woodward as to the mental condition of his client during the incident, asked Ethan Perry to relate a bizarre incident that had occurred many years ago. The witness told the court that when he was a small boy, the defendant and his father, Samuel Perry, visited his home. The witness offered his opinion that the defendant was deranged and related how during the visit, Seth placed a door hinge against his grandfather's neck and tried to choke him. Seth's father and Ethan's father intervened and then sent Seth to a bedroom where he remained until Samuel Perry left the house.

DA Clifford cross-examined Perry about his inspection of the defendant's shop. The witness told the court that Seth Perry was with him that morning and he pointed out one of the bludgeons, picked it up and handed it to him with a remark. (The remark was not allowed by the court as it was hearsay.)

The court excused Ethan Perry from the witness stand upon completion of his testimony. At 8:00 p.m., Chief Justice Shaw adjourned until 8:00 a.m. the next day.

≈

On Thursday, June 19, the defense resumed its examination of witnesses at 8:00 a.m. Once again, the defense intended to show the jury that Perry had sustained severe injuries and suggest that he had been in fear of his life. Four witnesses, Joshua Studley, Jr., Lebbeus Stockbridge, John N. Dwelley and Allen Clapp all testified as to Seth Perry's physical appearance on March 17.

Simmons then called Benjamin White to the witness stand. White told the court that he had known the defendant for over forty years. He related that when Seth was about sixteen years old, he was deranged. "He went round the streets, bare-headed, drumming on a tin pail," White said. White didn't know if Perry used intoxicating liquors at that time, but he knew him to be in the habit of drinking afterwards.

Defense counsel next summoned Dr. Samuel Woodward of the Worcester Lunatic Hospital. The defense hoped, through Dr. Woodward's testimony, to establish Perry's impaired mental condition at the time of the shootings. Simmons asked Dr. Woodward what effect a blow upon Perry's head would produce on the brain. Justice Shaw interrupted at this time and ruled that no foundation had been laid by the defense for such a question and would not allow any further examination of Dr. Woodward. The defense must have been dismayed at this ruling, as they had hoped to prove that Perry had experienced a temporary insanity during the assault on him.

The defense next called a witness to discredit the previous testimony of John Connor who said he had seen Perry descend on a ladder from a loft with a gun in his hand. John Crahan, who was at Perry's on March 17, told the court that he left Perry's place after being there only a few minutes. He was in the road in front of Perry's place when the firing began and was not in a position to see the shop's entryway. He believed that Connor may have been able to see the door because he was on the other side of the road and was closer to the shop than he was.

On cross-examination, Crahan stated that he had not seen a disturbance inside the shop when he was there. He did see Bates and the two Stapletons scuffling outside, but he was some distance away and couldn't tell who was on top.

The district attorney recalled Charles Dyer to confirm that Connor was capable of seeing Perry in the shop doorway. Dyer stated that the door on Perry's shop was hung on the right post and opened inward. If a person were in the road, it was possible for him to see someone going up or down the ladder to the loft inside.

The defense moved to impeach Dyer by questioning him about his participation in the destruction of Perry's shanty and property on the night of the shooting and his animosity toward Perry because of his rum-selling activities. The court ruled that the defense could not question Dyer on these points and he was dismissed from the witness stand.

The defense called Judson Bates to the stand. He testified that he had seen blood on Perry's shirt and face shortly after the shooting. He said that Perry ate supper at his house at about 9:00 p.m. the same evening and had a hearty meal that included three cups of tea.

Dr. Winslow Warren, a 50 year-old physician from Plymouth, told the court he examined Seth Perry at Plymouth Jail on March 19. Dr. Warren said he observed a bruise over Perry's left eye, extending up the forehead. He did not see any evidence of a cut on the forehead. In his opinion, if the cut had been deep, the marks would have been visible.

He sensed that if there had been a cut there at all, it had probably been a scratch.

DA Clifford recalled Dr. Fobes and asked him about his treatment of Pierce Dowlan. Fobes stated that two or three days after he had extracted the ball from Dowlan's jaw, he noted that Dowlan was suffering a fever and had considerable swelling about the jaw. Dowlan was in a stupor due to these conditions.

The defense rested its case and Attorney Coffin, senior counsel, began his closing arguments. Coffin told the jury that the prosecution had failed to prove its case. He said that the witnesses for the prosecution had provided contradictory testimony and attributed the discrepancies of their testimony to their lack of ingenuity in concocting a consistent account of the events that led up to and during the March 17 tragedy. In his opinion, they were determined to show that Perry had shot their friends without provocation by denying there was a disturbance inside the rum shop or that anyone had beaten Perry.

Coffin argued that after the shooting, Perry had evidence of violence upon his face and clothing and that testimony verified that there was a disturbance inside the shop where bloodstains were found on the floor and on the birch sticks used during the affray. There was also testimony that Perry had ordered Patrick Stapleton from the premises when he refused to stop his loud singing and that Patrick attacked Perry, knocking him to the floor. Tempers flared and the skirmish continued, now with both Perry and Enos Bates fighting, two against ten, for their lives. Perry, in great fear, saw three men upon Bates outside his shop, one beating him with a birch stick. Perry believed that the Irishmen would kill his friend then turn upon him. Perry's only recourse was to exert deadly force against the assailants and save the life of his friend and his own. Coffin theorized that after shooting Patrick Stapleton, James Stapleton rushed him and that Perry didn't fire at first, but tried to poke James with the muzzle of the gun and keep him at bay. But James persisted and left Perry with no choice but to fire upon him. Perry was being attacked in his home, his "castle." Coffin argued that given the odds against him and his right to protect his home, his person and his goods from the assault of a person or persons unlawfully present, Perry was justified in his actions.

DA Clifford then rose and described the defendant as of, "a brooding, vindictive and lawless disposition, (who) had familiarized his mind to the idea of inflicting summary vengeance on those who might offend him." Clifford questioned Perry's use of firearms to resolve the conflict. Rather than threatening the men fighting with Bates or firing a warning shot to break up the struggle, Perry, "having no respect for human life, deliberately fired upon the deceased, one after the other, with as much indifference as if they were nothing more than so many noxious animals." Clifford argued that Perry's only reason for shooting Dowlan, who was running away, was to eliminate him as a witness to the killings.

Clifford commented on Dr. Warren's testimony, pointing out that the physician had not seen any serious injury upon Perry. Since there was no evidence to show how Perry might have received the marks observed by witnesses, the jury was left to only one conclusion – that Perry self-inflicted the injuries. How else could Perry disprove that he had shot three men in cold blood? He had to show that he acted in self-defense, so he bruised his own eye, daubed the floor and birch sticks, his face and clothing with blood, then went to as many houses in his neighborhood as he could to exhibit himself.

Clifford spoke of Perry's trip to the magistrate to seek warrants against the Irishmen for assaulting him, pretending that he had been injured. He pointed out how Perry had lied to the magistrate about refusing drink and how he had failed to mention that he had shot three men. At the conclusion of his argument, Clifford appealed to the jury to set aside any religious or ethnic prejudices they might hold against the victims and rely only on the facts as presented during trial.[91] He then asked the jury to find a murder verdict against Perry and took his seat.

Chief Justice Shaw delivered the charge to the jury and explained the general principles of the law in cases of homicide. He then turned his attention to the evidence and instructed the jury not to consider any references to insanity as a defense.

In 1843, an English court established the standard for insanity in the *McNaughton* case. McNaughton shot and killed the British Prime Minister's secretary and was acquitted during trial "by reason of insanity." The "McNaughton rule" created a presumption of sanity, unless the defense proved "at the time of committing the act the accused was laboring under such a defect of reason, from disease of the mind, as not to know the nature and quality of the act he was doing, or if he did know it, that he did not know what he was doing was wrong."[92] The rule became the standard for insanity in the United States and is still the standard in some states today.

A year before Seth Perry's trial, Chief Justice Shaw presided over the Abner Rogers murder trial. Rogers had murdered the Charlestown State Prison's warden, Charles Lincoln. Dr. Isaac Ray, American founder of forensic psychiatry, whose work was cited in the McNaughton case, testified on behalf of the defense and claimed that Rogers could differentiate between right and wrong, but was driven by an "irresistible impulse" to murder the warden. According to Ray, Rogers believed that what he had done was right, because of his mental state.[93]

Rogers' attorney, George Bemis, pleaded with the jury to abandon the "common opinion" that a plea of not guilty by reason of insanity was nothing more than a clever excuse for getting away with murder. The prosecutor in the case argued that medical opinion should not be trusted and that the methods used by so called experts could not lead to the truth.[94]

Chief Justice Shaw relied on Ray's "irresistible impulse" argument during his charge to the jury. If the defense has proven that the defendant's mind is, in fact, diseased, the jury must then consider "whether the disease existed to so high a degree, that for the time being it overwhelmed the reason, conscience and judgment, and whether the prisoner acted from an irresistible impulse." Simply put, Shaw wanted the jury to decide whether Rogers's criminal actions were the result of his mental disease, or if Rogers was overwhelmed by emotion, deterring him from making a rational decision. The jury found Rogers not guilty by reason of insanity.[95]

In Shaw's opinion, Perry's actions did not meet the "irresistible impulse" standard. Shaw believed that Perry acted with uncontrolled emotion and was fully capable of making a sound decision before he acted.

He dismissed the defense's theory that the killings were justified, based on self-defense, and explained the legal aspects of man's right to defend his own home. He explained the difference between murder and manslaughter and asked the jury to consider whether Perry's acts were done in "the 'heat of blood,' and if so, he is guilty of manslaughter and not homicide." Shaw fully recognized that testimony presented by many of the witnesses was vague, which he attributed to their state of intoxication during the incident. But if the testimony convinced the jury that there had been a fight inside the shop and that the struggle outside the shop was a continuation of this fight, it was their burden to determine whether such circumstances would likely cause "heat of blood, which in the eye of the law extenuates even an unlawful killing, and reduces it to manslaughter."[96]

≈

At 8:00 p.m., the jury retired to deliberate on the evidence. At about 10:00 p.m., they informed the court that they had reached a verdict and filed into the court room. Jury foreman Samuel Thompson rose and announced that they had found the defendant, Seth Perry, guilty of manslaughter.

After the court clerk recorded the verdict, DA Clifford asked the court to delay sentencing until the next morning. Clifford did not want to proceed with a trial against Perry for the murder of James Stapleton, as he feared the verdict would be the same. He realized that eyewitness testimony was weak and difficult to overcome. His only alternative in securing a conviction against Perry for killing James Stapleton was to discuss a plea bargain with Perry and his counsel.

The next morning, after a conference with DA Clifford, defense attorney Coffin notified the court that the defendant would retract his plea of not guilty of the murder of James Stapleton if the district attorney entered a nolle prosequi (from the Latin, "we shall no longer prosecute") as to the allegation of "malice aforethought," and reduced the charge against Perry to manslaughter. Clifford then informed the court that the state wished to enter a motion to dismiss the charge against Perry for the murder of James Stapleton. Chief Justice Shaw allowed the motion. Perry then retracted his plea of not guilty. The court clerk told him that the charge had been reduced to manslaughter and asked Perry how he would plead to it. Perry replied, "guilty," and the clerk entered his plea into the record.[97]

The District Attorney decided not to prosecute Perry in the Supreme Judicial Court on the indictment of assault with intent to kill Pierce Dowlan. According to the June 28, 1845 edition of the *Quincy Patriot*, the indictment "was returned to the Court of Common Pleas and will not be called up by the District Attorney."[98]

A condensed transcript of the record of indictment, trial and conviction of Seth Perry from the Supreme Judicial Court, Plymouth County record book follows:

"The Jurors for the said Commonwealth, on their common oath present, that Seth Perry, of Hanover, in the County of Plymouth, Laborer, at Hanover...on the seventeenth of March, last past.... feloniously and willfully and of his malice aforethought did make an assault in and upon the body of one Patrick Stapleton...Perry, then and there discharged a shot...did strike, penetrate and wound Patrick Stapleton, giving him, the said Patrick Stapleton, one mortal wound...of which said mortal wound, he, the said Patrick Stapleton, then and there instantly died...the said Seth Perry, harm(ed) the said Patrick Stapleton in the manner and by the means aforesaid, feloniously, willfully and of his malice aforethought, did kill and murder against the peace of said Commonwealth and contrary to the law of the State in such case made and provided."

"This Indictment was found at our Court of Common Pleas...and the prisoner is set to the bar, and hath the indictment read to him whereupon he pleads and says thereof he is not guilty and at our said Supreme Judicial Court holden at said Plymouth in the County aforesaid...on the seventeenth day of June...the said Seth Perry, the prisoner, is again set to the bar and the cause, after a full hearing, upon the offense aforesaid, is committed to a jury duly empanelled and sworn to try the same, who return their verdict therein and say, that thereof the said Seth Perry is not guilty of murder and is guilty of manslaughter."

As to the charge against Perry for the murder of James Stapleton, the record reflected that he:

"...feloniously, willfully and of his malice aforethought, did kill and murder...James Stapleton." The transcript continues, "...and at our said Supreme Judicial Court holden at said Plymouth in the County aforesaid...on the seventeenth day June... the said Seth Perry, the prisoner, is again set to the bar and the District Attorney makes entry on said indictment in the words following, to wit: 'nol pros as to the malice,' thereupon, the said Seth Perry retracts his plea of not guilty by him heretofore made and again pleads and says thereof he is guilty (of manslaughter)."[99]

≈

On June 21, 1845, the *Boston Courier* also reported on the conclusion of the trial. The *Courier* correspondent recounted that the jury had deliberated for three and a half hours, as opposed to the two hours reported by the *Post*, before jurors returned with their verdict. He disagreed with the jury's finding and believed that Chief Justice Shaw's charge had persuaded them to arrive at a manslaughter conviction. The correspondent offered his opinion that Shaw had left them "free to finding as they did, upon the ground that Perry and Bates might be considered one party in the affray, and the Irishmen the other, and that the act was committed in the heat of blood, occasioned thereby." The reporter emphasized, once again, that although he believed "Perry was undoubtedly somewhat abused by the Irishmen during the day," he witnessed "no direct proof of the fact."[100]

The *Quincy Patriot*, on June 28, 1845, gave another account of the trial's outcome and contradicted the *Courier's* story. The correspondent for the *Patriot* stated evidence had been submitted at trial that "inferred that he (Perry) acted in self-defense." He related that "Perry had been maltreated, his clothes were sprinkled with blood and his house gave evidence of a severe and desperate struggle..."[101]

Commenting further on the verdict in the June 21, 1845 article, the *Boston Courier*'s correspondent wrote, "The great and increasing reluctance, in this community, to capital punishment, has, undoubtedly, much influence in cases of this kind."[102] His dismay with the verdict and his reference to "cases of this kind" suggests that the writer perceived an element of ambivalence among juries to convict and execute those accused of murder. His perceptions were justified, as a movement to overturn the state's right to impart capital punishment was gaining momentum during this period.

The hesitation by juries to convict defendants of crimes punishable by death is evidenced by the outcome of trials conducted between 1835 and 1849, when twenty-one men were tried for murder. In the twenty-one capital cases tried during the fourteen year period, jurors convicted five men. Three had their sentences commuted to life in prison and two were hanged. Jurors acquitted eight men and another eight, including Seth Perry, were convicted of the lesser crime of manslaughter.[103]

Existing law required a mandatory penalty of death upon a conviction for murder. The only option available to jurors who were reluctant to impose this penalty was either acquittal, or conviction for manslaughter. It wasn't until 1858 that the Massachusetts legislature abandoned the common law definition of murder (cited by Blackstone, above) and divided the crime of murder into two degrees. First-degree murder had to include the elements of deliberately premeditated malice aforethought; or in the commission of, or attempt to commit, any crime punishable with death or imprisonment for life; or committed with extreme atrocity or cruelty. First degree murder was punishable by death. Second degree murder was defined as an offense that did not fit the definition of murder in the first degree and was punishable by life imprisonment. The trial jury determined what degree of murder had been committed by the defendant.[104]

About 1830, a crusade to raise public support for the abolishment of capital punishment began with Robert Rantoul, Jr., a graduate of Harvard College and an attorney. Rantoul was born in Beverly in 1805 and was admitted to the Middlesex bar in 1831. In 1834, he was elected as state representative for Gloucester. During his term, he filed a measure to abolish the death penalty, but the bill never passed.[105]

Rantoul believed the government had no legal right to take the life of another. He insisted that the United States Constitution and the laws of Massachusetts prohibited capital punishment. He contended that man no longer lived in an uncivilized, savage society and had the power to "affect the 'general progress of society' and the freedom "to use 'knowledge, reason and reflection' to change any law, including that 'remnant of feudal barbarity,' the death penalty."

Rantoul also inferred that the death penalty was not a deterrent to crime, nor did it provide "the best protection for society." Rantoul insisted that the death penalty "diminished the 'natural sensibility of man for the sufferings of his fellow man' and generally promoted 'cruelty and a disregard of life.'"

Rantoul questioned those who would rationalize capital punishment on religious grounds. He admitted that the Old Testament justified the death penalty, but believed that the circumstances of that time did not apply in today's society. He asserted that an enlightened and pragmatic society should not base the laws of punishment on revenge, but on the Christian precept of "Thou shalt not kill."[106]

In a further indication that public debate about capital punishment was changing attitudes and values during this period, Massachusetts voters elected a Democratic governor in 1840 who was a proponent for elimination of the death penalty. The candidate, Marcus Morton, based his platform for capital punishment abolishment on arguments proposed by Rantoul.[107]

When Charles Spear, a Universalist minister, published his *Essays on the Punishment of Death* in 1844, he became New England's foremost proponent for the abolition of capital punishment.[108] Spear firmly believed in the benevolence of God, freedom of the will, and the salvation of all men. According to Spear, these three principles "would overcome every existing evil." He suggested that "All criminals, including murderers, could, and should, be reformed."[109]

In 1845, Rantoul and Spear, along with other Boston reformers, initiated a campaign to dissuade capital punishment proponents and place political pressure on elected officials to eliminate the death penalty by organizing the Massachusetts Society for the Abolition of Capital Punishment. In the same year, the society published the first issue of the *Hangman*, a weekly newspaper used to promote an organized effort against the death penalty through essays, meeting announcements, news about the plight of convicted murders and calls to action, such as the circulation of petitions asking for commutation of punishment.[110]

If not their reluctance to impose capital punishment, what other factors may have influenced the jury's decision to acquit Perry on a murder charge? Did the social atmosphere that existed at this juncture in American history influence the outcome of the trial? Is it possible that prejudice filled the minds of judges, jurors and attorneys in this case, preventing a fair and impartial judgment of the facts? Established society resented the growing population of immigrants and considered them the lowest of classes. Yankees freely voiced public criticism and directed their hate and bias toward foreigners in general and Irish Catholics in particular. Boston College professor of history Alan Rogers, in his book, "*Murder and the Death Penalty in Massachusetts*," commented on the influence of racial bias and ethnic hatred in capital trials. He observed that "A community's social and political imperatives and its values and biases affect the way in which justice is defined and administered."[111] One can only hope the evidence spoke for itself, neutrality and candor prevailed during deliberations, and open-minded jurors returned a dispassionate verdict.

≈

The court sentenced Perry to ten years in the State Prison at Charlestown for the death of Patrick Stapleton. He was to serve the first three days of his sentence in solitary confinement. For the death of James Stapleton, he received a consecutive sentence of three years in the State Prison, to be served on and after the ten years he received for the death of Patrick Stapleton. He was to serve three days of his three year sentence in solitary confinement.[112]

After sentencing, authorities transported Seth Perry to the State Prison in Charlestown, Massachusetts (now the site of Bunker Hill Community College), where he was received on June 28, 1845. Prison officials placed an entry into a commitment register that included Perry's age, birth place, physical description, the reason for his conviction and the length of sentence. The prison entered Perry's date of discharge into the register upon his release.

Officials assigned Perry to convict number 3880. They described him as being 52 years of age, 5' 6 ½" tall, with blue eyes, brown hair and a dark complexion. He had a large wen on the back of his head and two colored moles on his right breast. He also had two small scars on the middle of his back and a large scar on his left knee.[113]

In 1804, Massachusetts started construction of a prison in Charlestown on four acres at Lynde's Point. "The prison was to be 'for the reformation as well as the punishment of convicts.'"[114] It was completed at a cost of $170,000.00 (or $47 million in today's economy)[115] and opened on December 12, 1805. The prison was 200 feet long. Its physical layout included a central section sixty-six feet long and twenty-eight feet wide, rooms for the warden and prison officers, a kitchen, chapel and hospital.

On each end of the main building was a four-story wing that contained the prison cells. The first and second stories contained fifty-eight cells measuring eight feet by eleven feet. Thirty-two cells on the third and fourth floors were more spacious, measuring seventeen feet by eleven feet.

The prison walls were four feet thick. Officials believed it to be impenetrable, fireproof, and impossible to undermine. A stone wall, fifteen feet high, surrounded the 375 feet by 260 feet prison yard.[116]

When Perry entered the prison in 1845, it held 287 prisoners. He was one of three convicts between the ages of fifty and sixty and one of ten persons serving time for manslaughter. Principal employments in the prison included stonecutters, shoemakers, cabinet makers, tailors, blacksmiths, brush makers, whitesmiths and tin workers.[117]

In his book, *"Prison Discipline in America,"* Francis Calley Gray reported that "the prison at Charlestown resembles a great manual-labor school."[118] The prison's warden in 1845, Frederick Robinson, assigned convicts to various occupations and required them to work in silence. Rules maintained order in the workspace and supervisors quickly reported violations to the warden.

All of the prisoners were held in solitary confinement at night and began labor at sunrise in the summer and at first light in the winter. They worked for an hour to an hour and one half before breakfast, which they retrieved and ate in solitude in their cells. After forty-five minutes, they went to the prison chapel for worship for ten to fifteen minutes, then returned to the workshops.

At 12:30 p.m., the prisoners proceeded to the "cook-room," received their meals and went to their cells, again to eat in solitude. Again, the prisoners were allowed forty-five minutes to consume their food, although in summer, in periods of extreme heat, they were allowed an hour. After the meal, the prisoners returned to their work where they toiled until about 6:00 p.m. The prisoners then filed into the chapel for services, singing and Scripture readings, then collected their dinners and retired to their cells for the evening. This schedule remained constant every day of the week except Sunday, which was set aside as a day of rest and reflection.[119]

A "master of the shop" supervised the inmates during the course of the day. When he observed an infraction of a rule, he sent the offender to a place where he awaited the warden. The warden would hear the complaint, ask the offender for an explanation or defense of his actions, then mete out a punishment, if necessary. A first or minor offense usually called for a warning and chastisement, after a promise by the offender to behave.

For more serious or repeat offenses, the warden banished the offender to solitary confinement with meager rations of food. The warden also meted out floggings, which never exceeded ten lashes for each offense. Between 1843 and 1847, the warden authorized the flogging of forty-five convicts. The warden ordered a total of two hundred and forty-two lashes during this period, fifty of which were received intermittently by one prisoner.[120]

≈

Even with strict disciplinary procedures in place, prison officials found it extremely difficult to maintain order and prevent violence within the prison walls. On June 14, 1853, about two years before Seth Perry was remanded to the prison, Abner Rogers, a convict serving time for larceny, killed Warden Charles Lincoln as he passed through the shop where Rogers was assigned to make shoes. Rogers stabbed Lincoln in the neck with a shoe knife and he died instantly.

James Wilson, a convict serving time for breaking into and robbing the City of Boston's treasurer's office, was scheduled for release on July 19, 1853. Early in the morning of that day, he was marching with other prisoners from the prison to the workshops, when he set upon a fellow inmate, William Adams, stabbed him in the neck with a knife and killed him instantly. Wilson was found guilty of murder and was sentenced to hang, but his sentence was commuted and he served a life term at Charlestown.

On December 15, 1856, James Magee, a chronic offender and disciplinary problem at the prison, attacked Deputy Warden Galen C. Walker in the prison chapel with a sharpened shoe knife. Magee stabbed Walker in the neck below the left ear, then in the abdomen. The prison chaplain, present at the time, hit Magee over the head with a Bible, then called for help, whereupon Magee was restrained. Walker died almost immediately after the assault.

Two weeks later, on December 29, 1856, Charles Decatur, also known as Charles Cater, an inmate serving time for assaulting with intent to kill a prison guard at the South Boston House of Correction, stabbed and killed Warden Solon H. Tenney. Officials were at a loss to explain Decatur's actions, as he had never been a disciplinary problem during his sentence.

Magee and Decatur faced murder charges during a trial in the Supreme Judicial Court and both were found guilty and sentenced to hang. Officials hung Magee inside the rotunda of the Suffolk Jail in Boston. Decatur died in prison before his execution.[121]

There is no indication that prison officials ever disciplined Seth Perry, nor are there any reports that he was involved in any violent confrontations with fellow inmates during his incarceration. Within days of Perry's arrival at Charlestown, every inmate knew that Perry had murdered two men and nearly killed another. It is probable that he escaped injury or death during his imprisonment because other inmates feared him.

≈

Along with punishment for rule infractions came some privileges for prisoners. Prison authorities gave each inmate time to exercise, once in the morning and once in the afternoon, and always alone. Inmates were permitted to bathe once a week, except in the winter, "…when the bathing is regulated by the physician"[122] (likely due to drastic temperatures and risk to the prisoner's health). The warden granted permission for some of the inmates to maintain gardens near their workspace where the inmates could tend to two foot square boxes of soil containing "tomatoes, lettuce, cucumbers, onions and other vegetables for their own use."[123] He also authorized time for Sunday religious services and evening prayer in the prison's chapel. Some inmates were allowed to receive musical instruments for use in the services and could practice every Saturday for an hour. Also permitted was time to read and write, and a slate and pencil were furnished to each inmate so he might learn to "write and cipher." Inmates were given access to the prison library, which was funded each year with $100.00 of prison earnings.[124]

Upon discharge from prison, a convict received one pair of socks, one pair of shoes, one pocket handkerchief, one shirt, one pair of pants, one coat and five dollars. He also received the assistance of an agent for discharged convicts, "Boston Society in Aid of Discharged Convicts" – both counsel and help in securing employment.[125]

In 1846, John Ross Dix published a collection of observations entitled "Local Loiterings in the Vicinity of Boston, by a Looker On." During a visit to the State Prison in Charlestown, Dix encountered Seth Perry and provided a graphic account of Perry's description and demeanor.[126]

Dix and Warden Robinson passed through the prison yard and into a spacious shed where convicts, dressed in red and grey prison clothing, were engaged in masonry work. As he passed them, Dix "could observe furtive glances, and ferocious looks, and sullen scowls," and wondered what prevented the men, armed with hammers, from attacking him or the prison guards.[127]

Dix and the warden passed on into the next workshop, where men convicted of more serious crimes, including murder, were assigned. As they entered the shop, the warden pointed out a man Dix described as being about sixty years old, with grey hair and "an athletic form," who was making kegs for white lead. The warden informed Dix the man "had killed two men and almost massacred another."[128]

"Seeing that he was an object of attention, he paused amidst his work, and turning round looked me full in the face, and so repulsive a countenance I have very rarely seen. The grotesque prison cap which he wore was stuck on the summit of his head, and the point of it standing up over his forehead, and the two side pieces of the rim projecting over his ears, somewhat like horns, made him look not unlike the pictures of Mephistopheles in Restch's Outlines of Faust. His eyes were very large, of a light color, and impudently diabolical in their expression; he had a small nose, a large mouth, and a pointed chin. Altogether he looked the very incarnation of evil."[129]

Dix was appalled as Perry stood "unabashed, unconfounded, and apparently as unconcerned as if the blood of his brethren had not gone up to God, with a cry of vengeance."[130] As Dix turned to leave the shop, he looked back and saw Perry's head "resting on a stone, his great grey eyes staring at me, his lips compressed, and his brow knit up as if in defiance. He looked perfectly frightful. If ever there was a heart which could or would not repent, it must, I think, have been the one which had the breast of that hardened-looking old man."[131]

≈

Upon his indictment in April, 1845, officials remanded Perry to Plymouth Jail pending the outcome of his trial. When he was convicted several months later, Perry was sent to Charlestown State Prison to serve his thirteen-year sentence. Although he didn't arrive at Charlestown until June 28, 1845, prison officials credited Perry with time served at Plymouth Jail and released him on April 24, 1858.

Shortly after his release, Perry returned to Hanover. On November 15, 1858, Perry purchased land on Broadway in South Hanover from his brother, Cephas, for one dollar. The property, roughly seventy-five yards by fifty yards, abutted the property of his brother, Levi Perry, on the west, Joshua Mann on the north, his brother Cephas on the east and Broadway on the south. Perry constructed a small dwelling on the land and earned a living at various trades until his death on November 25, 1874 at the age of 81.[132] The registrar listed his cause of death as "old age."[133] Perry was a widower. According to testimony given by Enos Bates during the trial in 1845, Perry's wife died sometime before the incident. Bates also informed the court that Perry's house consisted of one room with a shed attached. When Perry's wife was alive, she lived in this house with him. After she died, Perry generally lodged at his sister's house next door.[134]

Perry's minor children were cared for by members of his family while he was in prison. They lived for a time with Perry's brother-in-law and sister, Albert and Wealthy Stetson.[135] Five years before his release, his two daughters married in Hanover. In the spring of 1853, his daughter Caroline married Nathan Turner, a shoemaker from Hanson, Massachusetts.[136] During the fall of the same year, Julia married James Turner (a distant relative to Nathan) of Hanover, also a shoemaker.[137] Perry's son, John, also plied the shoemaking trade. He was boarding with the Jeremiah Soper family in North Hanson when the Civil War broke out.[138] He enlisted with the Massachusetts Fourth Regiment Volunteer Infantry on April 16, 1861. He later served with the Seventh Infantry Regiment. He died of disease on October 31, 1862 in Hampton, Virginia.[139]

Seth Perry died intestate. On December 9, 1874, Perry's daughter, Caroline Turner, filed a request with the Plymouth Probate Court to appoint Edward Y. Perry as administrator of her father's estate. Edward, a second cousin to Seth, was a justice of the peace and an influential businessman in Hanover. On December 13, the court appointed him as administrator and ordered an inventory of Seth Perry's estate, which Edward filed on December 14, 1874.

According to appraisers appointed by the court, Seth left a dwelling on one-quarter acre of land in Hanover valued at $150 and a personal estate of $745.52. The personal estate included $600.27 in cash, a silver watch, two beds, household furniture, a shoemaker's bench and tools, a wheel barrow; three guns; stone tools; farming tools; a grind stone, lumber; split-stone; wood; an old iron and sundry articles, all valued at $80.25. After an auction of Perry's property and payment of debts for auction services, taxes, burial and expenses of administration, Caroline and her husband, Nathan Turner, and Nathan's brother, James Turner, husband of her late sister, Julia Ann (Perry) Turner, received $735.14, the balance of Seth Perry's estate.[140]

≈

Enos Bates lived on his family's farm on Centre Street, South Hanover, with his mother until her death in 1852.[141] Enos continued to maintain the farm and by 1860, to supplement his income, rented living space to John Larkum, a shoe maker, his wife, Mercy, and their four children.[142]

Just after the Civil War began, John and his eldest son, John F. Larkum, enlisted in the 18th Regiment, Massachusetts Volunteer Infantry. The son survived the war, but John, Sr. died on April 14, 1862, at Lookout Point, Maryland, and was buried at Arlington National Cemetery.[143]

On June 21, 1863, Mercy Larkum gave birth to an illegitimate child, Minnie Leland Larkum.[144] On August 18, 1864, Enos married Mercy Larkum at the First Congregational Church in Hanover. It was the first marriage for 54 year-old Enos.[145]

Shortly after, Mercy gave birth to a son, Everett Lincoln, and a daughter, Rosa. Rosa died on April 7, 1870, a year after her birth.[146] Enos tended the farm and plied trades as a shoemaker and stone mason to support his family. By 1870, his real estate was valued at $2,000.00 and his personal estate at $1,800.00,[147] far exceeding Seth Perry's combined real and personal property worth.[148]

Enos Bates died on May 9, 1886, in Hanover at the age of 76. His cause of death was certified as "old age."[149] Mercy died in Hanover on February 16, 1899 of "hepatitis."[150] Both are buried in Hanover Centre Cemetery.

Enos also died intestate. On August 23, 1886, Judge Jesse E. Keith of the Plymouth Probate Court appointed Jedediah Dwelley of Hanover, a selectman and Plymouth County commissioner, as administrator of Enos Bates' estate. Dwelley informed the court Bates had left a widow,

Mercy, and two children, Everett Lincoln Bates and Minnie L. Bates, both of Hanover.

Dwelley filed an inventory of Bates' estate including a house, a stable and a shop on a lot of seven acres as well as an additional nineteen and three quarter acre lot of swamp land, altogether valued at $1,850.00. He also filed a list of personal property valued at $318.00, which included the following items: household furniture, a buggy, a covered wagon, sleigh, oxcart, lumber and boards, stone tools, farming tools, a bellows and vice, a horse, hay and stones.[151]

≈

It is clear Perry was a lawless character and a nuisance to residents in his community. His unlawful activities drew the attention of local officials when, on two or more occasions, they filed criminal complaints against him for violating the liquor laws. Residents considered Perry's establishment "the terror of the neighborhood, and which has set at defiance the most vigorous efforts to obtain its discontinuance by any legal course."[152] Outraged by the St. Patrick's Day tragedy, residents flocked to his house, which they threatened to demolish, and destroyed all of the liquor remaining within.

A threat allegedly uttered by Perry that he expected one day to see blood stain his yard and his alleged remark that he had twelve guns in his house, suggested Perry's propensity for violence. A search of his home after the tragedy confirmed this assertion. This violent nature came to the fore when Perry killed two unarmed men and seriously wounded another fleeing man who posed no threat to him.

Accounts of the tragedy tend to show that Perry had been provoked and enraged when he fired at the men scuffling with Enos Bates. It is unclear if any of the Irishmen actually set upon Perry, or if any of them were armed, although defense counsel insisted both Perry and Bates had been in fear of their lives. One newspaper correspondent reported neither the prosecution nor the defense had submitted evidence that Perry had been struck, although after the killing, he was found bruised and his face was bloody.

Another reporter related that evidence at trial had revealed Perry's maltreatment, the blood-stained condition of his clothes and the signs of a frantic struggle at his house. DA Clifford had elicited testimony from one witness who testified that he had seen an Irishman named Cummings strike Bates with a birch stick, but did not see anyone assault Perry. It was only Enos Bates, Perry's first cousin, who testified, somewhat dubiously, that Patrick Stapleton had "taken hold of Perry," and when asked to elaborate, said, "I mean twitching hold, and throwing him down, and jamming him, or something to that amount." Physically assaulted or not, Perry's reaction on that fateful day was ruthless and unjustifiable.

≈

Perry met ridicule and condemnation upon his return to Hanover. Residents never forgave him for the barbarity he had exacted on that infamous Saint Patrick's Day in 1845. He was a pariah who had disgraced his family and his community. Townspeople vilified and shunned him until the day he died.

Peace and tranquility returned to the little town after Perry's imprisonment and residents enjoyed a period of accord and prosperity. It would be nearly thirty years before the town was rocked by another tragedy – a murder perpetrated by the manager of a hotel in Hanover's quaint Four Corners Village.

A Tailor's Goose

Nor is there any law more just, than that he who has plotted death shall perish by his own plot.

Ovid – Ars Amatoria (I, 655)

On a pleasant Sunday afternoon, May 24, 1874, two men strolled onto the Quincy Avenue toll bridge overlooking the Monatiquot River in East Braintree. Locals knew the span as Whitmarsh's Bridge, as the Whitmarsh family lived in a house at one end and collected tolls from travelers passing over the span.[1] The bridge connected East Braintree with the village of Weymouth Landing, otherwise known as Washington Square.

Whitmarsh's Bridge (Courtesy of Braintree Historical Society)

The companions stopped on the bridge and looked down into the gently flowing stream as churchgoers made their way home from services. The water sparkled in the bright sunshine. The men fully expected to see debris in the river, as a surge created by a week of inclement weather had disrupted the river's natural confluence.[2] One of the men, thirty-three year-old Alexander White, a shoe maker who lived at Weymouth Landing, suddenly noticed what appeared to be a human form in the water. He nudged his companion, David Pelleran, and frantically drew his attention to what he saw submerged below. "There's a foot in the water!" he cried. "You've got the jim-jams!" said Pelleran. But it was no illusion, and as the men peered more closely, they saw two legs protruding above the water line swaying with the river's current. They shouted to others near the bridge. John Bates, a boot maker, and Thomas South, a blacksmith, who lived near the bridge in East Braintree, heard the cries and ran to help. Bates and a man named Leach retrieved a boat and paddled toward the body. A crowd had gathered during the commotion and with great anxiety they watched as the men secured the body with a boat hook, and struggling with the weight of their ominous load against the outgoing current, slowly rowed back to shore.[3]

As Bates, South, Leach and several other men pulled the body to the river's banks, the crowd saw the body was that of a woman, clothed in a dress and wearing one shoe. With the exception of the legs from the knee down, her body was completely covered in mud. Her head was wrapped with a carriage robe, double-folded and tied tightly with a manila rope looped three or four times around her neck and tied with a half-hitch knot. The robe had red, white and black striped lining on one side and solid red lining on the reverse.[4]

A second rope tied to her neck was attached to a linseed gunny bag. The men opened the bag and discovered a twenty-four pound tailor's goose, a heavy flat iron used to smooth material. The goose's weight held the body to the bottom of the river.

A tailor's goose (Photograph by author)

The men left the body on the shore until the arrival of Norfolk County Coroner George W. White and Samuel Curtis, a mortician from Weymouth who had an office on Washington Street near Washington Square. White instructed Bates, South and others to remove the body to a fish shanty about ten yards away. The men gently lifted the body into a handbarrow and wheeled it inside.

White and Curtis examined the body briefly and then ordered the men to place the body in a wagon and move it a short distance to the Union Fire Company No. 1 engine house in East Braintree (located on present day Allen Street). Officials at the scene notified state and local police. Town constables and state constable Napoleon B. Furnald arrived to investigate.

At the engine house, White and Curtis inspected the bloated, decomposing corpse more closely.[5] Curtis cut the rope encircling the neck, as it was tied too tightly to loosen. Removing the carriage robe, the men observed the facial features of a woman with dark hair, dark complexion and a broad forehead.[6] None of the men recognized the woman.

The men estimated her to be about thirty-five years of age. On the left side of her head Curtis and White saw an apparent gun shot wound. Since there were no punctures in the carriage robe, the men surmised she had been shot before the robe had been placed over her head. An impression on the third finger of her left hand suggested a missing ring. The woman was about five feet tall, and was clad in a black and brown striped dress with a black alpaca overskirt, a felt skirt, a flannel underskirt and ribbed hose. On her right foot she wore a size three low cut shoe, commonly known as a "Newport tie." The woman had only a stocking on her left foot. She wore a jade earring in the shape of a ten pointed star on her right ear.[7]

The body's bloated condition was due to the effects of immersion and degradation. After death, the human body's temperature falls and the process of decay begins. A human corpse submersed in water will cool twice as quickly as a body found on land. The water's lower temperature slows the decomposition process. Post-mortem lividity, or discoloration of the skin, occurs within six to twelve hours. The effects of rigor mortis may not disappear until four days after death. If the body has been in the water for more than a week it will exhibit signs of bloating, as gas accumulates in the abdomen. The tailor's goose tied around the woman's neck secured her upper body to the river's bed, but not her lower body, and as bloating progressed, the torso and lower extremities floated to the surface.[8]

Several hundred people passed through the engine house to view the body and identify it. No one had ever seen the woman before.[9]

Coroner White summoned and empanelled a jury to investigate the woman's death. After jurors viewed the body, they adjourned until 2:00 p.m. on Tuesday, May 26, to conduct an inquest.

White requested the assistance of local physicians Francis F. Forsaith and Granville W. Tinkham for purposes of an autopsy. Dr. Forsaith was a fifty year-old New Hampshire native and graduate of Dartmouth College and Vermont University. Dr. Tinkham was a twenty-six year-old native of North Bridgewater, Massachusetts and a Harvard Medical

School graduate. Coroner White asked the two physicians to focus on two points – whether death was caused by a pistol shot; and if the woman was pregnant.

Constable Furnald telegraphed state police headquarters in Boston, informed superiors of the situation and his belief that a homicide had been committed. He requested additional resources to assist in the investigation. Chief Constable George Boynton detailed every available detective he had except one and responded to the scene with Detective Bailey. When they arrived, the officers canvassed the area in search of witnesses. They also conducted a search on the bridge and the adjacent area along the river's banks for further evidence of the crime.[10]

Newspaper correspondents arrived at the scene to question witnesses and gather facts about the gruesome discovery. The next day, daily papers printed a story about the tragedy and included a description of the deceased woman.

≈

That evening, as the body lay in the engine house, Drs. Forsaith and Tinkham conducted their examination. The doctors described the deceased as a thirty-five to forty year-old well-developed woman. They noted black marks under her eyes and an abrasion about a half inch above one eye, as well as bruises on her abdomen. The doctors noticed that there was no evidence of rigor mortis, suggesting that the woman had been dead for at least four days. Dr. Forsaith inserted a probe into the woman's skull and found a bullet had passed diagonally through her brain. He removed the upper portion of the skull and dissected the brain, and as he did so, a flattened pistol ball fell from the skull's membrane. Both doctors agreed the woman had been pregnant at one time, but was not at the moment of death.

The doctors ruled out drowning as a possible cause of death. A drowning victim characteristically displays a frothy mixture of water, air and mucus about the nose and throat. The same frothy mixture appears in the victim's windpipe and lungs and water is found in the throat and stomach. The lungs are spongy, swollen and soft to the touch. The doctors observed none of these characteristics on the body.

Both doctors conclusively ruled that the pistol wound had caused the woman's death and that she was dead before she entered the water. [11]

After the autopsy, Samuel Curtis took custody of the body and conveyed it to his funeral parlor on Washington Street. He summoned Ephraim Chamberlain, a photographer with an office at nearby Weymouth Landing, to take pictures of the woman's features. Curtis then preliminarily prepared the body, placed it in a coffin, and deposited it in a receiving tomb at the East Braintree cemetery.

≈

Mrs. Jane Smith, a Wollaston Heights, Quincy resident, reading an account of the Monaticquot River incident in a Boston newspaper on Monday evening, May 26, recognized the description of the woman's clothing and contacted undertaker Curtis. The next morning, Mrs. Smith, accompanied by her sister, Mrs. Margaret Garibaldi, met with Curtis and police officials and told them her suspicions about the deceased woman's identity. Mrs. Smith informed Curtis that the newspaper descriptions of the deceased's clothing closely matched attire worn by her friend, Mrs. Julia A. Hawkes. Curtis showed her the garments and she immediately recognized them. Mrs. Smith and her sister described Julia's features and also told Curtis that Julia had two false teeth on one side of her jaw.[12] Curtis told them their description matched the dead woman's appearance and asked if they'd accompany him to view the body. The two women assented and Curtis, along with Dr. Alexander Nye, escorted them to the receiving tomb where they positively identified the body as that of their friend, Mrs. Hawkes.

Upon their return to Curtis' office, the ladies told Curtis, Nye and state constables about Mrs. Hawkes' background. Mrs. Smith related that Mrs. Hawkes, a widow with one child, was a Saint John, New Brunswick native. She informed the men she had known Mrs. Hawkes since 1853. She told them the deceased had worked in a number of reputable homes in the Boston area as a domestic servant. When her services were no longer required at various places, Mrs. Hawkes stayed with Mrs. Smith, or found lodging at her sister's home on Oxford Street in Boston. Up until May 1, Mrs. Hawkes had been employed by a man named Costley at a hotel known as the Howard House in Hanover's Four Corners village.[13]

Mrs. Smith told the men that Mrs. Hawkes had visited her at her home in Wollaston on Tuesday, May 5 and had stayed until Friday, May 8. On Friday, she boarded an 11:00 a.m. train bound for Boston. Mrs. Smith said she hadn't seen Julia since then. She also stated that before Mrs. Hawkes left her home, Mrs. Smith had noticed a considerable amount of money in her pocketbook.

Several others identified the body of Julia Hawkes at the receiving tomb. These included Mrs. Smith's sister, Miss Joanna Randall of Boston; Annie White of Newton, a former resident of the Howard House; and Michael Flanagan of Boston.

≈

Mrs. Hawkes was of French extraction and was born Julia Brazeau about 1835 in or near Saint John, New Brunswick.[14] She married and gave birth to one child. Upon the death of her husband, Julia sought employment to support the child, who was left in the care of grandparents. Friends considered her industrious and frugal.[15]

About 1853, Julia was employed as a domestic servant at the Medford House in Medford, Massachusetts. She met Jane Randall (later Smith) during her tenure there. Julia remained at the Medford House for several years until she assumed domestic duties in the home of Isaac Rich at 9 Linden Street, Brookline, Massachusetts. After leaving the Rich family, Julia worked at the Mont Vernon House in Mont Vernon, New Hampshire, where she reconnected with Jane Randall Smith who was also employed there as a cook. Julia soon left Mont Vernon and obtained a position in the Daniel B. Stedman home in Savin Hill, Dorchester, Massachusetts where she was employed for seven years. She left the Stedman household about 1872 and secured employment at the Bowditch estate on Moss Hill in Jamaica Plain, Massachusetts. She remained there until August 1873, when James Henry Costley hired her as a hotel cook at Hanover's Howard House.[16] Julia remained in contact with her friend, Mrs. Jane Smith and Mrs. Smith's family, the Randalls, during her twenty years in the Boston area. The Randalls emigrated from Nova Scotia and settled in Boston in the 1850s. Julia boarded with the Randalls whenever she found herself between positions and unemployed. The Randalls regarded Julia as a member of their family.[17]

In 1872, Julia opened a savings account at the Union Institution for Savings on Bedford Street in Boston.[18] She made six deposits between July 3, 1872, and October 15, 1873. On April 3, 1874, she withdrew $268.05 and closed her account. Jane Smith's mother, Mrs. Deborah Randall, who lived on Oxford Street about a block from the bank, occasionally deposited money on Julia's behalf. Mrs. Randall told police Julia had consulted her about the prospect of buying a home in Hanover, but Mrs. Randall had dissuaded her from pursuing it.[19]

≈

On Tuesday, May 26, after interviewing Mrs. Smith and her daughter at Curtis' undertaking establishment, State Detectives Hollis C. Pinkham and Chase Philbrick and State Constable Napoleon Furnald suspected that James Henry Costley, Julia's employer, was involved in her death. The officers took a train to Hanover to conduct an investigation at the Howard House hotel, hoping to find Costley there.

Pinkham, age thirty-eight, and Philbrick, age fifty, were New Hampshire natives, Civil War veterans and experienced investigators. Furnald, age forty-five, was a native of Quincy, Massachusetts. Governor William Washburn appointed him to the State constabulary force in 1872.[20]

At about 1:00 p.m., the officers disembarked at the Hanover Branch Railroad's depot on Broadway. They engaged an open carriage at Randall's Livery and drove toward the Four Corners Village. Along the way, the men saw two women, Mrs. Harriet McLaughlin and Mrs. Adeline Lindsay, standing outside a home on Broadway and stopped to ask if they knew Mrs. Hawkes or Mr. James Costley. Mrs. McLaughlin told them she knew both and had spoken to Costley about an hour before. She directed the men to the hotel where Costley could be found.[21]

Pinkham, Philbrick and Furnald went to the Howard House hotel at Washington Street and Broadway. The old hotel had been in existence since 1797, when the owner, David Kingman, converted his

Constable Napoleon B. Furnald
(Courtesy of Thomas Crane
Public Library)

Howard House Hotel (Courtesy of Hanover Historical Society)

private residence into a lodging house. A number of other proprietors operated the hotel until August 12, 1870, when Franklin Howard purchased it from Elijah Barstow and named it the Howard House. In November 1872, Howard leased the hotel to Costley, who took over the business as the hotel manager. Costley paid Howard an annual rent of $475.00.[22]

Upon arriving at the Howard House, the officers found Costley packing a trunk. There were no other persons present at the hotel. They estimated him as between thirty-five and forty years of age, five feet eight inches in height, with a muscular build and dark complexion. He wore a beard and a moustache.

The officers asked Costley if Julia Hawkes had been in his employ and if so, had she left any trunks at the hotel. Costley told them Mrs. Hawkes had worked at the establishment until it closed after a furniture auction on May 1. Costley suggested she had gone "down east" to visit some friends the day before the auction. He said he had arranged, at Julia's request, to have her trunks shipped by train to Boston.[23]

Philbrick questioned Costley as to his whereabouts during the past month. Costley told him he had gone to Boston on Saturday, May 2 and returned to Hanover on May 4. He went to Boston again on May 6 when he accidentally encountered Julia Hawkes on Beach Street. He told Philbrick that when he saw her on that day, he gave her the baggage checks for the trunks he had shipped for her.

The officers noticed the hotel's unkempt condition. Pinkham brought this to Costley's attention during his questioning and Costley admitted nothing had been done at the hotel since Mrs. Hawkes' departure.

Examining the hotel more closely, the officers came upon a room in which traces of what appeared to be blood were evident on the walls, the door and the door latch. They also discovered a bloodstained towel in the corner of the room. They noticed someone had obviously made an attempt to clean an area on the floor, perhaps with the blood-stained towel. The officers immediately suspected Mrs. Hawkes had been shot at the hotel.[24]

In another small room, the officers found a pair of women's rubber overshoes. The officers surmised the shoes had belonged to Mrs.

Hawkes. The shoes were caked with mud that had not dried. Near the overshoes the officers found three handkerchiefs, one embossed with the initials, "J. H. C."

As the search progressed, the evidence against Costley began to mount. Constable Furnald lit a candle and explored a dark recess under a ladder leading to the attic. He found a clothes line, consistent in appearance with the rope found around the neck of Mrs. Hawkes. The rope's end showed evidence of having been recently cut.[25]

Near the end of the search, Costley asked the officers, "I suppose you're here in regard to the body found at Weymouth?" Detective Philbrick then said to him, "We shall have to take you into custody," and Costley replied, "Very well, gentlemen, but I should liked to have got away on the 4 o'clock train."[26] The officers searched him and found a wallet, (called a pocket-book at the time), containing $238.00, wrapped in a paper band marked, "Union Institution for Savings."[27] In his pockets, they discovered a pistol cartridge, a set of keys and a pocket knife. They found another cartridge in the room. Pinkham asked Costley if he owned a pistol. Costley told him he had bought one in Boston but had given it as a gift to Miss Sarah Cushing of Hanover, his fiancée. He said the cartridge was one of several the officers might find around the hotel. He told them the proprietor of the hotel, Franklin Howard, had brought them home from the service after the war.[28]

Detective Pinkham and Constable Furnald searched Costley's trunk and found three letters, two pocket handkerchiefs, a hand stamp (used for postal markings) and a bottle of ink. When Detective Philbrick took custody of the letters, Costley asked for them back. He said they were of a personal nature and had been written by his fiancée. Philbrick assured him if the letters were not important or material to the case he was investigating, he would be sure no improper use would be made of them.[29]

After the search, the officers secured the hotel with Costley's keys. They then escorted Costley by train to Plymouth where they jailed him on suspicion of murder pending a hearing in Plymouth County Court the following day.

≈

On Wednesday, May 27, Detective Pinkham and Constable Furnald appeared at Plymouth County Courthouse for Costley's hearing and arraignment. Court officers brought Costley before Justice Arthur Lord to answer a charge against him for the murder of Julia Hawkes on May 24, 1874. Costley entered a plea of not guilty and Judge Lord ordered Costley held without bail at Plymouth Jail. Detective Pinkham, without submitting any evidence before the court, requested a continuance of the case until Friday, June 5. Justice Lord granted the continuance and ordered all parties to appear at 11:00 a.m. on that date.[30]

Following Costley's appearance at court, Detective Pinkham and Constable Furnald proceeded to the Howard House to continue their investigation. The officers searched a shed attached to a barn on hotel property and found a tailor's goose on a dusty shelf. The goose, marked with the numerals, "88," perfectly matched the implement tied around the neck of Mrs. Hawkes. Next to the goose, the officers noticed an outline in the dust. Apparently, the goose they found had a mate that had been removed, leaving a matching imprint behind.[31]

In the same shed, the officers also found a linseed gunny bag, consistent in appearance and texture to the sack used to enclose the tailor's goose tied around Mrs. Hawkes' neck. The officers later learned that some time ago, railroad officials had hired a man to make roof repairs at the nearby Hanover railway station. The man had boarded at the Howard House during the course of his work. The man, referred to as "Brackett," had carried the sand and gravel needed to make the repairs in gunny bags similar to the bag found at the hotel. Police never considered Brackett a suspect.

The officers performed a more detailed examination inside the hotel and found an envelope addressed to Costley, stamped with a recent Boston postmark, in a stove pipe hole in the kitchen chimney. Pinkham and Furnald inspected the envelope's contents and found four pistol cartridges that matched those found on Costley the day before. The bullets in the cartridges were the same caliber as the bullet found imbedded in Mrs. Hawkes' brain.[32]

The officers seized the trunk Costley had been packing the day before and along with all the other evidence they had found in the hotel that day, took it back to Chief Boynton's office at state police headquarters in Boston.

≈

On Thursday, May 28, the state's Chief Constable, George Washington Boynton, Detectives Pinkham, Philbrick and Constable Furnald visited Costley in the Plymouth Jail. They questioned Costley with regard to his whereabouts during the past month and tried, in vain, to get a confession from him. He expressed sympathy about Mrs. Hawkes' death, but denied any involvement. Costley repeated his story of May 26 about his visits to Boston and his encounter on May 6 with Mrs. Hawkes on Beach Street in Boston.

The officers asked him if he owned any horses. Costley told them he had owned several, but sold them when he auctioned his hotel property on May 1. When asked if he had hired any recently, Costley said he hadn't. The officers inquired if Costley owned any carriage robes and he said he had owned several, but had sold them to a peddler. Pinkham showed Costley the robe taken from Mrs. Hawkes' body. Costley said, "That's my robe," but quickly retracted his statement and remarked, "No, that don't look quite like mine, the stripes are different."[33]

Pinkham showed Costley the gunny sack found at the hotel and asked him if he recognized it. Costley said he had seen similar bags at the hotel. He told Pinkham a man named Brackett had done some roofing on his hotel and had left them there.

Probing further into his movements, the officers asked Costley if he had traveled to Boston anytime after seeing Mrs. Hawkes on May 6. He told them he had only gone there on two other occasions. He said on the first occasion, he had stayed at a hotel called the Jefferson House at 18 North Street on May 9 and May 10 and returned to Hanover on May 11. He believed he had registered his name at the hotel. He stayed in Hanover until the sixteenth, when he went to Boston and took a train to New York. He told the investigators he had stayed at the Metropolitan Hotel in New York City and returned to Hanover on Tuesday, May 19.[34]

≈

As Costley continued to make his way through the criminal justice system, investigators remained hard at work investigating Costley's background and his steps up to the days prior to the murder. Chief Constable Boynton also assigned a squad of detectives and constables to interview friends of Mrs. Hawkes to ascertain her movements up until the day of her death. He directed them to develop more information on evidence found at the crime scene in Braintree.

Constable Furnald spent considerable time in Hanover interviewing persons familiar with Costley. He learned many people liked and respected him. Most felt confident the police had arrested the wrong man and Costley would be vindicated.

Furnald learned Costley had first arrived in Hanover around 1870. Costley had immediately secured work as a laborer on the farm of Mr. Stetson. After a short time, Franklin Howard, owner of the Howard House, hired Costley to work in the hotel's stable. Before long, Howard had Costley working inside the hotel as a waiter and bartender and provided him with room and board during his employ. Costley had eventually taken control of the hotel when he leased it from Howard in 1872.[35] Costley apparently spent time in social circles and had become involved in the Phoenix Masonic Lodge in Hanover's Four Corners. Residents told Furnald Costley had been seeing a local girl, Miss Sarah E. Cushing, for a considerable time and they were allegedly engaged to marry. Cushing was the daughter of a wealthy sea captain, John Cushing, who died in 1871. She lived with her mother on Church Street near Four Corners and had inherited a substantial amount of property upon the death of her father. Cushing refused to believe Costley was guilty of the murder, or for that matter, any crime. She was deeply in love with him and was determined to marry him.

≈

As Furnald and other investigators spent more time in Hanover, they heard a story about another housekeeper employed by Costley at the hotel who had mysteriously died the previous December. Townspeople suggested Mrs. Love Congdon, a thirty-five year-old divorcee from

Hyannis, had welcomed the attentions of Costley and eventually had an affair with him.

On the night of December 28, 1873, Mrs. Congdon retired for the evening at the hotel and the next morning was found dead in her bedroom. Her sudden demise raised questions, as she had displayed no indications of illness or discomfort the night before.

Eben Waterman, a Justice of the Peace in Hanover, called a coroner's jury and held an inquest into Mrs. Congdon's death. Waterman summoned a number of witnesses. Among these were Julia Hawkes and James Costley. Jurors questioned Costley about his knowledge of the circumstances surrounding the death. Mrs. Hawkes, then a cook at the hotel, corroborated Costley's testimony. Townspeople in Hanover believed Mrs. Hawkes' testimony allayed suspicion about the death and prevented a post-mortem examination of Mrs. Congdon's body. Residents told Furnald that Mrs. Hawkes, after her testimony, "shed tears copiously and otherwise acted very strangely."[36]

The jury rendered a verdict that "death had been caused by poison administered by her own or another's hand." No autopsy had been conducted for purposes of deliberation, which residents found odd. Many believed a thorough medical examination of Mrs. Congdon's remains could have confirmed or refuted evidence of foul play.

Hanover officials filed a death record for Mrs. Congdon shortly after the inquest. The town clerk recorded Mrs. Congdon's name as Love M. Fondell*, aged thirty-five, a married female residing in Hanover who was born to John Fondell in Lebanon, New Hampshire. The document reflected her cause of death as "colic."[37] Colic is a condition of acute abdominal pain caused by poisoning and may result in death.

---

*Note: A review of civil records in Massachusetts suggests Mrs. Congdon's maiden name was Fernald. It is possible the Hanover clerk recorded the name as he heard it, i.e., "Fondell" as opposed to "Fernald." Or perhaps the informant on the death record provided him with the incorrect spelling. It was common knowledge among those who knew her in Hanover that Mrs. Congdon was separated or divorced from her husband. Perhaps this clarifies the use of her maiden name, but still leaves unexplained why the clerk listed her as married on the record.

Love Congdon grew up in Barnstable and lived with her parents, John and Elizabeth Fernald, and her two sisters, Belinda and Maria.[38] On August 15, 1855, when she was 16 years of age, Love married Francis Congdon, a twenty-two year-old Rhode Island native and fisherman.[39] After the birth of their daughter, Agnes, in Barnstable in

1856, Francis and Love Congdon moved to Easton, Massachusetts. By 1870, the couple had returned to Barnstable and shortly thereafter, Francis and Love separated. In 1873, Love obtained employment at Howard House as a domestic until her death the same year.

≈

As Furnald continued his investigation, he learned that during his brief tenure as the hotel lessee, Costley had been found in violation of the state liquor laws. Plymouth County deputy constables George Pratt and Uriah McCoy had cited Costley on more than one occasion for illegally providing distilling liquors on the hotel premises. During one search of the hotel police discovered a surreptitious device designed to dispense liquor without notice. Costley apparently carried on a large "bottle trade" on the premises. Costley had placed a large barrel full of ardent spirits on a staging between the hotel stable and a shed. He inserted a tube into the barrel, buried the tube along the ground and behind partitions, and then threaded it through the hotel's exterior wall and under a broad shelf in the pantry. The tube was inserted into a pipe to which was attached a nozzle small enough to fit inside a bottle. Over the pipe, and coming just flush with the top of the shelf, was the handle of a stop-cock.

Costley placed a pail containing white beans that had a hole in the bottom of it over the stop-cock. The beans would fall from the bottom if an unsuspecting or unauthorized person lifted it. This would naturally cause the person to put the pail down, while a person familiar with the setup would gently push the pail to one side along the shelf, disclosing the stop-cock without disturbing the beans.[40]

Constable Furnald initiated an inquiry into Costley's assertion that he did not own a horse and had not rented a horse and carriage around the time of the murder. Furnald canvassed stables in Hanover,

Weymouth, Braintree and Quincy and had no success in finding a person who could confirm a team rental by Costley, nor could he verify that Costley owned a horse.

Furnald interviewed Miss Mary A. McCurdy who told Furnald she first met Mrs. Hawkes in August 1873. She informed Furnald she had last seen her at the Hanover depot on April 30, 1874 with two trunks. She watched Mrs. Hawkes board the 4:00 p.m. train.[41]

While Constable Furnald continued his probe in Hanover, State Detective Christopher Bailey followed up with Mrs. Smith and her sisters to trace Mrs. Hawkes' footsteps prior to her death and to uncover the reasons for her trip to Boston after leaving Wollaston Heights. Mrs. Smith recounted once again how Mrs. Hawkes had visited with her in Wollaston Heights between the fifth and the eighth of May. She told Bailey Mrs. Hawkes had left for Boston on the 11:00 a.m. train on the eighth.

Bailey determined Mrs. Hawkes had called on the Daniel B. Stedman family on Savin Hill Avenue in Dorchester on Monday, May 11. Mrs. Hawkes had been a maid in the Stedman household for seven years. Stedman was a wealthy crockery importer with several stores in Boston proper. Detective Philbrick visited Mrs. Stedman who told him Julia entrusted her financial affairs to her, leaving several bank books in her care. Inspecting the documents, Philbrick noted a withdrawal of $268.05 by Mrs. Hawkes from the Union Institution for Savings at 37 Bedford Street in Boston on April 3, 1874.[42] Costley possessed a packet of bills in the amount of $238.00 bound in a Union Institution for Savings paper band at the time of his arrest. Detectives later verified Mrs. Hawkes' account activity through bank records.

Bailey went to 109 Albany Street, Boston, to interview Michael Flanagan, one of the persons who had identified Mrs. Hawkes' body. Flanagan told Bailey he was a friend of Julia Hawkes and he had seen her on May 11 when she stopped by his home for a visit with his mother. He hadn't seen her since that day.

The detective went to Oxford Street to interview Mrs. Deborah Randall and her daughter, Joanna. He was able to determine that on Tuesday, May 12, Mrs. Hawkes stopped by Mrs. Randall's home on

Oxford Street, near Beach Street. Mrs. Randall, Jane Smith's mother, lived there with her daughter, Joanna. While there visiting, Mrs. Hawkes told the Randall women she needed to shop for a thimble and left the house. She did not return. Mrs. Hawkes had told the women she was boarding at "a friend's house at the South End."[43]

The women told Detective Bailey that Mrs. Hawkes had seemed dejected and anxious, not her usual buoyant and happy self.[44] She had told them that when Costley closed the hotel in Hanover, he had arranged temporary employment for her in Weymouth Landing. She told them of his plans to eventually open a hotel in Oregon and how he had asked her to accompany him on this new venture, along with his brother.[45]

Bailey learned from the women the "friend's house" was located at 63 Camden Street, on the edge of Roxbury. Bailey went to the house and met the proprietor, Mrs. Mary A. Day, the wife of Boston Police officer James Day. When he asked Mrs. Day about Mrs. Hawkes, she confirmed Mrs. Hawkes had boarded at the address for nearly two weeks. She said a man named James Costley had appeared at her door on Monday, April 27, and had asked to engage a room until June 1 for a lady friend. He told Mrs. Day the woman had lost her position and room at her last place of employment and needed accommodations until she had secured a new situation. He explained to Mrs. Day the woman had friends in Boston, but she didn't want to reveal her whereabouts to them, at least temporarily.[46]

Before agreeing to Costley's request, Mrs. Day asked for a form of reference. Costley produced a flyer advertising the auction at the Hanover Howard House on May 1, telling her he was the manager of the hotel and a legitimate business man. Satisfied with Costley's explanations, Mrs. Day handed him a room key after Costley paid her a one week advance of $2.00 for the room. Costley told Mrs. Day he would persuade Mrs. Hawkes not to bring her trunks or at least maybe a small one, as the room was at the top of a long flight of stairs. Mrs. Hawkes arrived on May 1 with the key and her belongings and stayed until May 13. Mrs. Day never saw her again after that date.[47]

Mrs. Day rented another room at the house to Miss Minnie Arbuckle. Investigators learned that Miss Arbuckle had moved from Boston to Chicago. When they located her, Miss Arbuckle told them she had first met Julia on May 2 at the rooming house on Camden Street. She remembered James Costley had stopped by the boarding house on three separate occasions between May 2 and May 13 to visit Julia at her room.

Miss Arbuckle informed investigators that on May 13 she and Julia left their rooms on Camden Street and walked along Washington Street to Chester Park in Boston's South End. During their stroll, Julia had told Miss Arbuckle she was going to Weymouth Landing that evening for several months.[48] They departed company at about 5:15 p.m. Miss Arbuckle remembered Julia had worn a bonnet and cloak, a brown and black skirt and Newport tie shoes on that day. It was the last time she saw Julia.[49] Police never recovered a cloak or bonnet during the crime scene search in the days following the discovery of Julia's body.

≈

Investigators gathered at police headquarters to compare notes and review the case. Based on Costley's movements within Boston, they decided to concentrate their efforts on locating a livery near Camden Street or the hotel where Costley had claimed he had stayed. After interviews with several stable owners, the detectives finally located a livery at 9 Van Rensselaer Place, where stablemen confirmed Costley had hired a team. Riedell's Stable was located around the corner from the Creighton House, 245 Tremont Street, where detectives later determined Costley had rented a room on May 9 while in the company of a woman. Costley signed the hotel register as "J. H. Costello and wife, Duxbury, MA."[50] Police suspected that Julia Hawkes was the woman who had accompanied Costley that evening.

This information discredited a statement made by Costley during an interview with police at the Plymouth Jail on May 28. During the interrogation, Costley had told investigators he had stayed at the Jefferson House on May 9 and May 10.

Detective Pinkham interviewed the stable owner, James A. Riedell, as well as Riedell's employees, Joseph Neas, Frank Wills and James

Spillane. Pinkham showed the men a photograph of Costley and asked if they recognized him. All of them identified him and Riedell told Pinkham the man had given the name James Costley and had hired a bay horse and piano box buggy on May 9, saying he wanted to take the team to Weymouth Landing.[51] Riedell told Pinkham Costley returned with the team at about midnight. Costley left two valises at the stable with Joseph Neas and told the stableman he'd retrieve them when he returned later. Several of the stablemen told Pinkham they had lifted both bags and found one to be unusually heavy.[52]

At about 6:30 p.m. on Wednesday, May 13, Costley returned to the livery alone and reclaimed the two valises. He asked for another team and requested a quiet horse. He told Riedell he intended to take the buggy to Weymouth Landing and expected to return at about midnight. Riedell harnessed a dark bay horse to a square box buggy for Costley.[53] As Frank Wills, the foreman at the stable, lifted the heavy valise into the buggy he said to Costley, "What have you got in here, gold?" Costley replied, "I wish it was."[54] After both valises had been placed into the buggy, he drove away just before 7:00 p.m.

At about 1:00 a.m., Thursday, Costley returned the horse and buggy. At 5:00 a.m., James Spillane, an employee at Riedell's stable, began to clean out Costley's rented carriage and found a ladies shoe and a new claw hammer on the floor. Riedell turned both articles over to Pinkham. Pinkham noted the shoe bore striking similarities to the footwear worn by the murdered woman when her body was discovered. He also noticed the hammer was new and wrapped in paper from the Thomas B. Barnes Hardware Store in Boston. Pinkham later visited the hardware store and spoke with the manager, Justin Harris, who told Pinkham he had sold a .22 caliber pistol there on April 27.[55]

At about 10:00 a.m. the same Thursday, May 14, Costley appeared at Mrs. Day's boarding house. He had the key to Julia's room. He told Mrs. Day he had come for Julia's belongings. Mrs. Day accompanied him to the room and helped him pack a small bag. She found a bottle of hair oil on a bureau and presented it to Costley for packing. He told Mrs. Day it wasn't necessary stating, "Oh, no, she won't want that." Mrs. Day also found a night dress and when she showed it to Costley, he told her not to bother with it. She pressed Costley to take the item. Finally, Costley said, "Well if you insist on it, put it in."[56] He then left the house with the effects.

Once again, Costley was caught in a lie. During his interview by police on May 28 Costley said he had stayed in Boston from May 9 through May 11 when he returned to Hanover. He stated he had not returned to the city until May 16 when he took a train from Boston to New York.

≈

On June 4, 1874, Coroner White summoned a jury of inquest to investigate and determine the facts of the tragedy. Under Massachusetts law at that time, the coroner possessed the same power as a judicial officer. He was empowered to compel the attendance of jurors and any person whom he believed had knowledge relating to the death he was investigating.

The verdict of the jurors, after deliberation, carried the same weight as a grand jury indictment and empowered the coroner to issue a warrant for the arrest of an accused person, unless he was already in custody. Since Costley was confined to Plymouth Jail, the law required a grand jury indictment before trial proceedings against him commenced.

After careful consideration, Coroner White selected Elias Richards, Albion Hall, Henry Gardner, Phillips Curtis, Dr. Alexander G. Nye and Thomas South, all residents of Norfolk County, as jurors. He swore the members of the jury and began the inquisition with the presentation of evidence and the testimony of witnesses. All of the jurors had viewed and examined the body of the deceased at the engine house on May 24. They had inspected her clothing and made note of the shoe and earring she wore, as well as the impression made by a missing ring on her left hand.[57]

Jurors heard the testimony of witnesses acquainted with Mrs. Hawkes, persons who found and retrieved the body from the river and the physicians who conducted the autopsy. State constables also testified before the jury and presented the evidence they had gathered during their investigation of the crime.

Coroner White, upon completion of testimony and the introduction of evidence, instructed the jurors in the laws of the Commonwealth and dismissed them to deliberate upon the facts presented.

≈

On Friday, June 5, deputy sheriffs assigned to the Plymouth Jail brought Costley to Plymouth County Court. A large crowd of onlookers gathered at the court house hoping to get a glimpse of the prisoner.

At 11:00 a.m., Costley appeared with counsel before Justice Arthur Lord. Detective Pinkham, acting under instructions from District Attorney Asa French, asked the court for a one week continuance on the matter. Counsel for the defense made no objections and Judge Lord scheduled a further hearing for Saturday, June 13 at 11:00 a.m.[58]

DA French expected a decision from the coroner's jury within days and did not want to proceed with his case until the inquest concluded. He also needed more time for his investigators to collect evidence. French already knew that investigators no longer believed that Costley had committed the murder at Hanover in Plymouth County. He planned to prosecute Costley in Norfolk County, where the body was found. This would necessitate the dismissal of the complaint against Costley in Plymouth County and the issuance of a new complaint in Norfolk County.

On Saturday, June 6, the jury of inquest informed Coroner White of their verdict. "That the said Julia Hawkes came to her death on the night of the thirteenth of May last past, by means of a pistol ball willfully discharged from a pistol through her brain; and the jurors further say that upon the evidence before them they believe that James Henry Costley of Hanover, MA, is guilty of the murder of the said Julia Hawkes."[59] The jurors also believed that Costley had committed the murder somewhere between Braintree and Weymouth in Norfolk County.

As scheduled, Costley appeared at Plymouth court on Saturday, June 13, before Trial Justice Lord. Jailor Captain A. K. Harmon brought Costley into court and placed him in a dock in the Probate Court room, as the Criminal Court room was not available. The courtroom was packed with spectators.

Detectives Pinkham and Philbrick requested that Justice Lord dismiss the complaint against Costley. Justice Lord, not hearing any further evidence from the officers, complied with their request and discharged Costley. People in attendance watched in bewilderment as Costley and Detective Philbrick rose to leave the courtroom. What the onlookers didn't know was that the detectives, anticipating dismissal of the murder charge by the Plymouth County court and prior to Costley's arraignment there, had sought an arrest warrant for Costley from Justice Everett C. Bumpus at the Eastern Norfolk District Court in Quincy. Detective Pinkham approached Costley, put his hand on his shoulder and said, "Mr. Costley, in the name of the Commonwealth and by virtue of this warrant I arrest you on the charge of murder and shall proceed to take you to Norfolk County." According to a *Weymouth Gazette* reporter, "Costley's eyes dropped and his face showed mental discomposure."[60]

The officers boarded a 3:55 p.m. train and escorted Costley to Quincy where they turned him over to court officials. Justice Bumpus entered the courtroom and the clerk read the complaint against Costley. Costley, represented by Baylies Sanford, Esq., a former Bristol County district attorney, listened attentively and when asked if he was guilty or not guilty of the charge against him, he replied in a distinct tone that he was innocent. Sanford waived any further examination and Justice Bumpus committed Costley to Dedham Jail pending the action of the Norfolk County Superior Criminal Court Grand Jury. District Attorney Asa French represented the Commonwealth at the arraignment.[61]

≈

On September 10, 1874, the Norfolk County Grand Jury returned an indictment against James Henry Costley for the murder of Julia Hawkes. The indictment charged the murder had been committed in Braintree and the weapon used had been a pistol, the ball of which entered Mrs. Hawkes' head and caused a mortal wound. Justice Putnam, accepting the indictment, scheduled further action at the Massachusetts Supreme Judicial Court for trial on the capital crime.[62]

≈

State detectives continued their investigation of Costley and his movements before and after the murder of Mrs. Hawkes on May 13. Although the evidence presented to the Grand Jury was sufficient for an indictment, the state prosecutor needed insurmountable evidence to secure a conviction at trial. Detectives interviewed hundreds of persons to uncover the slightest detail of damaging testimony or evidence helpful to the case.

Investigators learned Costley had registered for a room at the Jefferson House, 18 North Street, Boston, between 1:00 a.m. and 2:00 a.m. on May 14, shortly after returning the horse and buggy to Riedell's stable. Hotel manager Joseph Flatley produced the hotel register and pointed to a signature by "John H. Costley, Hanover, MA," on the date in question.[63] Once again, Costley's statements to investigators at Plymouth Jail were refuted. Costley had told them he had not been in Boston between May 11 and May 16.

≈

Detectives were in a quandary as to the whereabouts of two russet-colored trunks owned by Mrs. Hawkes that Costley allegedly shipped on her behalf. A witness in Hanover had seen her at the Hanover depot on April 30 with two trunks. The witness said Mrs. Hawkes had left for Boston on the 4:00 p.m. train.

Detectives went to the Old Colony Depot in Boston where they met Charles Everdean, baggage master. Everdean told investigators he had received two russet-colored "Saratoga" trunks from Hanover on May 4. On May 14, Everdean released the trunks to express man Daniel Lynch, who presented the two baggage checks for the luggage.

Police located Lynch at the corner of Court and Brattle Streets, Boston, where he had a stand. Lynch told the officers he went to the Old Colony Depot on May 14 after being engaged by Peter Warner of Dow's Stable at 20-22 Portland Street. Warner gave Lynch two baggage checks and asked him to pick up two trunks at the depot and bring them back to the stable. Lynch retrieved the trunks and returned them to Warner.

When the officers spoke with Peter Warner at Dow's, they learned Costley had visited the stable on the morning of May 14. Warner told them Costley appeared with two baggage checks, which he gave to Warner, and asked Warner to have someone pick up the two trunks at the Old Colony depot, bring them back to the stable, and store them until Costley returned for them. Warner then hired Lynch to retrieve the bags.

On May 16, Warner released the bags to Cornelius Sullivan, another express man. When police contacted Sullivan, he told them James Costley had approached him at about 6:00 p.m. on May 16 and had hired him to pick up two trunks at Dow's and transport them to the Boston and Albany depot. He informed the officers Costley had accompanied him to the stable. After loading the trunks on his wagon, he and Costley drove to the depot. During the ride, Costley told Sullivan he was boarding a train to New York the same night.[64] Sullivan unloaded the trunks at the depot and Costley took them inside. Sullivan never mentioned a black valise, but police later suspected Costley had the valise in which he had kept the robe, goose and rope had placed it inside one of the trunks after he entered the depot.

≈

Prosecutors considered several motives for the murder of Mrs. Hawkes, but settled on the two they felt were the most plausible. The first motive centered on the death of Mrs. Love Congdon. Although

District Attorney Asa French
(Courtesy of Braintree Historical Society)

officials lacked evidence to prove that the death of Mrs. Congdon in December 1873 was a homicide, questions still lingered. Norfolk County District Attorney Asa French and Massachusetts Attorney General Charles R. Train speculated her demise had been at the hands of Costley. Perhaps Mrs. Hawkes had some knowledge about the crime that would implicate Costley. Maybe Mrs. Hawkes had promised to keep Costley's role secret, but Costley feared she would reveal the facts and expose him and so had to eliminate Mrs. Hawkes.

A second theory was that Costley had made a promise of marriage to Mrs. Hawkes but had reconsidered the proposal when he recognized the pecuniary advantages of marrying the wealthy Sarah Cushing. Mrs. Hawkes' refusal to break her engagement placed her in a perilous position. Costley became determined to marry Miss Cushing and Mrs. Hawkes stood in his way. Only by eliminating Mrs. Hawkes could Costley realize his selfish interests.

Train and French believed this motive was the most plausible. They believed Costley had taken Mrs. Hawkes from the South End boarding house to Weymouth, a distance of about eleven miles, and had stopped at a secluded site along the route where, under the cover of darkness, he coaxed her from the carriage and shot her. Constable Furnald later theorized the most isolated area and probable murder location was "… just over the town line of Hingham, between Nash's Corner, Weymouth, and Queen Anne's Corner."[65] Although there were no witnesses to the crime, both prosecutors felt the circumstantial evidence gathered by investigators provided more than enough proof for a first degree murder conviction against Costley.

≈

By Monday, December 28, 1874, the first day of trial, the prosecution team was prepared to present the case before the Supreme Judicial Court's special session in Dedham with the testimony of sixty witnesses and numerous evidentiary exhibits. The court ordered that all witnesses remain outside the courtroom until called to testify. No witness was allowed to overhear the testimony of another, nor was a witness allowed to discuss his/her testimony with other witnesses.

The courtroom was overflowing with spectators. At about 10 o'clock, Justices John Wells and Charles Devens entered the court room.

Justice John Wells was born in Rowe, Massachusetts in 1819 and graduated from Williams College in 1838. He studied law at Harvard Law School and was admitted to the Franklin County, Massachusetts, bar in 1841. He was appointed to the Massachusetts Supreme Judicial Court in 1866.[66]

Justice Charles Devens was born in Charlestown, Massachusetts in 1820. He graduated from Harvard in 1838 and was also admitted to the Franklin County bar in 1841. Justice Devens served in the Union Army during the Civil War and was engaged in some of the most significant battles of the struggle. He was brevetted Major General in 1865 and was mustered out in 1866. In 1867, the governor of Massachusetts appointed him to the Superior Court and in 1873, to the Supreme Judicial Court. He left the bench in 1877 to accept an appointment as Attorney General of the United States under President Rutherford B. Hayes.[67]

Attorney General Charles Russell Train was born in Framingham, Massachusetts in 1817. He graduated from Brown University in 1837, studied law in Cambridge and was admitted to the Suffolk County bar in 1841. He held various political offices between 1847 and 1871 and became Attorney General of Massachusetts in 1872.[68]

District Attorney Asa French was born in Braintree, Massachusetts in 1829 and graduated from Yale in 1851. He received a bachelor of laws degree from Harvard Law School in 1853. After he was admitted to the bar in the Supreme Court of New York at Albany in 1853, he returned to Boston where he set up a practice. In 1870 Massachusetts Governor Claflin appointed him as District Attorney for Norfolk and Plymouth Counties.[69]

As in the case against Seth Perry, the Supreme Judicial Court still maintained judicial authority and responsibility for trying capital cases, but several changes in court procedure had occurred since that time and prior to Costley's trial. Perry's trial was heard before three justices in 1845. In 1872, the legislature amended the law so that only two justices of the Supreme Judicial Court were required to preside over capital trials.[70]

Jurors were compelled in Perry's trial to decide whether Perry, if guilty, had committed murder or the lesser crime of manslaughter. In 1858, the Massachusetts legislature enacted a statute that changed the definition of murder by dividing it into two degrees. An offense committed with "deliberately premeditated malice aforethought, or in the commission of, or attempt to commit, any crime punishable with death or imprisonment for life; or committed with extreme atrocity or cruelty" constituted murder in the first degree. A murder that did not meet the definition of first-degree murder was second-degree murder. The new law directed that the jury decide the degree of murder. If the crime did not include the elements of murder in the first and second degrees, then jurors might consider a conviction of manslaughter. The punishment for a conviction of first-degree murder was death. Second-degree murder carried a penalty of life imprisonment.[71]

Another important procedural change came about in 1866 when the legislature passed a law that allowed a defendant to testify on his or her own behalf. If the defendant did not testify, a jury could make no presumption as to his or her guilt.[72]

During Perry's trial, he was permitted, as a capital defendant, the right to a limited number of peremptory challenges based on no more than "sudden impressions and unaccountable prejudices we are apt to conceive upon the bare looks and gestures of another."[73] The law, enacted in 1836, also allowed Perry the right to challenge prospective jurors for cause in order to uncover and eliminate those who held biases against him, the prosecution, or the case. The law also required the trial judge to excuse a potential juror for cause if he opposed the death penalty. This system of challenges allowed for the empanelment of a "death qualified" jury, or a jury in which capital punishment opponents had been purged.[74]

In 1845 the law prohibited prosecutors from challenging prospective jurors peremptorily. The law required that the prosecutor establish a legitimate reason, or cause, before he could eliminate a potential juror. In 1869, new legislation allowed prosecutors a limited number of peremptory challenges in capital cases. A prosecutor could now strike a prospective juror if he merely suspected the individual might acquit the defendant based on some real or supposed predisposition.[75]

The legislature made no changes in the defendant's right to peremptory challenges and challenges for cause. The law still required the court to challenge a potential juror for cause to discover whether the person had "conscientious scruples or such opinion on the subject of capital punishment as to preclude him from finding a defendant guilty."[76]

Attorney General Train and District Attorney Asa French immediately moved for trial. It was common during the late 19th century for the state's attorney general, in concert with the county district attorney, to prosecute murder cases.

Attorneys Baylies Sanford and Horace Cheney represented the defendant. Sanford was born on Cape Cod at Dennis, Massachusetts in 1825. He studied at Amherst Academy, Amherst, Massachusetts, and was admitted to the Massachusetts bar at Taunton in 1851. He practiced law in Taunton from 1851 until 1860 and was District Attorney for the Southern District of Massachusetts from 1859 to 1860. He left Massachusetts in 1860 to practice law in New York City where he remained until his return to Massachusetts in 1869.[77]

Horace Cheney was born in Parsonsfield, Maine in 1844, the son of Oren Cheney, founder of Bates College. Cheney graduated from Bates in 1865 and from Harvard Law School in 1868. He tutored at Bates College for a time and later pursued the study of law. Before setting up his own law practice, Cheney, for a brief period, was an assistant district attorney in Suffolk County.[78]

Jury empanelment was the first order of business for the court. When defense counsel, the prosecution and the court completed their challenges, the twelve jurors who were selected took their places in the jury box. Among the jurors were five farmers, a house painter, a carpenter, two laborers, an auctioneer, a grocer, and a business man. Justice Wells then summoned District Attorney Asa French to address the court with his opening statement. French summarized the details of the case and the court recessed until 1:00 p.m.

During the afternoon session, DA French called Alexander White, Thomas South and John Bates to describe how they found the body. Coroner George White then testified as to the condition of the body and the results of his examination. Drs. Forsaith and Tinkham were the next witnesses and they revealed the results of their autopsy. Counsel for Costley cross-examined each witness to solicit contradictive or exculpatory testimony.

The last witness on the first day was Mrs. Jane Smith who described her relationship with Mrs. Hawkes and shared her knowledge of Mrs. Hawkes' movements prior to her death. DA French introduced a russet-colored Saratoga trunk with "J.H. Costley" written across it and asked Mrs. Smith if she recognized it. Mrs. Smith told the court the trunk belonged to Mrs. Hawkes. She also identified a comb found inside the trunk as Mrs. Hawkes' property. The court allowed DA French's request to mark the trunk and comb as evidence. DA French showed Mrs. Smith several articles of clothing, including the Newport tie shoes, and asked her to identify them. Mrs. Smith told French the items looked like clothing worn by Julia Hawkes the last time she saw her. The clothing was also marked as evidence. The court then adjourned until 9:00 a.m. the next day.[79]

≈

On the second day of trial, Mrs. Smith completed her direct testimony. Attorney Sanford conducted an extensive cross-examination of Mrs. Smith, focusing on Mrs. Hawkes' clothing, the trunk and the personal effects found in it. The defense gained nothing helpful during this questioning.

Mrs. Smith's sister, Margaret Garibaldi, testified next and told the court when she had last seen Julia and described the clothing she had been wearing at that time. She was followed by her sister, Elizabeth Fillebrown, Michael Flanagan, Mary McCurdy and Mrs. Deborah Randall. All testified as to their relationship with Mrs. Hawkes and what she was wearing the last time they had seen her. DA French presented the clothing previously marked as evidence during Mrs. Smith's testimony to each witness and all identified the clothing as the same attire Mrs. Hawkes had been wearing the last time they saw her.

Miss Joanna Randall, another of Mrs. Smith's sisters with whom Julia Hawkes occasionally boarded, testified about her knowledge of Julia's two trunks and the personal effects they contained. The DA showed her the russet-colored Saratoga trunk that had been previously identified by her sister, Jane Smith. She identified it as belonging to Mrs. Hawkes. She also identified the contents, including a comb she had given to Mrs. Hawkes. Miss Randall was the seventh witness to identify the clothing previously introduced as evidence as belonging to Mrs. Hawkes. Mrs. Deborah Randall, mother of Joanna, corroborated her daughter's testimony and also identified the trunk as belonging to Mrs. Hawkes.

Mrs. Mary Day, owner of the boarding house at 63 Camden Street, provided the court with important testimony regarding Costley and his appearance on May 14 to collect Mrs. Hawkes' property. Mrs. Day told the court that Costley had the key to Julia's room. Costley's remarks to her that Mrs. Hawkes "wouldn't want" personal items left in the room proved damaging to Costley.[80]

The court recessed until the afternoon when Mrs. Day returned to the witness stand to testify about her confrontation with Costley when she appeared before the Norfolk County Grand Jury. Mrs. Day related that when she saw Costley she said, "How do you do?" Costley replied, "You have the advantage of me." Mrs. Day responded, "Don't you remember Mrs. Day of Camden Street?" Costley answered, "I don't know Mrs. Day and I don't know where Camden Street is."[81]

The government called Miss Sarah Cushing to testify. She was not in the court room. Dr. Woodbridge R. Howes and Dr. John O. French, both of Hanover, appeared on her behalf and told the court Miss Cushing was unable to appear due to "continued mental excitement and neuralgia pains in the spine." The doctors told the court that if Miss Cushing traveled from Hanover to Dedham it might endanger her life. DA French advised the court that the government intended to request a capias warrant if Miss Cushing continued to disregard the court's summons to appear. (A judge may order a capias warrant [from the Latin, to seize] for the arrest of a person who refuses to appear in court.)

The government summoned Miss Minnie Arbuckle to the stand. Miss Arbuckle testified about her acquaintances with Mrs. Hawkes and the defendant. She told the court she had met Mrs. Hawkes at the rooming house on Camden Street on May 2 and last saw her at 5:15 p.m. on May 13 in the South End of Boston. She met Costley several times when he visited Mrs. Hawkes in her room. During a walk on that evening, Mrs. Hawkes had told her she was going to Weymouth Landing for two weeks and if Costley should come to Camden Street for her things, to let him have them. She described the clothing Mrs. Hawkes wore on May 13. Her description was consistent with the clothing worn by Mrs. Hawkes the day her body was found in East Braintree. When DA French presented the witness with the apparel and Newport tie shoes previously identified and marked as evidence, she recognized them immediately as part of the ensemble worn by Mrs. Hawkes on May 13.

James Riedell, owner of the stable where Costley had rented a horse and buggy on May 9 and May 13, testified as to his knowledge of Costley's actions and remarks on both occasions. He also testified about the lady's shoe and hammer found in the carriage Costley had rented. His testimony was followed by stablemen in his employ who corroborated Riedell's statements. All of the witnesses identified the "Newport tie" shoe and the hammer presented to them in court.

Employees of Dow's stable on Portland Street, Boston, testified that on May 14, Costley appeared at the stable and asked that someone pick up two trunks at the Old Colony railroad depot, return them to the stable, and store them there until a future date. One of the employees, John Brown, testified Costley had paid him for the trunk storage.

Cornelius Sullivan, express man, was asked if the Saratoga trunk bearing Costley's name, which had been previously entered as evidence, was one of the trunks he had transported with Costley from Dow's stable to the Boston and Albany Depot on May 16. Sullivan told the court he believed it was one of them.

Testimony concluded with direct and cross-examination of the Creighton House hotel clerk, George A. Balch, and Jefferson House hotel clerk Joseph P. Flatley. Balch confirmed Costley's registration at his hotel on May 9 and Flatley swore to Costley's registration at the Jefferson House on May 14.[82]

≈

The third day of trial began with a motion by Attorney General Train to compel Miss Cushing's attendance and testimony. Train requested the court appoint a Boston physician to visit Miss Cushing in Hanover and diagnose her condition and capability. The court allowed Train's request and sent Dr. F. S. Ainsworth to Hanover.

Meanwhile, John Burke, owner of Burke's Saloon, 176 Tremont Street, testified Costley had been in his establishment on May 13 and left a black valise and umbrella there. Three days later, on May 16, Costley returned to the bar, in the company of Cornelius Sullivan, express man, and retrieved the valise, but left the umbrella. Another employee at the saloon, John Kalbskopl, corroborated Burke's testimony.

The prosecution next summoned three expert witnesses to testify about Costley's handwriting. Each compared Costley's signature on the hotel registers with a known sample of Costley's handwriting and verified the signatures were in Costley's hand. DA French showed handwriting expert George A. Sawyer the Saratoga trunk previously identified by several witnesses as belonging to Mrs. Hawkes. On the trunk was written, "J. H. Costley." Sawyer testified the signature on the trunk was written by the same hand that had signed the hotel registers.

Franklin Howard, proprietor of Howard House, was called to identify letters written to him by Costley while Costley was incarcerated. James H. Williams, a photographer from the Hanover area, testified he and Costley had practiced their signatures at the Howard House on a number of occasions. DA French presented the witness with Costley's letters to Howard and he testified that the signatures and handwriting on the letters were Costley's.

The prosecutors turned their attention to the "Newport tie" shoe found in the carriage returned by Costley to Riedell's stable on May 14. Investigators had been able to track down the man who made Mrs. Hawkes' shoes. Jason H. Knight, employed by Lucius B. Evans at his shoe factory in Wakefield, Massachusetts, told jurors he began making

Newport tie shoes about two years before. He positively identified the two shoes in evidence as shoes he had made. There were characteristics about the shoes that were unique to Knight's methods. His employer, Mr. Evans, told the court his shop had produced about 1600 pairs of Newport tie shoes between December 1873 and January 1875 and that he had placed these shoes on the market in Boston, Taunton, Charlestown, Saco, Maine and Cleveland, Ohio.

Parker W. Cushing was the next witness called by the prosecution. Cushing (no relation to Sarah Cushing) testified that while working for Franklin Howard at the Howard House last September 1874, he found a Wesson and Harrington pistol hidden in a storage room above the stable office. The pistol was secreted behind a beam by the side of the chimney. He gave the pistol to Howard. About a week later, he found a baggage check, #2549, in the same spot. He also turned this over to Howard. When he was shown the two items in court, he said he could not recognize them. It's not known why Cushing couldn't identify the items, unless his memory had seriously faded, or he was intimidated by Costley's presence.

When the court returned from recess at 1:00 p.m., DA French called Franklin Howard back to the stand. Howard told the court he was the proprietor of the Howard House and had leased the hotel to Costley from November 1872 until May 1874. During this time, Costley had asked Howard for a rent reduction. After leasing the hotel to Costley, Howard moved to Danvers, Massachusetts. About April 1874, Costley visited him in Danvers and told him he wanted to give up his lease and get out of the hotel business. Costley wanted to sell his personal property from the hotel, so asked Howard for permission to conduct an auction on the premises before he terminated his lease. Howard agreed to release Costley from the lease and allowed him to conduct the auction at the end of April. DA French showed Howard a poster and he identified it as the poster Costley had used to advertise the auction.

Howard told DA French he returned to the Howard House in May 1874 after Costley sold out. He hired Parker Cushing for odd jobs and verified Cushing's discovery of the pistol and baggage check #2549 last September. Howard identified both items when DA French presented them to him. Howard stated he had kept both items locked in his office desk but later placed both items back where Cushing found them. He kept quiet about the gun and check. He wasn't certain he wanted to get himself involved in the murder investigation. He testified he had a change of heart when two men, who he did not identify, came to his office and told them that Cushing had informed them he possessed the two items. Both men urged him to turn the gun and check over to the police, as both might prove critical to the case against Costley. Howard acquiesced, contacted police, and turned over the fully loaded gun and the claim check to Chief Constable Boynton.

Howard had placed himself in jeopardy with this testimony. Howard admitted secreting two important pieces of evidence. French could have charged him with being an accessory after the fact of murder, but whether he was prosecuted at a later time is unclear.

Baggage Master George Ingalls of the Boston, Hartford and Erie Railroad, testified that he received a russet Saratoga trunk bearing baggage check #2549 on the morning of May 20 at the Boston depot. Written on the trunk was "J. H. Costley." The trunk had been sent from New York via the Norwich line. The trunk remained in the depot's baggage room for seventeen weeks until Chief Boynton appeared with the matching check and claimed it. Ingalls identified the Saratoga trunk already entered as evidence and identified by previous witnesses as the trunk he had received.

DA French called Chief Constable George Boynton to the witness stand and after he was sworn in, Boynton told the court about his involvement in the murder investigation. Boynton provided an account of his interview with Costley in Plymouth Jail on September 28. He identified the pistol and baggage check he had recovered from Franklin Howard at the Howard House last September 15. He related how he had removed the five cartridges from the pistol. He told the court he had submitted several of these cartridges to a pharmacist for analysis. DA French showed Boynton the Saratoga trunk bearing Costley's name that had been previously introduced as evidence. Boynton identified it as the trunk he had claimed at the depot on September 16 with claim check #2549, which he had recovered from Franklin Howard.

He testified there were two shirts in the trunk and two handkerchiefs, both monogrammed "J.H.C." He also testified that a black valise was found in the trunk and that the interior of the valise was stained with what appeared to be blood. Boynton believed this was the black valise Costley used to conceal the carriage robe, tailor's goose, and rope on the night of the murder. He had earlier theorized that Costley, upon his return to Boston after the murder, stopped at Burke's saloon and left the valise there, then brought the horse and buggy back to Riedell's Stable. Costley then returned to Burke's, picked up the valise, and placed it in the Saratoga trunk before shipping it from the Boston and Albany Depot on May 16. Boynton told the court Mrs. Hawkes' second trunk was never found. Defense attorneys subjected Boynton to extensive cross-examination but elicited no new information or contradictions.

After Boynton was excused from the witness stand, the government summoned Dr. Edward S. Wood to testify. Dr. Wood was an assistant professor of chemistry at Harvard Medical University (so-called at the time) who specialized in bloodstain identification. Dr. Wood testified that he had received the stained valise from Chief Constable Boynton and found several stains in an upper pocket of the valise and another stain in a lower pocket. Other stains were found in the valise and Dr. Wood subjected them to chemical analysis. Even though a fail-safe method for confirming whether blood was human or not had not been developed by this time, he testified the stains were, in his opinion, consistent with the characteristics of human blood. Attorney Cheney cross-examined the witness about the validity of the tests he performed and how exact they could be in differentiating between human blood and that of "fish and fowl" in an attempt to discredit his testimony.[83]

By 1874, scientific analysis of human blood had not been legally embraced by the courts. The courts did not believe science could conclusively determine, beyond a reasonable doubt, the difference between human blood and the blood of animals. Analytical chemists, testifying about blood evidence during this period, used chemical and microscopic examination to establish the presence of human blood. In 1868, Samuel M. Andrews was placed on trial in Plymouth County for a murder he had committed in Kingston, Massachusetts. Chemists testified about the process used to determine evidence of human blood on a number of exhibits offered by the Commonwealth. A chemical analysis called the guiacum test involved placing a suspected stain into a mixture of glacial acetic acid and chloride of sodium. The test confirmed the presence of blood, but did not allow the chemist to conclude whether the blood was human or animal.

In order for the chemist to determine whether the stain was human blood, he soaked the blood-stained item for several hours in glycerine and water, and then scraped the suspected blood stain from the garment or other object onto a microscopic slide. The chemist inspected the slide for particles of starch and fat globules and circular, biconcave, disc-like bodies that corresponded in appearance, due to their shape and size, to human, red blood corpuscles. Chemists compared these corpuscles with known blood corpuscle samples from humans, horses, cows, dogs, rabbits and pigs by inspecting their shape and measuring their size. But the size and shape of the human corpuscle could present itself in so many variations that chemists were unable to conclusively state that a blood stain examined by them was, in fact, human blood.[84]

In 1895, Joseph H. Linsley, M. D., professor of pathology and bacteriology at the University of Vermont, published an article in the *Medical Record – A Weekly Journal of Medicine and Surgery*, about the scientific examination of suspected human blood stains. Dr. Linsley did not believe that a physician, however expert, could go on the witness stand and conscientiously swear that blood stains examined by him are "even probably human blood corpuscles." Linsley asserted that microscopic examinations used to measure the exact size of corpuscles in blood specimens could not conclusively determine whether the specimens are human blood. He found it regrettable that certain medical men, posing as experts, would give testimony and declare that they could positively identify a suspected blood stain as originating from a human source.[85]

It would be six more years before chemists could positively confirm whether a blood stain was human blood, when, in 1901, a German bacteriologist developed the precipitin test, a failsafe chemical method for distinguishing human blood from animal blood by the presence of unique proteins. In the same year, the naming and standardizing of blood groups was established. The precipitin test is still used today by forensic scientists to verify the presence of human blood.

After Dr. Wood completed his testimony, he was excused from the witness stand. The jury was left to decide if Dr. Wood testified credibly and that the tests he performed for the existence of blood were valid. Court then adjourned until the next day.

≈

Detective Hollis C. Pinkham, lead investigator in the Hawkes murder case, took the witness stand when court opened on Thursday morning, December 31. Pinkham told the court he began his investigation at East Braintree on May 25, 1874 after being notified of the discovery of Mrs. Hawkes' body. He provided details about his meeting with Costley at the Howard House on May 26, Costley's arrest on the same day, and evidence collected since that time. Pinkham also testified about his interviews with Costley while he was in custody in Plymouth.

Pinkham's testimony was briefly interrupted so the court could hear from Dr. F. S. Ainsworth about his examination of Miss Sarah Cushing. Dr. Ainsworth told the court he and Dr. Moreland visited Miss Cushing in Hanover yesterday and found her not ill but suffering from "nervous excitement." In his opinion, her traveling from Hanover to Dedham would not jeopardize her health, regardless of her back pain.

Defense Attorney Sanford protested against Dr. Ainsworth's conclusion. The court suggested a compromise and instructed counsel to discuss a possible alternative to Miss Cushing's presence in court. The court suspended Detective Pinkham's testimony shortly thereafter and took a half-hour recess to enable counsel to confer.

When the court reconvened, the attorneys told the court they had reached an agreement. They had decided they would secure a written statement from Miss Cushing that could be presented in lieu of her testimony in court. Judge Wells asked Costley if he was in agreement with the arrangement and Costley told him he was. Judge Wells then authorized the written statement in lieu of Miss Cushing's testimony and directed Detective Pinkham to continue his testimony.

Detective Pinkham outlined how he had taken a buggy from Riedell's stable to Weymouth Landing along the carriage road by way of the Neponset River and Quincy and returned. He testified it took him four hours and twenty minutes with a ten-minute stop along the way.

He described the geographical setting along the route. The area between the stable and Neponset was thickly settled. From Neponset to the Monatiquot Bridge in East Braintree the region became more rural and homes were spaced from a half-mile to three-quarters of a mile apart. The road from Quincy to the bridge was heavily wooded.

Attorney Sanford objected to Pinkham's testimony about the carriage ride and the geography. The court sustained his objection as to the route taken by Pinkham and the duration of the ride, but not Pinkham's description of the route. The court recognized that many various routes existed between Boston and Weymouth Landing, and Pinkham's buggy ride was only one of the possible routes. The court also acknowledged that any attempt to estimate the time of travel was mere speculation. The court allowed Pinkham's testimony of the area's description, ruling it competent, and stated the evidence might be considered by the jury in connection with other evidence in the case.

The court recessed until the afternoon. At that time, Attorney Sanford began his cross-examination of Detective Pinkham. He questioned Pinkham about the blood found at the Hanover Hotel on May 26 and asked why Pinkham had discounted it as human blood. Pinkham told the court he had first considered it human blood as his initial inclination was to assume the murder had been committed at the hotel. But he said that after he examined the substance at the scene more closely, he believed it to be something other than blood. Although no mention is made in newspaper accounts of the trial, Sanford probably did not pursue this matter any further with Pinkham. His co-counsel, Cheney, had already disputed Dr. Wood's testimony and challenged the validity of blood testing.

Sanford's intent in questioning Pinkham about the blood evidence was to obtain an acquittal for his client based on an error in the indictment, which alleged the crime had been committed in Norfolk County. He hoped, through Pinkham's testimony, to cause doubt in the jury's minds about where the murder was committed. If he could convince jurors the murder happened in Hanover, which lies in Plymouth County, a legal technicality could free Costley.

After Sanford concluded his cross-examination, DA French called Albert L. Sawyer, a druggist with an apothecary shop at Washington and State Streets, Boston, who gave testimony about the ballistics evidence. Sawyer explained that a cartridge consisted of a bullet, shell casing, powder and primer. The hammer of a pistol, upon striking the cartridge, ignited the primer and powder and expelled the bullet from the shell casing. He told the court he had weighed the bullet taken from Julia Hawkes' head in the presence of Chief Boynton and Francis Green and determined its weight as seventy-seven and one-half grains. He then weighed two cartridges given him by Boynton and found them to measure eighty-one and eighty-two grains. Sawyer testified that the fatal bullet had probably been fired from a cartridge consistent in weight with the two cartridges provided by Boynton.

Francis Green, a firearms dealer in Fanueil Hall Square established himself as an expert witness. He told the court he was present when Sawyer weighed the evidence. He was of the opinion that all of the cartridges were consistent with ammunition used in the .22 caliber Wesson Harrington pistol that DA French showed him. This was the pistol found hidden in the Howard House stable by Parker Cushing.

Judson D. Harris, manager at the Thomas B. Barnes hardware store in Dock Square, testified about the sale of a .22 caliber pistol on April 27, 1874. DA French showed Harris the Wesson Harrington pistol found five months later at the Howard House and Harris identified it as similar to the one he had sold in April. Harris was unable to identify the second pistol, the one given to Miss Cushing by Costley as a gift. He described this pistol as a half-plated "Tycoon" revolver. Harris could not positively identify James Costley as the man who had purchased the .22 caliber pistol.

Upon the dismissal of Mr. Harris from the witness stand, the prosecution and defense approached the justices' bench and informed Judges Wells and Devens they had agreed on a statement that conveyed the substance of Miss Cushing's testimony. The court then instructed

Attorney General Train to read the statement. In it, Miss Cushing swore to the following facts: she had known Costley ever since he had lived in Hanover and that she was engaged to marry him. She and Costley were to marry on May 13, 1874. She owned property in excess of $12,000.00, which in today's economy is equivalent to $1.3 million.[86]

She acknowledged writing and sending letters found by Detective Pinkham in Costley's trunk at the hotel. She admitted that she had addressed them to "Thomas I. Thomas, Boston, MA," but that the letters had actually been sent to Costley using the fictitious name of Thomas she and Costley had previously arranged. Why she and Costley corresponded in this way was not revealed in newspaper accounts. It's possible she addressed her letters to "Thomas" to prevent her mother from discovering her relationship with Costley. It's also possible that she and Costley used the fictitious name to hide their relationship from Julia Hawkes.

She also acknowledged writing and sending a letter dated May 28, 1874, to Detective Pinkham, in which she explained how Costley had given her a pistol. She later turned this pistol over to Detective Pinkham.

The statement concluded with Miss Cushing's admission that Costley had told her he was in New York from May 15 to May 19. She also stated that she had received a letter from Costley purportedly written by him in New York.

The court accepted Miss Cushing's statement and entered it as evidence. The prosecution then called Constable Napoleon B. Furnald to the witness stand.

Furnald corroborated the previous testimony of Detective Pinkham as to their visit to Howard House and evidence found there, and offered information solicited from witnesses during his investigation. He also testified about geographical conditions in the vicinity of Weymouth Landing. No new evidence was obtained during cross-examination and the court adjourned until the next day.[87]

≈

The court opened for the fifth day of trial on Friday morning, New Year's Day. It was the practice of the courts at that time to remain in session during capital trials regardless of holidays. The government called Detective Chase Philbrick to testify. Philbrick's testimony bolstered evidence already submitted to the court. He underwent a lengthy cross-examination that elicited no new facts.

DA French recalled three witnesses, James Riedell, the stable owner, Cornelius Sullivan, the express man, and Franklin Howard, owner of the Howard Hotel, to clarify issues in their previous testimony. Riedell related Costley had given him his name on both May 9 and May 13. Sullivan told the court about an encounter he had with Costley at the Plymouth Jail last June. He said to Costley, "You have got me into a scrape about those trunks I moved for you." Costley replied, "You never moved anything for me." When Howard was called again, he told the court he hadn't left any pistol cartridges at the hotel, nor did he know of a tailor's goose about the premises. Howard's statement refuted Costley's allegation that the cartridges and tailor's goose found by investigators at the hotel belonged to Howard. Attorney General Train and DA French then rested their case against Costley.

Attorney Horace Cheney, counsel for the defense, addressed his opening statement to the court. Cheney attacked the government's attempts to connect the carriage blanket, tailor's goose and trunk to Costley. He also assailed the forensic testimony, stating the government never proved the bullet recovered from the victim's head matched the cartridges found on Costley's person and at the hotel. He dismissed the notion Costley had hidden the baggage check and pistol in the barn at the hotel and suggested some other person had placed them there to implicate the defendant. Cheney commented on the government's failure to properly issue the indictment against the defendant and questioned the court's authority to take jurisdiction in the case, since no evidence had been submitted to prove the crime occurred in Norfolk County. Cheney continued to note other technical aspects of the case and shared his definitions of circumstantial evidence and reasonable doubt with jurors. As to circumstantial evidence, Cheney said, "...no living witness had testified to seeing anything done, and they (the jury) would have to distinguish between circumstantial and direct evidence. You are asked to infer certain proved facts, or certain facts claimed to be proved and from them you are asked to infer certain other facts which usually accompany and attend them..."

As to reasonable doubt, Cheney cited Massachusetts Supreme Judicial Court Chief Justice Shaw's definition, which was first introduced in the Parkman-Webster murder trial of 1850 in Boston. Shaw defined reasonable doubt as: "that state of the case, which, after the entire comparison and consideration of all the evidence, leaves the minds of jurors in that condition that they cannot say they feel an abiding conviction, to a moral certainty, of the truth of the charge. For it is not sufficient to establish a probability, though a strong one arising from the doctrine of chances, that the fact charged is more likely to be true than the contrary; but the evidence must establish the truth of the fact to a reasonable and moral certainty; a certainty that convinces and directs the understanding, and satisfies the reason and judgment, of those who are bound to act conscientiously upon it. This we take to be proof beyond reasonable doubt."[88]

The defense's first witness was John F. Lovell, a Boston firearms dealer with forty years experience. Lovell testified the cartridges found by police at the hotel were .32 caliber, not .22 caliber as testified to by previous experts, and could be fired from twenty to twenty-six different pistols on the market at the time.

Attorney Cheney called Eben C. Waterman to the stand. Waterman, a store clerk and assistant postmaster at Hanover Four Corners, told the court he had known the defendant for two years. He testified he had accompanied Costley before noon on May 9, 1874 to the Hanover depot in a wagon driven by express man Horace Tower. He recalled Costley having a black valise that he passed to Waterman who put the bag in the wagon. Waterman said he didn't notice anything unusual about the bag's weight. When they arrived at the depot, Costley and Waterman took their belongings from the wagon and boarded a 10:00 a.m. train for Boston.

Upon cross-examination by Attorney General Train, Waterman told the court he left Costley at the Old Colony depot and didn't see him for two days. He wasn't sure if Costley took the black valise with him or had placed it in the depot's baggage room.

Attorney General Train then questioned Waterman about Mrs. Love Congdon's death in Hanover in December 1873. Train wanted the jury to hear about her death and the rumors that suggested Costley's involvement. Congdon's death had never been officially ruled a homicide, but Train hoped to arouse suspicion in the minds of the jurors about Costley and suggest his propensity for violence. At first, Waterman told the court he had never heard anything in connection with Costley and Mrs. Congdon and he didn't recall hearing it said Costley had poisoned her. Waterman then regressed and said he might have heard it suggested Costley had killed Mrs. Congdon. Many people talked about the death, he testified, and there were varying opinions about Costley's involvement. He told the court that in addition to his other town duties, he was Hanover's coroner, and he had assembled a coroner's jury to investigate Mrs. Congdon's death. He presented the inquest's testimony before a magistrate in Plymouth Court and the magistrate took no action. This, in his mind, closed the case and any further inquiry.

The defense called Horace S. Tower to testify. Tower told the court he worked as an express man for Hiram Randall in Hanover. He testified that on May 9, 1874, he took Costley and Waterman to the depot, corroborating Waterman's testimony. Tower told jurors he had known Costley for about five years and considered him a kind and humane man.

When cross-examined, Tower stated he hadn't seen the contents of Costley's black valise on the day in question, nor could he estimate its weight. He didn't remember taking any other baggage to the depot for Costley on any other day. He didn't remember anyone discussing Mrs. Congdon's poisoning and Costley's possible involvement.

Mrs. Adeline Lindsay, who lived a short distance from the Howard House and had been questioned last May 26 by Pinkham, Philbrick and Furnald before they went to the hotel to investigate, testified next about the day of Costley's arrest. Mrs. Lindsay said several officers stopped in front of her house and questioned her and Mrs. Harriet McLaughlin, who boarded in Mrs. Lindsay's house with her husband, as to Costley's whereabouts, then walked toward the hotel. Mrs. Lindsay testified she had seen Costley before his arrest and had asked him if he had heard about Mrs. Hawkes' death. She had a newspaper in her hand that detailed the incident. Mrs. Lindsay said she watched Costley as he read the article and didn't see any change in his expression.

The defense team introduced six other witnesses to testify as to Costley's good character. Abner Stetson of South Scituate, Costley's first employer when he arrived in Hanover; Francis P. Arnold of Pembroke, a shoe manufacturer and Grand Master of the Phoenix Masonic Lodge; John P. Ellis; Michael R. Sylvester; George H. Bates; and Edward M. Sweeney; all residents in the Four Corners neighborhood of Hanover and members of the Phoenix Masonic Lodge, said they knew Costley as a quiet, peaceable and humane man. DA French cross-examined each of the men in an effort to discredit their testimony about Costley's reputable character. He asked them what they knew about the death of Mrs. Congdon and asked if they had heard any rumors about Costley's involvement in her poisoning. All of the men admitted hearing rumors about Costley and his suspected involvement in Mrs. Congdon's demise, but considered it gossip and unfounded speculation. None believed Costley was in any way responsible for her death and all believed him incapable of foul play. But French accomplished what he had set out to do by presenting the Costley/Congdon rumors before the jury once again, nourishing the seed of suspicion he had planted during the direct testimony of previous witnesses. He was determined to convince jurors that Costley was an evil man, capable of violence and murder.

The court recessed for the morning and after Justices Wells and Devens opened the afternoon session, defense counsel, once again, set out to cast doubt as to the location of the murder. Attorney Cheney recalled Dr. Forsaith to clarify his observations during the autopsy. Costley's team hoped to convince the jury Mrs. Hawkes' death was not instantaneous and that she could have survived the pistol wound for an indeterminate time.

Attorney Cheney presented Dr. Forsaith with a skull and asked him to point out the location of the fracture on Mrs. Hawkes' head. Forsaith indicated the fracture was on the right side of the head at the juncture of the parietal bone and with the temporal and frontal bones. DA French approached Dr. Forsaith for cross-examination. French recognized the intent of Cheney's line of questioning and wanted to prevent the defense from establishing that Mrs. Hawkes' wound was not immediately fatal. French asked Forsaith if there were differences between the skull presented in court and the skull of Julia Hawkes. Dr. Forsaith admitted that the skull exhibited in court was unlike Mrs. Hawkes,' stating, "Mrs. Hawkes' was much higher and a very different proportioned skull." DA French then asked Forsaith if he knew where Julia Hawkes was buried. Forsaith replied that he did not know. Forsaith's statement suggested that without Mrs. Hawkes' skull, he could not competently comment on the specifics of her cause of death. Dr. Forsaith was then excused from the witness stand.

Attorney Cheney called Dr. William C. B. Fifield of Dorchester, a graduate of Harvard Medical School, who testified he reviewed the autopsy notes of Drs. Forsaith and Tinkham. He asserted the wound received by Mrs. Hawkes was not necessarily fatal; that she could have survived from such a wound, as the path of the bullet did not strike "...any important veins, arteries or sinuses, the destruction of which would lead to such effusion of blood upon the brain as to indicate speedy death there from..."[89]

Attorney General Train, on cross-examination, got Dr. Fifield to state Mrs. Hawkes' wound may or may not have proved fatal. He said each case had its own individual consequences. He admitted the wound received by Mrs. Hawkes could have caused instantaneous death. This skillful interrogation by Train completely defused the defense team's attempt to prove the murder had occurred in another place and at a later time.

No evidence was offered during the course of the trial to suggest that drowning, strangulation, suffocation, or any other cause contributed to, or was the actual cause, of Julia Hawkes' death. The issue was whether or not the victim died from the gunshot instantaneously, or over the length of a certain period of time. Defense attorneys requested the court rule on a number of exceptions, including "That the government must prove with the same moral certainty that the proximate immediate cause of the death of the deceased was a wound from a pistol, not suffocation, strangulation, drowning, or any other cause," and "That although the deceased may have received a mortal wound from a pistol, yet, if before death had actually resulted there from, though the deceased remained entirely insensible, any other cause of death intervened so as to hasten her death in any degree, then, in contemplation of law, the pistol wound was not the cause of death; and if the jury are left in doubt whether such additional cause of death did intervene, the prisoner cannot be found guilty on this indictment."

The court ruled that:

…the government must prove, in the way all necessary facts are proved in criminal trials, that the pistol wound given by the prisoner, if given by him, was the cause of the death of Julia Hawks (sic). If other circumstances came in to prevent any recovery that might otherwise have taken place, or to aggravate, even, the effect of the wound, yet, if the wound was the cause of which she died, the fact that such other circumstances hastened or retarded the effect of the wound, does not prevent the wound from being the cause of death; but if, while alive, another cause came in, which, independently of the pistol wound, caused the death, so that the death resulted from that, and not from the pistol wound, then the jury cannot here find a verdict of homicide from the cause alleged in the indictment.[90]

Evidence was offered by the defendants from Dr. Fifield, Dr. Cheever and Dr. Gay, tending to show that the wound as described by the witnesses, Dr. Forsaith and Dr. Tinkham, was not necessarily instantly or at all fatal; that the ball in its course did not involve any important veins, arteries or sinuses, the destruction of which would lead to such effusion of blood upon the brain as to indicate speedy death there from; that it was probable that the deceased may have lived an indefinite period of time, it might be three hours or ten hours, or longer, after the infliction of the pistol wound; and that she would have been rendered unconscious by the wound.[91]

This was another effort by the defense to have the case against Costley dismissed by convincing the court and the jury that Julia Hawkes' death occurred outside Norfolk County and therefore, beyond the court's jurisdiction. His lawyers argued that he had been brought to trial in Norfolk County because the victim's body had been found there. But they insisted that if her murder occurred in some other county, be it Suffolk or Plymouth, then his case must be dismissed – he was not being prosecuted in the appropriate jurisdiction. The court dismissed this exception, but agreed to clarify, for the jury's consideration, the issue of where the crime occurred and its connection in the case. When the court charged the jury, the following summation was given, "As I said in the outset, it is necessary for the government to prove, as it is necessary for them to prove all the other facts in the case to your satisfaction, beyond a reasonable doubt, that the offense was committed in the county of Norfolk. If the pistol was fired in Suffolk County, but she died in Norfolk County, or within one hundred rods of the line, the offense may be prosecuted in the county of Norfolk. The statute is, 'If a mortal wound is given, or other violence or injury inflicted, or poison administered, in one county, by means whereof death ensues in another county, the offense may be prosecuted and punished in either county.' This may or may not have a bearing upon the case, according as you may give effect to the evidence which tends to show where it may have been committed, and to the evidence as to the continuance, for some indefinite period, of life in the body of Julia Hawks (sic). As already suggested, the body being found, with the bullet wound in the head, dead, within the body of the county of Norfolk, although that does not prove that she was shot in the river where she was found, still may be taken with all the other circumstances in the case, and if other circumstances are consistent with it, they may authorize you to find that she was shot, and came to her death from the wound, in the county of Norfolk. But in this case, it is argued that there are some other circumstances which affect the probabilities. You are to consider those in connection with the place where she is found. You are to consider, of course, the distance to this place from the county line, either in one direction or the other, as you may be satisfied from the evidence as to the direction from which the party came to the point where she was found. You will consider the probabilities from the difficulty of transporting after death. You will also consider the place where she was last seen, which was in the county of Suffolk, and her declarations there, also, as to where she was going; and you will consider the whereabouts of the prisoner, because this investigation as to where it occurred may be affected by the question whether this prisoner committed the offense, and therefore you may consider his whereabouts, and his declarations as to where he was going, and the time of his return."[92]

Attorneys Sanford and Cheney called two other physicians as expert witnesses to corroborate and bolster Dr. Fifield's claims. They also called several witnesses to describe the layout of roadways and common routes taken from Boston to Weymouth, suggesting that a number of areas along the road would have been suitable for a man to commit murder without being detected. In other words, the murder could have been committed in Suffolk County, not Norfolk County.

They decided, with Costley's consent, not to place Costley on the witness stand in his own defense. They then closed their case and the prosecution offered no rebuttal witnesses. At this, the defense moved that the court find a directed verdict of not guilty, because the Commonwealth had failed to provide evidence that the murder was committed within Norfolk County, or within one hundred rods of its boundary line and failed to produce evidence that would be competent for the jury to find beyond a reasonable doubt that the murder was committed within the same Norfolk County, or within one hundred rods of its boundary line. The court declined to rule in favor of a not guilty verdict and the defense team informed the court it would file an exception to the ruling.[93] The court then adjourned until the following day.[94]

≈

The next day, Saturday, January 2, the court reconvened at 8:00 a.m. It was not uncommon, in capital cases in this era, for the court to continue capital trial proceedings into Saturdays. The American work week during the nineteenth century was typically six days.

Defense attorney Baylies Sanford rose at 8:30 a.m. to address the court with his closing argument. Sanford's remarks consumed five and one half hours, not an unusual length of time during this era. His goal was to raise doubt in the juror's minds about the location of the murder and the cause of death. He told jurors that his review of the case opened only one or two conclusions: "...either his client must be acquitted because the Government failed to show where the offense was committed, or because they had failed to show that the offense was committed by him."

Sanford first asked the jury if the prosecution had established Costley's guilt "beyond a reasonable doubt in the manner prescribed by law." If the jury could not determine that the murder had been committed within Norfolk County, they had no right to convict Costley. If they were uncertain about the cause of Mrs. Hawkes' death, they must find Costley innocent. Sanford tried to convince the jury that the prosecution never proved that the pistol shot killed Mrs. Hawkes instantly. She could have been shot elsewhere and survived until she had been deposited in the river. He also argued that Mrs. Hawkes' death could have been caused by drowning, strangulation, or some other means, not by pistol shot alone.

Sanford then attacked the evidence presented by the prosecution. He argued that the carriage robe found about Mrs. Hawkes' head had never been identified as belonging to his client. He also questioned the ownership of the russet colored trunk, stating it had never been positively identified as Mrs. Hawkes.' He challenged the testimony of handwriting experts who told the court that the handwriting on the trunk, "J. H. Costley," belonged to his client. Sanford dismissed the government's assertion that the pistol and baggage claim check found in the Howard House stable had been placed there by Costley and suggested that some other person, possibly the real murderer, had put the items there. He said the detectives who searched the hotel and stable when they first visited Hanover never found the pistol and check. How could Costley have secreted them there after his arrest, when he had been confined since that time?

Sanford discredited the testimony of the constables in the case, focusing particularly on the conversations they had with his client in Plymouth Jail. He believed their comments and reports were untruthful stating, "...testimony coming from prosecuting officers was necessarily tinged and colored by the enthusiasm and zeal with which a man follows all such circumstances, which necessarily affects the workings of his mind, and render him absolutely unable – though it may be honestly unable – to report exactly what is said under the circumstances."

He believed it incredulous that after seven months, when the officers first interviewed Costley at the jail, that they could recall everything that was said. The officers, "...are prejudiced witnesses, having an interest in the result of the case."

Sanford then moved to motive. He told the jury his client's reputation had been untainted before May 26, except for "an idle, evanescent rumor that Costley's former housekeeper died suddenly." When he was arrested, Costley was engaged to marry "an accomplished lady in Hanover possessed in her own right of more property than ordinarily falls to any human being."[95] Why would Costley jeopardize his future with this woman by murdering Mrs. Hawkes and risking imprisonment or death? He also tried to convince jurors that the woman who was said to live in the rooming house on Camden Street had never been proven to be Mrs. Hawkes. He tried to discredit Miss Arbuckle's testimony that Julia, in the afternoon of May 13, had told her she was leaving with Costley that evening for Weymouth Landing. He also questioned the testimony of the stablemen at Riedell's, alleging that they didn't know for sure that Costley had returned the buggy on that evening of May 13. If they didn't know for sure, how could the Newport tie shoe found in the buggy be connected to Costley?

Seated in the court dock, Costley remained composed during the summation, as he had during the entire trial. On many occasions he laughed and smiled at spectators and conveyed a cavalier and confident demeanor. Costley was arrogant and manipulative. Even with his life at stake he remained confident that his charm and deviousness would convince both spectators and jurors of the absurdity of the charges against him. He was always smartly dressed and usually wore a navy blue suit. His physical appearance had changed little since his incarceration, although he had lengthened his "side whiskers."

At about 3:00 p.m., Attorney General Train presented the closing argument for the prosecution. Train summarized the prosecution's case, highlighting the testimony and physical evidence introduced during the course of the trial that contradicted statements made by Costley during his interrogations with police. He delivered a powerful and convincing rebuttal to the defense's closing remarks. He employed simple logic and reasoning as he carefully reconstructed the planning and execution of the crime.

Admitting the government's case was strictly circumstantial, Train told the jurors, "It is true the evidence is circumstantial, but it is more satisfactory than if four or five men from Quincy had testified that they were in a piece of woods on the night of the thirteenth of May and had seen, on that misty night, the woman shot down by a man resembling the prisoner, because they might have been mistaken if they didn't catch him in the act. There is no break in this chain of evidence, and it does not only constitute a chain made of iron links but a cable made of strands of hemp, from which no hypothesis, beyond a reasonable doubt, can be assumed that it is not consistent with the guilt of the prisoner." Upon the conclusion of Train's remarks, the court recessed until 7:15 p.m.[96]

When the court reconvened, but before the jury was seated in the courtroom, Baylies Sanford submitted twelve exceptions for consideration by the court on points of law. Judge Wells allowed some of the exceptions, but dismissed the majority. The most important (and disappointing from a defense standpoint) of the rulings concerned the issue of venue. Costley's attorneys filed an exception stating that the court must acquit the defendant if the government failed to prove that the offense charged had been committed in Norfolk County, "or within one hundred rods of the line…" Judge Wells ruled, "…it is necessary for the government to prove, as it is necessary for them to prove all the other facts in the case to your satisfaction, beyond any reasonable doubt, that the offense was committed in the county of Norfolk. It is not necessary to prove that the pistol was fired within the county of

Norfolk. If the pistol was fired in Suffolk County, but she (Hawkes) died in Norfolk County, or within one hundred rods of the line, the offense may be prosecuted in the county of Norfolk."[97] At this point Judge Wells made reference to Massachusetts General Statutes, Chapter 171, Sections 17 and 18. "The statute is, 'If a mortal wound is given, or other violent injury inflicted, or poison administered, in one county, by means whereof death ensues in another county, the offense may be prosecuted and punished in either county.'"[98]

The defendant asked the court to instruct the jury during its charge "...that the fact, if they should find it, that there was no evidence tending to show that the homicide was committed in either of two counties adjoining, was not to be considered by the jury as evidence as to whether the homicide was committed in the county alleged." The court overruled this exception and did not give this instruction to the jury. The court ruled, "...that the point was to be considered by the jury upon all the circumstances of the case, and if they thought that, if it had been committed elsewhere, the defendant would have the means of showing it by other witnesses, they might consider the absence of evidence that it was committed in another county."[99]

After Judge Wells ruled on the exceptions, the jury was brought into the courtroom and seated. Judge Wells then addressed the defendant, advising him of his privilege to make a statement to the jury if he wished. Costley told the judge he had nothing to say. Judge Wells then charged the jury, explaining the law as it pertained to the degrees of murder, jurisdiction and circumstantial evidence. Judge Wells concluded his charge at about 9:00 p.m. and the jury was dismissed to begin deliberation.

Many spectators remained in the court room as the jury considered Costley's guilt or innocence. Costley stayed in the prisoner's dock and chatted and laughed with some of the men in the room as if he were disinterested in the case's outcome. But some recognized his false confidence, watching as Costley occasionally stroked his beard or twirled his moustache. It was evident to them he was on the "ragged edge of anxiety and despair."[100]

≈

Two hours later, the court advised the prosecution and defense that the jury had reached a verdict. An eerie silence filled the court when at 11:12 p.m. the justices took the bench and court officers escorted the jury into the court room. The jury foreman announced to the court the jury had found Costley guilty of murder in the first degree in the death of Julia Hawkes. Costley, upon hearing the verdict, showed no emotion. His attorney, Horace Cheney, asked the court to poll the jury. The court told Cheney such action was not the usual custom and denied his request. Costley asked the court if he could make a statement to the jury, but this was also denied. The court adjourned at 11:20 p.m. and Costley was remanded to Dedham Jail to await sentencing.[101]

A newspaper correspondent later found an opportunity to question Costley about what he intended to say to the jury had he been given a chance. Costley told the reporter he wished simply to thank them and say that he had no hard feelings against them.

≈

On Saturday, March 13, 1875, Norfolk County Deputy Sheriff Warren escorted Costley into the prisoner's dock in Dedham court for sentencing. As Costley conferred with his attorney, Horace Cheney, the court clerk ordered Costley to stand and asked him if he had anything to say why sentence of death should not be pronounced. Costley replied, "I have nothing to say."

Judge Wells then pronounced sentence upon him declaring:

James H. Costley, it now becomes the painful duty of the Court to award against you the judgment which the law affixes to the crime of which you stand convicted. Under the humane provisions of the laws, there is but one offense the commission of which subjects the guilty party to the forfeiture of life. In the brief and simple, but expressive and solemn language of the statute, it is enacted that whoever is guilty of murder in the first degree shall suffer death. Of this high and heinous offense – the taking of human life with deliberate, premeditated malice aforethought – you have been found guilty by a jury carefully selected by yourself, and after a patient and impartial trial, in which you were defended by able counsel. To this verdict and to the sufficiency of the indictment, we have been able to find no valid objections by reason upon any error in law, nor upon a deliberate and careful survey of the case by the full bench. The verdict was the necessary and inevitable conclusion resulting from the evidence of your guilt. Nothing, then, remains for the Court but to pass the sentence of the law: which is, that you, James H. Costley, be removed from this place to the Prison of this County, there to be kept in close confinement until such time as the Executive Department shall, by their warrant, appoint, thence taken to the place of execution, and there to be hanged by the neck until you are dead. And may God, in His infinite wisdom, have mercy upon your soul.

Judge Wells scheduled Costley's execution for June 25, 1875. Costley bowed his head but showed no emotion. Deputy Sheriff Warren took custody of Costley and led him from the court room and back to the jail. Spectators noticed Costley smiling slightly as he passed by.[102]

≈

Costley spent much of his time in jail reading and writing. Prison officials considered him a model prisoner, as Costley had never caused a problem or been disciplined during his incarceration.

The only member of his family to visit him at the jail was a brother from California. Costley's parents and siblings had moved from Nova Scotia to California after the Civil War. His brother spent a number of hours with Costley and as he departed, promised Costley he would not tell his parents of Costley's fate.[103]

Costley's fiancée, Sarah Cushing, devastated by the verdict and sentencing, visited him frequently as did the prison chaplain, Rev. Zachariah A. Mudge and the rector of St. Andrew's Episcopal Church in Hanover, Rev. William H. Brooks. A Dedham florist, George E. Morse, in commiseration with Costley's fate, sent Costley a bouquet of flowers. Costley thanked Morse with the following note: "Mr. Morse, Respected Sir: I much appreciate the favors you have presented, and my true friend (Cushing) wished me to say that every kindness shown to me is increased tenfold to her. A blooming flower in a cell, so grim and dismal, seems to keep the soul awake, 'sweet thoughts alive, and sordid ones dead,' or it helps to bear a sorrow that often seems unbearable. But I do not want to mar the comforts of others by my cup of bitterness, as every heart has trials to endure. I know you give cheerfully. I feel it much. Will simply say, 'Thanks!' Ever grateful, J. Henry Costley."[104]

Costley had befriended his jailors and made every attempt to convince them he had not committed the crime. He developed a special relationship with jailor Isaac F. Porter, who, out of his good nature, sympathized with Costley and allowed him certain privileges. This friendship became such a bond between the two men that Costley believed he could trust Porter with his life.

≈

As June 25, the scheduled date of his execution neared, Costley and his fiancée became frantic. Cushing had funded Costley's legal representation through the course of the trial and continued to pay his expenses during appeal. Chances for a reversal of his conviction seemed bleak, so the two contrived an escape plan. They hoped to enlist the aid of their mutual friend, Isaac Porter, by offering him a bribe of $10,000.00, nearly all of her riches, an incredible sum and one that Sarah Cushing could only raise through the sale of her property or the contributions of others sympathetic to Costley's cause.[105]

Several days later, Costley approached Porter with the proposition. He felt confident that Porter was an ally who believed Costley was innocent and would sympathize with his plight. He offered Porter the money in exchange for his cooperation. Costley told Porter of two plots to gain his freedom. The first plan was to obtain tools to remove the bars on the window of his cell, which was located on the extreme west wing of the jail. The jail at that time was being remodeled and a portion of its western wall had been demolished. Once he had liberated himself from the cell, Costley planned to escape through the compromised wall and meet friends who would be waiting with a carriage.

Costley told Porter an alternative to the plan would involve the use of acid. Costley intended, after being released from the confines of his cell, to blind the prison guard with the acid, relieve him of the jail's outside key and make good his escape through the wall under construction. Porter agreed to Costley's proposal. Costley told Porter he would keep him apprised of further details of the escape plan.

On May 7, 1875, Sarah Cushing arrived at Dedham Jail to visit her lover. Cushing met Porter at the jail and he led her to Costley's cell. Prison rules prohibited visitors from approaching the prisoner, so Cushing had to remain a short distance from the cell. As she neared the cell, Cushing staged an episode of dizziness and nausea and collapsed on the floor close to the cell, allowing her to fall within reach of Costley. She furtively passed a package containing files, saws and acid through the bars to Costley. As previously agreed, Porter made no attempt to interfere. Porter rendered assistance to Cushing and after she had "recovered," accompanied her from the cell area to the prison exit.

Later that day, Porter had second thoughts about his complicity. He confronted Costley and told him he was reconsidering his promise of cooperation. Costley threatened Porter's life and warned him not to betray him. Porter sought a compromise with Costley. He feared the tools in Costley's cell would be discovered. It was agreed Costley would turn over the implements to Porter and Porter would make the tools available to him when needed.

Several days later, Porter, racked by guilt, confessed his role in the plot planned by Costley and turned over the tools in his custody to the head prison guard, or head turnkey, as he was also known, Henry White. Porter told White about the acid in Costley's cell. White retrieved the acid without Costley's knowledge and the plot was foiled. Porter then tendered his resignation and left the jail. Prison officials told Costley nothing of Porter's departure. When he didn't see Porter at the jail, Costley assumed Porter was biding his time, waiting for the right moment for the plan to unfold. Several days later, Costley found out that Porter had resigned his position and realized that his plot to escape had failed.[106]

On June 21, 1875, the full bench of the Supreme Judicial Court heard Costley's last appeal. Chief Justice Gray and Associate Justices Wells, Morton, Devens and Endicott presided over the hearing. Attorney Horace Cheney represented the defendant and Attorney General Train and Associate Attorney General Waldo Colburn represented the government. After listening to the arguments of both sides, the Court advised it would take the matter under advisement and the case was adjourned. Several days later, the court overruled the exceptions filed by Cheney.[107]

On Wednesday, June 23, two days before Costley's scheduled execution, Detective Hollis Pinkham contacted Norfolk County Sheriff John W. Thomas and told him he had received information regarding a plot to free Costley by force. Thomas considered the information valid and made arrangements to hire additional security to prevent the escape attempt.

That evening, a detail of officers from the Boston Police Department, led by Sgt. John Laskie, arrived to guard the exterior of the prison. The officers remained the following day and evening. On Friday morning, the day of execution, Captain Alexander McDonald of the Boston Police West Roxbury station arrived with Lieutenant Chase and thirty men to complement the officers already assigned to the jail.[108]

≈

The execution caused a stir of great excitement in the little village of Dedham and beyond. So many persons wanted to witness the hanging that Sheriff Thomas ordered the issuance of a limited number of permits for access to the gallows. Heavy cardboard tickets, bordered in black, were printed:

> **"Admit............TO THE JAIL, DEDHAM, On *Friday,*
> *June* 25, 1875, At 9 o'clock A. M. – No Admittance after 9
> 1-2 o'clock. John W. Thomas, Sheriff."**

These tickets were distributed to witnesses in the case and members of the press. The sheriff disseminated additional tickets on a case by case basis.

Winslow Drew, a carpenter from Plymouth, arrived at the jail on June 23 to begin construction of the gallows. Drew used the same design as the gallows he had built to execute another murderer, William E. Sturtevant, in Plymouth several weeks before.

The gallows consisted of two upright posts, eighteen feet high, securely stayed and put together by bolts. It was erected in the prison's vestibule, facing the entrance. The platform was only a moderate step from the prison floor. A manila hemp rope, attached to weights, ran over a wheel, the rise, or "lift," being about six feet. The rope was Italian hemp, half an inch thick.[109]

Costley was advised by his attorney that all attempts at reversing his conviction had failed. The prison warden, fearing suicide or another attempt by Costley to escape, assigned officers Goodwin, Bailey and Clifford to oversee Costley during the death watch.

Costley slept soundly on Thursday evening, getting up only once. He rose early on Friday morning. He ate a hearty beef steak breakfast prepared by the Sheriff's personal cook. Reverend Brooks of Hanover visited him in his cell and prayed with him. A *Boston Globe* reporter later wrote that Reverend Brooks had advised Costley to confess. Costley said, "I have nothing to confess. I did not commit the deed." "But," said the clergyman, "If you did not do it, you may be cognizant who did it, and are equally guilty." Costley answered, "Yes, I suppose I am. I do not want to tell who it was. It would only criminate (sic) others and not help myself. I am prepared to die, and at 11 o'clock I shall be happier than any whom I leave behind."[110]

Costley then took pen to paper and began to write several letters, including one to his fiancée, Sarah Cushing. He composed a letter to Chief Turnkey Henry White and thanked White for his kind treatment of him while in his custody. The letter read: "Mr. White, Respected Sir: I think you know my feelings without my expressing them in writing. But the very kind words and acts while under your care bids me say here that the respect I bear to you and Mr. Goodwin was stronger than all precaution that might surround me. I know you will act faithfully to all you have under your charge. I will not multiply words, but my trust and respect is second to that of a brother. Truly gratefully, J. H. Costley."[111]

Costley penned a letter to Detective Christopher Bailey of the state constable force. "Mr. C. Bailey, Respected Sir: You have asked me for information that is beyond my power to give in full, and betraying my word to give in part. I know you feel deeply for me, and would be pleased to do anything allowed by law that would benefit me. For all of which I feel extremely grateful. I will not multiply words, Mr. Bailey. But I feel as if you were an honorable friend. Good-bye. Very respectfully, J. H. Costley."[112] Bailey, during his conversations with Costley, apparently asked Costley to confess, or at least tell what he knew of the murder. Costley wouldn't confess to committing the crime and suggested to Bailey that someone else had been responsible, but he was not free to tell who this person was.

Costley then wrote his final statement, professing his innocence to the end. "These are my last words. I have the kindest wishes for the just laws of this Commonwealth, and the execution of the same. These laws would not allow my execution if my situation was made known. I assert no goodness, but in the fear, and almost presence of God, I say to one and all, I am innocent of murder. I now forgive my enemies, thank my friends, and submit myself to the mercy of God, and know my end shall be peace. I feel thankful to all the prison officers, and especially to Mr. White and Mr. Goodwin, in whose charge I have been for the last year. While strict to duty, they have shown every kindness allowed by law. I have no words to fully express my respects and good feeling to them. The many kind visits of Dr. Chase, the prison physician, are very dear to me. I am truly grateful to all the officers in whose charge I have been since my arrest. I am very thankful to all the followers of Christ for their sympathetic visits during these solitary hours, and am extremely grateful to Rev. W. N. Brooks of Hanover, and Rev. Z. A. Mudge of Dedham, the Chaplain of the prison. Friends not mentioned I thank again and again for every kindness. Gratefully, J. H. Costley - Dedham, June 25th 1875."[113]

By order of Sheriff Thomas, Timothy Smith, an undertaker in Dedham, delivered a coffin to the prison the same morning. Friends of Costley paid for its adornment, including a cover of black broadcloth and silver mountings.[114]

Sworn witnesses to the execution and members of the press began to arrive at the prison and seated themselves in front of the gallows. Officials estimated a crowd of three hundred were present for the execution. Shortly after 9:30 a.m., Costley entered the vestibule from the east wing of the prison with his arms strapped closely to his body. He was accompanied by Rev. Brooks, Rev. Mudge and Deputy Sheriffs White, Endicott, Wood and Warren. The sheriffs were dressed in blue broadcloth coats with brass buttons, silk hats and were equipped with side arms. Dignitaries included District Attorney French, Sheriff Sprague of Worcester, Sheriff Bradley of Springfield and Police Chief George W. Boynton.[115]

Costley, dressed in a black suit and white shirt, was unemotional, although somewhat pale. Deputies Paul and Twitchell wheeled sixty year-old Sheriff Thomas, who was suffering from rheumatism, in a chair to the left of the gallows. The four other deputies seated Costley in a chair directly beneath the gallows rope. Sheriff Thomas asked those in attendance if any person among them did not desire to remain for the execution, but no one left. Reverend Brooks offered a prayer, "commending the soul of the condemned man to the mercy and goodness of God."

The Sheriff then read the warrant of execution. When he finished, he turned to Costley and asked him if he had anything to say before he was executed. A *Boston Globe* correspondent present at the gallows heard Costley say, "I think what I intended to say I have committed to writing to my much honored and respected keeper, Mr. Henry White. I have no words that I can speak that can express anything of his kind attention and respect paid me at this place and now. This much I have to say and no more." The reporter then noted as Costley, "so speaking, in a quiet but firm tone, bowed and stepped back under the noose, the chair having been removed."[116]

Deputies fastened straps about his knees and ankles. Warden Henry White placed the noose over Costley's head and around his neck, securing the knot just behind his left ear. White then drew a black cap over Costley's face. Sheriff Thomas said, "I proceed to execute the law upon James H. Costley," and pulled the strap. The *Globe* reporter wrote, "Costley's body bounded straight up about six feet and settled back with a sickening jerk. There were some eight or ten convulsive contractions of the legs and shoulders, lasting for nearly a minute and a half, after which the inanimate corpse of the murderer hung without motion."[117] A witness to the execution, Mr. Ames of the Norfolk Fire Insurance Company, fainted and was carried outside the prison for fresh air. The body was lowered after twenty minutes and Dr. Chase and several other physicians present examined Costley's pulse and heart and pronounced him dead.[118]

≈

Deputies placed Costley's body in the coffin and at the request of Sarah Cushing, released it to Francis P. Arnold of Hanover for burial. Arnold carried the body by wagon back to Hanover where Costley was interred in an unmarked grave beneath a large maple tree at Hanover Center Cemetery.[119] Sarah wanted to bury Costley in her family's plot, where her father had been interred in 1871. But her mother forbade it. Her mother told Sarah if she persisted and buried Costley there, she would exhume her father's remains and find another burial plot.[120] She would not allow her husband to lay side by side with a murderer.

Few people attended Costley's burial. His betrayal and atrocity was rewarded by passersby, most of them townspeople, who, as they passed his grave site, threw stones upon it in condemnation. And as the memory of the tragedy faded, the heap of stones settled and the patient and deliberate effects of nature covered the stones with a blanket of moss. Today, as one glances at the largest oak tree in the oldest part of the cemetery, the mound beneath it still marks the murderer's remains.

≈

Sarah Cushing was never prosecuted for her attempt to liberate Costley from jail. Neither the district attorney, nor the attorney general for the Commonwealth saw a need to punish her. They perceived her as an innocent victim of Costley's wile and treachery.

Four years after Costley's death, Sarah Cushing married. On December 27, 1879, Rev. S. H. Winkley of Boston united Sarah and Godfried Turcotte, a cabinet maker from South Abington.[121] Sarah contracted pneumonia two months after the marriage and died in Boston on February 24, 1882.[122]

She was buried with her parents, Captain John and Sarah Cushing, in the family plot at Hanover Center Cemetery.[123] Her monument faces the unmarked grave of James Henry Costley, who is buried thirty yards away.

≈

So ended the saga of the murderer, James Henry Costley, a depraved and wicked man of cunning and deceit, convicted of Julia Hawkes' slaying and forever suspected in the poisoning of Love Congdon, whose death was never adequately investigated. During their preparation for trial and in consideration of motive, prosecutors had theorized that Costley had promised to marry Julia Hawkes, or at the very least, he had made some other type of promise or inducement to her. Attorney General Train and DA French never proved this relationship during trial, but they were convinced that Costley had become engaged to marry the wealthy Sarah Cushing sometime before May 13, the last day Julia Hawkes was seen alive. The prosecution firmly believed that Costley had eliminated Julia to expedite his plan of marriage to Miss Cushing.

The court never ruled on Costley's involvement in the poisoning death of Mrs. Congdon, as it was not a matter for consideration before it. Prosecutors alluded to Costley's connection to Mrs. Congdon's death through testimony of rumors and innuendo, but never introduced any material facts to confirm that Mrs. Congdon's life was taken by Costley's hand. But Attorney General Train and DA French must have considered and discussed the possibility that Costley had made the same promises, inducements or proposal of marriage to Mrs. Congdon as he had to Mrs. Hawkes. Had Costley disposed of Mrs. Congdon in order to court Mrs. Hawkes, just as he had eliminated Mrs. Hawkes in order to court and marry Miss Cushing?

The two prosecutors must have also wondered if Mrs. Hawkes held a secret about Costley's connection to Mrs. Congdon's death. Did she threaten to notify authorities about his involvement? Is it possible that Costley's real motive for killing Mrs. Hawkes was to keep her quiet about his role in the woman's demise?

Why an autopsy had never been conducted on Mrs. Congdon's body remains a mystery. The examination of her remains might have revealed whether she had, in fact, been murdered. If murder had been established, perhaps a thorough investigation may have led to Costley's arrest and put an end to his murderous actions.

JOHN F. GALLAGHER

Costley truly believed he could get away with murder by carefully planning every step in his nefarious scheme. Costley set his plans in motion by selling his interest in the Howard House hotel and telling Julia Hawkes that he was planning on setting up a new venture in Oregon with his brother and that he wanted her to accompany him. It's likely that Julia was either not aware of his affair with Sarah Cushing or that she did know about it and Costley had convinced her that he intended to end his relationship with Miss Cushing. Before closing the Howard House, Costley went to Camden Street to secure temporary housing for Julia. When he spoke to the landlady, he told her that the room was for a woman who did not want her friends to know she was there. Costley later gave Julia a key for the room and she arrived there about May 1, 1874. Costley told Julia he'd handle the transfer of her travel trunks by shipping them to the railroad depot. He later told investigators that he had given the baggage checks for the trunks to Julia when he accidentally met her in Boston. But he never gave them to her. He planned to keep the checks and conceal the trunks.

When anyone asked at the Hanover House about Julia's whereabouts, Costley falsely answered that she had gone to Maine to visit friends. Once he had disposed of her, he could tell those who asked that he never heard from her again, that she had apparently decided not to return.

Costley rented a horse and buggy on May 9 in Boston and traveled to Weymouth Landing and back so that he could search for an isolated place for the murder and estimate the length of time it would take him to ride to the Landing, commit the murder along the way, submerge Julia's body in the river, and return to Boston with the buggy. Upon his return to the stable in Boston that evening, he left a black valise containing the rope, a hammer, the carriage robe, and the tailor's goose he would need to anchor Julia's dead body to the Monatiquot river bed.

On the night of May 13, Costley executed his plan and rented a horse and buggy from the same stable, loaded the valise he had left there four days before and set out to retrieve Julia at the Camden Street rooming house. He and Julia drove from the city through Quincy and Weymouth and somewhere near Weymouth Landing, Costley stopped in a darkened, isolated area he had selected during his trial run, removed

138

the pistol he had concealed in his clothing and shot Julia in the head, killing her. Costley then removed any identifying papers and jewelry from her person, covered her head with the carriage robe, and tied the rope around her neck to secure the robe and attach the tailor's goose. He then drove a short distance to the bridge spanning the Monatiquot River and tossed her body into the water. Costley returned to the stable without the valise and left the horse and buggy in the care of the stableman. Costley had secreted the valise at Burke's Saloon and retrieved it after depositing the buggy.

Costley next had to conceal any trace of Julia's existence. The morning after the murder, Costley showed up at the Camden Street rooming house with the room key Julia used to enter and exit her room. Costley told the landlady he was there to pick up Julia's things. Costley took some of Julia's personal items, but not all. When the landlady tried to give a night dress to Costley, he told her to leave it, telling the woman that she wouldn't need it anymore.

Costley went to the railroad depot to present the baggage checks for Julia's trunks. He put the black valise he had used on the night of the murder into the trunks marked with claim check #2549, wrote his name on the outside of it, and then took both trunks by train to New York. Costley later shipped the trunk tagged #2549 back to Boston. The other trunk was never found. Costley kept the baggage claim check, #2549, but never intended to retrieve the trunk until he knew it was safe to do so. He hid the baggage check in Hanover, along with the pistol he used to kill Julia. Later in the murder investigation, the baggage check and pistol were found and were turned over to police. The chief constable went to the train station with the baggage check and retrieved the trunk with Costley's name written on it. Inside the trunk the constable found the black valise Costley had carried the night of the murder and a pocket handkerchief bearing the initials, "J.H.C." The valise was later found to contain blood stains, which Dr. Wood suggested during trial were consistent with the characteristics of human blood.

Costley felt confident that he had pulled off the "perfect crime." That was until constables came to visit at the Howard House hotel on May

25, asking questions about Julia Hawkes. Even before they got there, the investigators believed they had sufficient evidence to arrest Costley for Julia's murder. And as the investigation continued in preparation for trial, the evidence continued to mount. Costley was doomed.

Costley made two fatal errors: first, he failed to weigh down the lower part of Julia's body when he threw her into the Monatiquot River, leading to her discovery; secondly, he unknowingly left one of Julia's "Newport tie" shoes in the buggy he had rented at Riedell's. The shoe verified Julia's presence in the buggy on the night of the murder.

Attorney General Train skillfully summed up the facts of the case during his closing arguments when he told the jury that Costley's motive "…was to get rid of Julia Hawkes to gratify lust, or love of property, or jealousy." Train believed Costley had spent considerable time planning for Mrs. Hawkes' murder and had been caught in a series of lies trying to mask his intentions.

It is likely they discounted Costley's later assertion that another had been responsible for the murder and scoffed at his contention that he would not talk about the murder for fear that he would implicate others. Undoubtedly, there was never a hint of skepticism in their minds that Costley had been the lone killer in the Julia Hawkes affair. The evidence against him had been overwhelming and irrefutable. In this case, justice had been served.

Costley's conviction could never have been achieved without the skill and determination of the state constable force. Chief Boynton's men and their "good old-fashioned legwork," persisted in "beating the bushes" until they had found every possible witness and piece of physical evidence to tie Costley to the murder. The case was strictly circumstantial, as no one had actually witnessed Julia Hawkes' murder. But the testimony and evidence presented during the trial was overwhelming and left the jury, all men "tried and true" to quickly decide, beyond a reasonable doubt, that Costley was guilty.

The investigators and prosecutors in the case were without the benefit of today's forensic technology in proving Costley's involvement. It wasn't until the late nineteenth century that fingerprint evidence, for the first time, was used to convict a suspect. Dr. Henry Faulds, a Scottish scientist, succeeded in matching the fingerprints of a burglary suspect. Faulds had been studying fingerprints as a means of identification for many years. He called the science "dactylography" and his work introduced the potential use of dactylography in forensics. His studies were complemented by the work of Sir Edward Henry and Sir Francis Galton. Galton, an English anthropologist, determined that no two persons were likely to have the same fingerprints. He published a number of papers and books between 1888 and 1895 that explained and validated his findings. Henry, head of the Metropolitan Police in London from 1903 to 1918, built upon Galton's research and developed a method of fingerprint classification that has become the standard for law enforcement agencies throughout the world. Courts in many countries began to recognize and accept the reliability and validity of fingerprint comparison as a tool for proving that fingerprints found at a crime scene positively matched the fingerprints of a defendant. Police and prosecutors, through fingerprint evidence, achieved their first murder conviction in the United States in 1911.[124]

Through the years, technological advances allowed more conclusive and irrefutable proof. Scientists have devised instruments and chemicals to better detect and process fingerprints. Through computers, law enforcement has developed a nationwide database that includes the fingerprints of convicted felons. Investigators, lacking a known suspect, can now submit fingerprints found at a crime scene to the database for comparison with prints on file.

Developments in the area of ballistic fingerprinting have also advanced. In 1889, criminologists first considered the use of rifling patterns as a forensic science. During Costley's trial in 1874, the prosecution had to rely on the testimony of pharmacists to suggest the bullet removed from Mrs. Hawkes' brain resembled in weight the cartridges found on Costley's person and at the Howard House hotel. DA French had no other means by which to positively prove that the fatal bullet had been fired by the pistol found hidden in the hotel stable.

The barrel of every firearm is designed with grooves to improve the weapon's accuracy. The barrel's grooves are unique to every firearm.

When a bullet is discharged, the grooves make an imprint, or rifling pattern, on it as it spins through the barrel. Today, ballisticians fire a bullet from a suspected murder weapon and retrieve the bullet for comparison with a bullet found at a crime scene. Through a comparison microscope, the ballistician can positively state in a court of law that the bullet found at a crime scene was fired from a particular weapon. Ballisticians now enter their findings in a nationwide database that allows comparison with ballistic evidence throughout the country.

Fibers provide important trace evidence at many crime scenes. Every fiber bears characteristics that make it distinctive. Had the technological advances in microscopic examination been available to Constable Furnald, he could have submitted the rope found in the Howard House Hotel for comparison with the rope found coiled around Mrs. Hawkes' neck. Analyzing the color, diameter and other physical features of both ropes would have conclusively determined that the both sections of rope were part of the same length.

The substance found inside and outside the Howard House Hotel by Detective Pinkham on his first visit there had never been tested to determine if it was blood, or more specifically, human blood. DA French also had to rely on the testimony of Dr. Wood to convince the jury that the blood inside the black valise was human blood. A method for proving whether blood was human wouldn't be introduced until 1901, when the precipitin test provided the scientific means. This test would have allowed investigators to confirm or deny with certainty that the substance at the Howard House and the stains in the black valise were human blood.

Had DNA analysis been developed by that time, investigators, prosecutors and defense attorneys could have determined not only the existence or absence of human blood, but could have ascertained whether or not the blood was that of Julia Hawkes. It wasn't until 1987 that the first conviction using DNA analysis was secured in the United States. DNA typing or "genetic fingerprinting" is based on the theory that no two people are composed of the same genetic makeup. DNA-deoxyribonucleic acid-is often called the genetic blueprint of life. It is a double-stranded chain of molecules that winds it way through the nucleus of every cell in every organism. From organism to organism, the sequence in which molecules form the DNA chain differs.[125]

As research continues in the DNA field, the chances of a false match have become smaller, but the courts have not yet accepted it as absolute proof of identity. Whether the benefits of DNA analysis would have been another piece of evidence to link James Costley to the Hawkes murder will never be known. Certainly, it's another important forensic tool that would have confirmed for investigators, prosecutors, defense attorneys, judges, jury, friends of the victim and Costley himself, whether justice had prevailed or justice had been denied.

A Soap Box

Other sins only speak; murder shrieks out.

John Webster – The Duchess of Malfi, act 4, sc.2.

The butcher in the Four Corners Village of Hanover thought it peculiar when he noticed the door to Quong Sing's laundry shop open on that cold day of January 28, 1904. When he entered, he saw the shop in disarray. He called out, but no one answered. Walking to the rear of the shop, a sense of foreboding enveloped him. As he entered a room on the right, he froze. There, in the middle of the room was his Chinese friend, his head immersed in a wash tub, a heavy soap box on his shoulders. Quong Sing was dead.

The slightly built Chinese man had been operating a hand laundry business in the Four Corners Masonic Building for about two years. His kind demeanor and diligent ways endeared him to patrons, businessmen, and residents of the village. The people of Hanover, distressed and angered by the cruelty inflicted on their friend, acted swiftly to identify his murderer. Many who lived and worked in the village still recalled the murder of Julia Hawkes nearly thirty years before by James H. Costley, the manager of the Howard House hotel. They were dismayed that such senseless violence had once again descended upon their quiet community.

≈

Business flourished in Hanover's village of Four Corners at the turn of the twentieth century. The village derived its name from the four corners created by the intersection of Broadway and Washington Street. The area bustled with the commerce of hotels, dry goods and provisions stores, carriage makers, blacksmiths and wheelwrights,

149

barbers and clock makers, carpenters and shoemakers. Over the years, its hotels and taverns had accommodated and entertained such notables as Paul Revere and Daniel Webster.

Physicians and surgeons practiced in the village. Drs. William Grovestein, Clarence Howes and Andrew MacMillan each had offices there. William Curtis' drug store not only provided for the medicinal needs of area residents, but also their transportation and recreational needs, as he kept a stock of bicycles. John Loring, a plumber, sold stoves and ranges in his shop. M. E. Flavell and Company, "The Corner Store," specialized in dry and fancy goods, as well as "Kushion Kumfort" shoes for ladies.[1]

The Hanover Branch Railroad, completed in 1868, connected residents from its station, located a short distance from the Corners, to other parts of town and to the city of Boston and beyond by way of the former Old Colony Railroad, which was later absorbed by the New York, New Haven and Hartford Railroad in 1893. Ten trains operated every day from 6:00 a.m. until 6:00 p.m. The Southern Massachusetts Telephone and Telegraph Company had expanded its service in the area and had established a new telephone office in the village. Churches and schools completed the social fabric of the village, clergy conducted services at the Second Congregational Church and St. Andrew's Episcopal Church and teachers broadened the horizons of pupils at the Salmond School. Hanover was now a community of 2152 people.[2]

The North River Lodge of the Independent Order of Odd Fellows maintained a hall on Broadway, as did the Freemasons at the Phoenix Lodge Masonic Building. The Freemasons rebuilt their lodge in 1900 after it had been destroyed by an explosion and fire in 1898. They held their meetings on the second floor of the building. The first floor housed Snell's barber shop, Wilkinson and Paxton's provisions market, and Quong Sing's Chinese laundry in 1904.

Phoenix Lodge Masonic Building
(Courtesy of Hanover Historical Society)

≈

In 1882, the United States government enacted the Chinese Exclusion Act. The act's intent was to restrict the number of Chinese immigrants into the country for a period of ten years. In 1892, the government extended the law for an additional ten years. It was the first federal law banning immigrants based solely on the basis of race and nationality. Fleeing economic restraints, political and religious persecution, hunger, drought and disease taking place in their homeland, Chinese citizens immigrated to the United States hoping to find fortune during the 1849 Gold Rush in California. As their numbers increased and gold became more difficult to find, native-born competitors became resentful and eventually forced the Chinese from the mines.

The animosity continued as industrialists, exploiting the Chinese immigrants' willingness to work for low wages, employed them in the canning, timber and garment industries and in railroad and canal construction. Those Chinese who could not find employment established restaurant and laundry businesses.

Just as they had when the Irish streamed into the country during the nineteenth century, American citizens perceived the overwhelming influx of Chinese immigrants as a threat to their own job prospects and as a negative influence on economic conditions. Cultural differences only added to the level of social tension and discrimination. To biased Americans, the Chinese man's queue, which they mockingly called a pigtail, represented the vast differences between them. The Chinese man saw the queue as a symbol of loyalty to his country and his plan to return home.[3] Bostonians during the early twentieth century negatively stereotyped the Chinese, mostly due to press accounts that depicted the Chinese as dishonest, crafty, money grubbing, profoundly ignorant and naturally violent.[4]

Addressing the concerns of constituents, but risking diplomatic relations with China, President Chester A. Arthur signed the Exclusion Act into law on May 6, 1882. Although the law made immigration to the United States difficult, it did not make it impossible. Certain classes of Chinese people, such as merchants, diplomats or scholars, were exempt from the law. The only way for other Chinese immigrants to enter America legally was to prove he or she was the son or daughter of an American-born citizen. Upon verification of their legal right to be in the country, each Chinese immigrant was issued a certificate of identification. If a Chinese immigrant did not obtain a certificate or failed to produce one upon demand of a public official, he was subject to immediate deportation.

The Chinese immigrant living in America found ways to acquire false documentation to reflect his status as an American born citizen. Once his citizenship was officially recognized, he claimed he had a son or daughter in China who wished to immigrate to the United States. The Chinese-American citizen then created false documents that proved the relationship between him and the immigrant "son." The Chinese-American citizen would then sell the "papers" to a Chinese citizen seeking to immigrate. Once secured, the immigrant assumed the name that corresponded with the papers, carefully studied the documents of "proof," and prepared himself for questioning by immigration authorities. Once he had convinced officials of his identity claim, he was allowed to enter the country.

Those who gained entry into the United States in this manner became known as "paper sons" or "paper daughters." It is likely that Hanover laundryman Quong Sing, whose true name was Soo Hoo Yee Yoke, was a "paper son" who had secured the papers of "Quong Sing" and entered the country under that alias.[5]

Soo Hoo Yee Yoke, alias Quong Sing, probably immigrated to America sometime after 1882, when immigration laws changed, and before 1902, when his presence in Hanover was first documented. His surname, Soo Hoo, points to the Pearl River Delta region of Guangdong Province in Southern China as his place of origin.[6] Like so many of his countrymen, he fled the poverty and strife of his homeland to find peace and prosperity in America. He left his wife and four children behind and hoped some day to reunite with them.[7]

In 1916, a nephew of Quong Sing, Soo Hoo Tom Sing, also known as Tom Sing of Pittsburgh, Pennsylvania, applied to the U. S. Department of Labor's Immigration Service for a passport. Tom Sing had established himself as an American born citizen and received a certificate of residence from the Collector of Internal Revenue at Boston, Massachusetts on May 3, 1894.

Before U. S. officials would grant him a passport, it was necessary for Tom Sing to verify his citizenship. Soo Chong, also known as Soo Hoo Chong of Cambridge, Massachusetts testified on behalf of Tom Sing before Immigration Inspector J. McCabe on August 2, 1916. Soo Chong told Inspector McCabe that he had been born in Hon Gong Village, Hoiping District, which is in the Guangdong Province of China. Soo Chong asserted that he knew Tom Sing's father, Soo Hoo Yee Lon, from his home village of Hon Gong. According to Soo Chong, Soo Hoo Yee Lon was born in the same place. He also swore that Tom Sing was born to Soo Hoo Yee Lon and Wong She in San Francisco, California about 1880. Officials were skeptical of his account, but granted Tom Sing a passport.

Soo Chong made no mention of Quong Sing, alias Soo Hoo Yee Yoke, brother of Soo Hoo Yee Lon, during his interview. However, based on Soo Chong's testimony, it is likely that Quong Sing was born in the same village as that of his brother at Hon Gong, Hoiping District, Guangdong Province.[8]

≈

Along with another brother, Soo Hoo Yee Sing, Quong Sing opened a hand laundry business in the Masonic Building in 1902. Mrs. Emily J. Freeman of Washington Street in Assinippi provided the only other laundry service in Hanover at the time.[9] The brothers were industrious and dependable, and quickly built a reputable business. Soo Hoo Yee Sing eventually left the business in his brother's hands and opened his own laundry shop at 79 Cabot Street in Beverly, Massachusetts in 1903.[10]

Quong Sing's shop was typical of Chinese hand laundry shops in America during the nineteenth and early twentieth centuries. Around 1900, one in four ethnic Chinese men in the U. S. worked in a laundry, typically working ten to sixteen hours a day.[11]

A Chinese laundryman earned between $8 and $20 a week in 1903.[12] At that time, the Chinese hand laundry's charge for laundering shirts was ten cents apiece; for handkerchiefs, two cents each; for cuffs and collars, which during that era were detachable dress shirt accessories, also two cents each; and so on.[13] Sing made the shop not only his work place, but also his living quarters. His shop consisted of four small rooms, one where he washed laundry and cooked and ate his meals; one to dry laundry; another, a front room for ironing and wrapping finished laundry; and the last one was a bedroom with a small cot and his personal belongings.

A partition with a counter top divided the front and back of the shop. A small gate in the partition allowed entry and exit to both areas. Quong Sing placed his finished laundry in brown paper packages on shelves behind the counter, each package labeled with a ticket in Chinese to identify the customer. He paid his rent to William Bates, a Hanover merchant, in "fractional silver" (coins worth less than one dollar).

Residents from the area respected and liked the Chinese man. They Americanized his name and affectionately called him "John" He was meticulous about his work and generous in extending credit to customers. According to the *Rockland Standard*, in an article published nine days after his murder on February 5, 1904, "Quong Sing was highly spoken of by all who knew him. He was very quiet and inoffensive, minded his business steadily, and never sought a quarrel with anybody. He was of a very good Chinese family and had a wife and four children in China, to whom he had hoped to return as soon as he had earned a competence."[14]

≈

January 1904 brought arctic conditions to the South Shore area. It had been a winter unlike any other that year in Hanover. Temperatures in the ten to thirty below zero range were recorded and more than the usual amount of snow fell. On one night, "people had great affection for all stoves that gave out warmth and some slept in chairs with their feet in the ovens."[15] During the first week of January, a significant blizzard occurred with many inches of snow falling. The weekly *Rockland Standard*, in a January 15 article, indicated "storm piled up on storm until the 'oldest inhabitant' says he never saw the equal." Railroad lines and streets were impassable, plumbers were kept busy repairing frozen pipe lines, church attendance was down and schools were closed. The article went on to further relate, "The thermometer at Josselyn's grocery read thirty-four below zero on Tuesday morning, January 5. Mrs. Charles Winslow, aged ninety-six, says it was the coldest since 1856."[16] By January 28, 1904 at least fifteen inches of snow remained on the ground and the temperatures had "warmed" to a high of about eighteen degrees.[17] On January 31, twelve more inches of snow fell.[18]

But the harshness and severity of winter conditions quickly faded in the minds of the community of just over two thousand people. In that bitter month of January, the brutal murder of Quong Sing stunned area residents.

≈

Cyrus Lawrence Ryan was born on April 12, 1883, the son of Michael and Elizabeth (Pierce) Ryan, in Charlottetown, Prince Edward Island. He was the eighth child in a family of eleven.[19] Three days after his birth, he was baptized at St. Dunstan's Roman Catholic Basilica in Charlottetown by Rev. John Corbett.[20]

Ryan only attended school for six months as a youngster and never learned to read and write. His father held a low-paying position as a stevedore on the Charlottetown docks, so all of the Ryan children, at a very early age, were sent to work to support the family.[21] When Ryan was nine-years old, his father sent him to strip tobacco in the factories of Hickey & Nicholson and T. B. Riley.[22, 23] Due to his age and size, he had to stand on a box in order to reach the counter to do his work.[24] He continued to work in the tobacco factories until about 1903, when he took a position as third cook on the *Olivette* steamer of the Plant Line Steamship Company.[25, 26] He remained on the *Olivette* for three weeks until July 29, 1903, when he resigned from the crew and disembarked in Boston. In the city, Ryan bought some clothing and an overcoat on credit. He borrowed $17.00 from the Washington Credit Company at 503 Washington Street.[27] He agreed to pay the credit company $1.00 a week until his debt was paid in full.[28]

Ryan had made plans to stay in Hanover at the home of thirty-four year-old Frederick Pierce, his half-brother.[29] Ryan and Pierce were born to the same mother. Pierce's home was on Water Street, near Elm Street, which is less then a mile from the village of Hanover Four Corners. Pierce emigrated from Charlottetown, Prince Edward Island by rail and entered the United States at Vanceboro, Maine on September 21, 1895. He settled in Hanover shortly thereafter.[30] He worked briefly at the E. H. Clapp Rubber mill and later hired on with the Hanover Branch Railroad as a flagman at Curtis Crossing.[31]

After he settled in at his half-brother's home, Ryan looked for employment. Ryan did odd jobs until he obtained a position for $9.00 a week at the Clapp Rubber mill sometime in August. He stayed at Pierce's home until October, when he left to live with Richard Smith, a cousin, for some unexplained reason. He returned to Pierce's home in December and paid his half-brother $4.25 a week for room and board.[32]

≈

January 23, 1904, was an unusually mild day for that frigid winter, with temperatures reaching fifty degrees.[33] Two intoxicated men entered Quong Sing's laundry shop and started taunting him, then demanded money. Sing refused to comply and one of the men struck him in the face. Quong Sing, who weighed a mere ninety pounds,[34] produced a revolver and threatened the men, ordering them from the premises. The two men decided to avoid any further confrontation and fled.

The village community considered Quong Sing a quiet, peaceful man. After the altercation at his shop, they became acutely aware that if anyone provoked the slightly built man, he wouldn't hesitate to defend himself. The *Rockland Standard*, in an article six days later, summed up the general opinion of Quong Sing's character when it printed, "Quong Sing is very quiet, minds his own business, and will molest no one if they treat him decently, but he will not take many knocks from an assailant without showing that he is able to defend himself."[35]

≈

At about 10:00 o'clock Wednesday evening, January 27, Mrs. Solomon Russell of Elm Street answered a knock on her door. A man she did not know greeted her and told her he had a message from Boston informing him that Mrs. Russell's daughter, Lucy, had been killed in a railroad accident.

Mrs. Russell, a seventy-five year-old widow, lived alone in her house, which was a short distance from Frederick Pierce's home. She had no means by which to contact Lucy and was frightened to travel alone into the city at night. Frantic, she planned to take the 8:15 a.m. train to Boston the next day.[36]

Mrs. Russell walked to the Curtis Crossing railroad station in the morning and according to witnesses, Cyrus Ryan was with her. She later told newspaper reporters she was not sure if it was Ryan who notified her of her daughter's death, but she was sure he was the man who walked with her from her home to the depot.[37]

Mrs. Russell arrived in Boston and learned her daughter was alive and well. Confused, shaken and relieved, she left Boston on the 2:43 p.m. train and returned to Hanover. When she arrived home, she discovered someone had ransacked her house and had stolen some jewelry and trinkets. She was unsure if the thief had taken any cash. She immediately suspected that the man who had visited her the evening before was the man responsible for the burglary.[38] In an odd coincidence, sometime during the same day, someone had also burglarized the nearby home of Frederick Pierce. The perpetrator took small articles of value from the house.[39] Police never arrested anyone for the thefts.

≈

Quong Sing rose early on the chilly morning of January 28. The thermometer read four degrees.[40] He stoked the stove in his drying room and prepared for his day.

At about 11:10 a.m., Stanley Baker, a clerk at Phillips, Bates and Company, arrived at Quong's shop and dropped off some laundry. Baker saw Cyrus Ryan in the shop when he was there.[41]

Domingo Perry, a twenty-three year-old immigrant from the Azores who operated a barber shop on Broadway in Four Corners, saw Ryan at about 11:30 a.m. when Ryan came into his shop for a shave. Ryan changed his mind about the shave a few minutes later and left.[42, 43]

William Appleton, a twenty-three year-old Brockton resident and a grocery clerk at Little's Market in Pembroke was driving his team into town when he noticed Cyrus Ryan in the front room of the laundry shop. He knew Ryan and had seen him in the Four Corners area on a number of other occasions. He waved to him from his wagon as he passed the laundry and Ryan waved back. As he went by, the 11:45 a.m. Clapp Rubber Works whistle blew.[44]

That same morning, butcher William D. Paxton, owner of Wilkinson and Paxton, a provisions market in the Masonic Building (next door to Quong's Laundry), opened his shop. About 11:55 a.m., Paxton went into Quong Sing's shop to retrieve some water, as the water pump in his own shop had frozen due to the frigid overnight temperature. As he entered the shop, he noticed a young man he knew as Cyrus Ryan in the front room. Paxton saw Quong Sing eating a bowl of rice in the back wash room. Paxton asked Quong Sing if he could pump some water and with Quong Sing's consent, he filled his pail and returned to his market. Shortly thereafter, Paxton left the market for lunch.[45, 46]

At about the same time, Henry Snell, a barber with a shop next to Quong Sing's in the Masonic Building, and a friend, twenty-two year-old house painter William Handy, left Snell's shop to get a bite to eat. They noticed Cyrus Ryan and Quong Sing in the front room of the laundry. Quong Sing was ironing a shirt.[47]

Nineteen-year-old Frank E. Chamberlain, a hostler at Howland's Livery at Four Corners, said Ryan came to the stable at about 12:35 p.m. and requested a team to go to Rockland. Chamberlain couldn't authorize the rental on his own and told Ryan he'd have to wait until his supervisor returned. Ryan told Chamberlain he was in "kind of a hurry." He became impatient and soon left.[48]

Chester C. Hobart, a fifty-four year-old shoe peddler in the employ of his son-in-law Everett Damon, drove a cart in Hanover as part of his route. He was having lunch with Mrs. Josselyn at her home near Water Street, discussing debts owed him by some of the people in Hanover. He mentioned Ryan's name and at that very moment, Ryan was passing the house on foot. Hobart left Mrs. Josselyn's at about 12:40 p.m., and followed Ryan to the Pierce home near Curtis Crossing at Water and Elm Streets.

At the house, Hobart asked Ryan for the money owed him. "I would like to pay all of my bills as easy as I can this one," said Ryan, as he pulled a roll of bills from his pocket and handed Mr. Hobart five $1 bills and twenty-five cents in change. Hobart later said Ryan's hand trembled as he gave him the money. Other than that, he didn't notice anything unusual about Ryan's behavior or appearance but thought it odd that Ryan had the cash readily available. He gave Ryan a receipt, talked for a short time, then left the house.[49]

Elm Street residents John C. Levings, Margaret J. Barry, Sarah F. Christy and Catherine Ridgeway saw Ryan on the road from the Four Corners to Curtis Crossing at about 12:45 p.m. He was walking at a brisk pace.[50]

When William Paxton, the butcher, started back to his market from the post office just before 1 p.m., he noticed that on this blustery day, the front door to Quong Sing's laundry shop was ajar. He stepped inside the shop and called out, "Hello." He received no answer. Sensing something wrong, he went to Snell's barber shop and told Snell about the odd circumstances.

Paxton, Snell and Alonzo Whiting, a friend of Snell's who was visiting in Snell's shop, went to the rear of the building to see if Quong Sing was there. When they couldn't find him they returned to the front of the shop and as they entered, they noticed there had been a struggle. Quong Sing's belongings were strewn about the front and back rooms and a trunk in Quong's bedroom had been disturbed.

Paxton noticed Quong's slippers and a board eight by eighteen inches, which he last saw on the left hand set tub, on the wash room floor. Water from the set tubs had spilled across the floor into the drying room to the right.[51] Paxton realized he and the others had arrived soon after the murder because an iron Quong Sing had been using was hot and burning a hole in a shirt on the ironing board.[52]

Quong Sing's legs were protruding from the drying room on their right. Inside the drying room, they saw Quong Sing's head submerged in a portable tub filled with water. On his head was a soap box. The three men were shocked at what they saw. They noticed the body was still warm, but lifeless.[53]

Henry Snell immediately summoned Dr. William. P. Grovestein, who had an office in the Four Corners. He also telephoned the office of Massachusetts District Police Chief Rufus R. Wade. (In 1875, the State Constabulary Force was renamed the State Detective Force. The State Detective Force was reorganized as the Massachusetts District Police four years later. The District Police eventually became the Massachusetts State Police). He notified Wade's office about the murder and gave a description of Cyrus Ryan, the person he last saw with Quong Sing and who he believed was responsible for his death. A telegraph with a description of Ryan was sent to all of the railroad stations between Hanover and Boston with orders to point him out to police if seen.[54]

Eben C. Waterman, chairman of the Hanover Board of Selectmen, arrived at the laundry at about 1:25 p.m. He went to the wash room and saw a pair of slippers on the wet floor. He noticed two barrels of clear water in the room. In the drying room, Waterman saw Quong Sing's face, as far back as the ears, submerged in a tub containing six and one-half inches of water. Paxton, Snell and Whiting hadn't touched the body. They were likely convinced he was already dead. On top of Quong's head, Waterman saw and removed the soap box.[55] The soap box weighed about seventy-five pounds.[56]

Dr. Grovestein appeared then, and removed Quong Sing's head from the tub and tried to resuscitate him. The room was very warm. Dr. Andrew L. MacMillan, another physician with an office in Four Corners, subsequently entered the laundry and after repeated attempts by the two physicians to revive Quong Sing, they abandoned their efforts and pronounced him dead. Both doctors noticed marks on the windpipe and the left side of Quong's neck as if the fingers of a left hand had grasped it from behind.[57]

Hanover Chief of Police David H. Stoddard of North Hanover and Special Officer Thomas Tindale of South Hanover came to the laundry shop, as did Hanover Selectman Edward A. Bowker. The three men, along with Selectman Waterman, investigated the premises. As town officials, Bowker and Waterman were obligated to respond and assist in serious, unexpected events within their community. Joseph Tripp, owner of the Howard House at Four Corners, and Benjamin F. White, a house painter from Pembroke, also entered the crime scene.

≈

Today's investigator must take every precaution to ensure that strict procedures and guidelines are followed at every crime scene. Evidence contamination hinders the investigator's ability to establish the facts and circumstances of a crime. Therefore, every effort is made to curtail the number of persons who enter the scene in order to prevent the displacement, loss or tainting of evidence. The investigator of the early 20th century placed the same amount of value upon evidence, but hard and fast rules for proper identification and collection of evidence and the technology to process it did not exist. By the time Hanover

Police Chief Stoddard arrived at the laundry shop, no fewer than eleven persons had been inside. If Stoddard had been first at the scene he could have prevented unnecessary persons from entering. Each one tracked footprints into the shop, touched various items inside and otherwise corrupted the crime scene's integrity.

When Chief Stoddard entered the shop, he determined that Quong Sing had been removed from the wash tub and laid on the floor where doctors had tried to resuscitate him. It's likely that he asked witnesses already present if anything else had been moved in the room prior to his arrival. Stoddard knew that if Quong Sing's killer was apprehended, a trial would ensue and critical questions would be asked about conditions within the crime scene.

Like the state constables investigating the Hawkes murder, Stoddard lacked the forensic tools available to today's investigator. A legally accepted test for human blood identification had been developed by scientists in 1901, but fingerprint identification, hair and fiber recognition, ballistics identification and DNA analysis were beyond the imagination of early twentieth century lawmen. The first murder conviction in the United States based on fingerprint evidence was still seven years away.

≈

Back at the crime scene, investigators noted that someone had pried open a trunk inside Quong Sing's bedroom and strewn its contents around the room. The bed was disturbed, but apparently the perpetrator failed to search it thoroughly, as Waterman found $37.00 in silver and bills tucked between the bedding. The men looked for the revolver Quong Sing was known to have, but could not find it.[58] It was apparent to them that the perpetrator's intent was robbery and that the situation had gotten out of hand with the death of the laundry man.

William F. Bates, owner of Philips, Bates and Company near Four Corners, went to the Curtis Crossing station to take the 2:15 p.m. train for Boston. Bates hoped to find Quong Sing's relatives and notify them of his death. At the depot, Bates saw Ryan accompanying two women. Ryan was wearing a long black overcoat and a slouch hat and was carrying a small trunk and a satchel.[59] Bates thought Ryan seemed very uneasy. He saw him get up from his seat four times between Hanover and North Abington and go to another part of the car.[60]

The conductor on the train, who had obviously received the telegraph alert, told Bates state police officers were at South Station anticipating Ryan's arrival. They requested that Bates point Ryan out to them as he got off the train. Deputy Chief Joseph E. Shaw of the Massachusetts District Police dispatched forty-two year-old Captain William H. Proctor to South Station to wait for the train.

When the train arrived at 3:16 p.m., Bates disembarked and found state police Captain William Proctor on the platform. As Ryan descended from the steps of the train with his two companions, later identified as his fiancée, Catherine (Katie) Murray and his sister-in-law, Mary Pierce, Bates alerted Proctor and the captain placed Ryan under arrest.[61]

Proctor searched Ryan and his satchel and found a revolver in his coat pocket. The revolver contained three cartridges. Proctor also found a gold watch Ryan had in another pocket.[62]

Proctor escorted Ryan to the police offices a short distance away at the State House. Ryan's fiancé and sister-in-law accompanied him. At the State House, Proctor and Deputy Shaw interrogated Ryan. Ryan admitted under questioning he had visited the laundry shop in Hanover several times during the day. He told police he went to the shop to retrieve a shirt that had been laundered. When he got to the laundry, he realized he had lost the check for the shirt. He said the shop owner would not give him the shirt without it, so he left the shirt there. He told the officers he had heard of the man's death before leaving Hanover, but adamantly denied any part in the murder.

Further investigation by the state police revealed Quong Sing was left-handed. When Ryan was arrested he had scratches on his face and his clothing was torn. When the police questioned him about the scratches, Ryan told them he had received them during a good-natured scuffle with a co-worker.

Officers asked Ryan to show them just how the struggle with the co-worker occurred. After considering Ryan's demonstration, the officers determined the scratches and torn clothing could only have been inflicted by a left-handed person.[63]

Deputy Shaw surmised Ryan had entered the laundry shop expecting to pick up his shirt. When the Quong Sing wouldn't produce it, a heated exchange occurred between the two men. The situation escalated and Ryan assaulted Quong, killing him. Shaw believed Ryan had placed Quong's head in the tub with the soap box on it to give the appearance an accident had occurred. At that time, Deputy Shaw had no evidence robbery was the motive because he had not as yet verified the gun and watch belonged to Quong and had been notified that the cash drawer in the shop had been left secure.[64]

Ryan told the officers he had planned yesterday to leave Hanover today with his fiancée, Katie Murray. He said Murray had packed his trunk earlier in the day and Ryan had given it to the station master at Hanover to load onto the train. Officers retrieved Ryan's trunk from the baggage room at South Station. Inside the trunk they found clothing belonging to Ryan and Murray. When officers questioned Ryan and Murray about their final destination, they received conflicting statements. Ryan told them they intended to stay at his sister's house in Brookline. Murray said they planned to stay at her sister-in-law's house in Cambridge.[65]

At the State House, police allowed Katie Murray to speak with Ryan at his cell. Proctor suspected that Ryan had slipped something to Murray during their conversation. He confronted her later and demanded that she turn the item over to him. Apparently, Proctor had not searched Ryan thoroughly at South Station. She reached into the bosom of her dress and handed Proctor a silver watch. She also turned over $18.00 Ryan had given her. Police never charged Murray for complicity in the deception. Proctor later confirmed that Quong Sing had purchased a similar watch six months before at W. S. Curtis' store in Four Corners. It was an inexpensive, silveroid, open-faced timepiece.[66]

Ryan asserted he owned the revolver and both watches. He told Proctor and Shaw he had bought the silver watch from a crew member on the *Olivette* who was hard up for cash. He said he had purchased the revolver from a man on a street in Rockland for $1.00. The gold watch was a gift from his sister.[67]

Stanley Baker, William Paxton, William Handy and Henry Snell boarded a train for Boston after receiving a call from the district police about the arrest. The police requested the presence of the men to interview them about the murder and to seek their assistance in identifying the suspect in custody. Upon their arrival, the four men met William Bates and all five went to the police offices where the four men identified Cyrus Ryan as the man they had seen in the laundry shop earlier in the day. William Paxton identified the revolver seized from Ryan as the same gun owned by Quong Sing. The men could not identify the watch.[68]

≈

Massachusetts Governor George Robinson appointed Dr. Henry Watson Dudley as Medical Examiner for the Second Plymouth District in 1890. Dudley was born in New Hampshire in 1831 and graduated from Harvard Medical School in March 1864. By 1904, Dudley had been practicing in Abington for forty years.[69] He arrived at the laundry shop at 3:30 p.m., and after inspecting Quong Sing's body, scheduled an autopsy for the next day.

≈

On Friday morning, January 29, police brought Ryan to the Plymouth County Second District Court at Hingham where he was arraigned before Judge George W. Kelley. He entered a plea of not guilty to a charge of murder. Captain Proctor, present at the arraignment, requested the court continue the case until February 6 at the Plymouth County Second District Court in Abington for a hearing. Judge Kelley granted the request and ordered Ryan held without bail. Sheriff's deputies then took him to Plymouth Jail. The court notified witnesses in the case to appear at Plymouth County Superior Court to give testimony before a grand jury.[70]

Two of Ryan's sisters arrived in Hanover before noon. They had mistakenly gone to the court house in Abington to support their brother at his arraignment and missed the proceedings in Hingham. Ryan's fiancée, Kate Murray, also failed to attend the arraignment. Later the same day, Ryan's sisters took a train to Boston with Frederick and Mary Pierce to seek legal counsel for Ryan.

On the same day, a *Boston Post* reporter interviewed Ryan's fiancée, who dramatically came to his defense. Murray told the reporter, "Poor Cyrus is accused unfairly. I know that some great mistake has been committed and before the matter is settled, justice will be gained. My Cyrus is a good, upright man and I will stand by him to the last." Murray told the *Post* correspondent she was seeking employment in Boston to help Ryan pay his legal fees. She added that she still intended to marry Ryan upon his acquittal.[71]

≈

Officials removed Quong Sing's body from the laundry shop, where it had remained overnight, to the medical examiner's office in Abington. Dr. Dudley, assisted by Drs. F. G. and L. F. Wheatley of North Abington, conducted the autopsy. Drs. Grovestein and MacMillan were also present. Captain Proctor attended the postmortem examination along with sixty-two year-old state detective Alfred B. Hodges of Taunton, who was assigned by Deputy Shaw to assist in the murder investigation. An inspection of the body by the doctors revealed slight wounds on the side of the head, neck and chin, perhaps caused by finger nails. There were four scratches on the neck. Scrutiny of the chest cavity showed a rupture of the right auricle of the heart, the wall of the organ being as thin as paper. The soap box placed on the body, the attempts at resuscitation, or attempts to breathe while asphyxiating, might have caused the rupture. Dr. Dudley issued his final ruling as death caused by drowning.[72] Quong Sing was forty-eight years old at the time of his death.[73]

The Medical Examiner's Office released the body to the Sparrell Funeral Home in Norwell.[74] Lewis Jones & Sons, undertakers at 50 LaGrange Street, Boston, later received the body and handled funeral and burial arrangements.[75]

Quong Sing's brother, Soo Hoo Yee Sing, arrived in Hanover by train the same morning with two other Chinese men. One man was fluent in English and was an interpreter for Yee Sing. Yee Sing saw Cyrus Ryan, in the custody of police officials, on the train from Boston as officials transported Ryan to Hingham for his arraignment at the district court. According to the *Boston Globe*, Yee Sing "expressed himself as very bitter against Ryan."[76]

Yee Sing had many questions about his brother's death. He had come to take custody of Quong Sing's body and inquire about the disposition of his property. Yee Sing and his companions met with Medical Examiner Dudley and he addressed their concerns. He explained to them that authorities would turn over Quong Sing's property after the conclusion of the criminal trial and settlement of his estate in probate court.[77]

Dr. Dudley authorized the return of laundry in Quong Sing's shop to the proper owners. Selectman Eben Waterman issued a notice asking patrons to contact him to claim finished and unfinished laundry.[78]

Captain Proctor, Detective Hodges and Eben Waterman accompanied Yee Sing and his companions to the laundry. While there, Yee Sing accounted for all of the laundry at the shop and deciphered the names attached to the laundry parcels ready for delivery.

Proctor, Eben Waterman, Yee Sing and his interpreter found a shirt corresponding in size, fourteen and one-half, to that claimed by Ryan as his. Yee Sing and his interpreter traced the shirt in an account book kept by Quong Sing. The book revealed Ryan had left the shirt for laundering nearly a year before January 28.[79]

Captain Proctor and Detective Hodges continued their investigation inside the shop. The officers found a box for a revolver in the bedroom trunk and one cartridge in the box. They also uncovered a roll of five-cent pieces in the trunk.

Proctor and Hodges came across another box in the lower part of the trunk. The box, designed to store fifty .44 caliber cartridges, contained only forty-seven. The cartridges were stamped with the Union Metallic Cartridge Company (U.M.C.) brand name. The company manufactured ammunition in Bridgeport, Connecticut.

The officers found a third box on the bed that contained a watch chain and $21.39 in cash. The officers located an additional $1.00 in Quong's clothing.[80] A combination lock secured a cash drawer in the front room. Officers forced the lock and found $9.00 inside.[81]

≈

Newspaper correspondents spent Saturday, January 30, in Hanover interviewing Cyrus Ryan's friends and relatives. His supporters refused to believe Ryan had committed the crime and told reporters that they had evidence to prove his innocence. Ryan's family secured the services of Attorneys John F. Callanan of Plymouth and Fred M. Bixby of Brockton to defend him.

Ryan's advocates asserted that witnesses who could testify to Ryan's movements on the day of the murder and could verify his location at certain times and places refuted the possibility that he was present at the laundry shop when Quong Sing was murdered.

Ryan's family alleged William Appleton had seen Ryan in the laundry with Quong Sing at 12:15 p.m. Frederick Pierce's wife, Mary, maintained Ryan had been in her house at 12:45. His defenders believed this half hour left little time for Ryan to have committed the murder, ransack the laundry shop, then reach the Pierce home. They reasoned a man could walk the only two routes between the Four Corners and Pierce's – the main road or the railroad bed – in a maximum of twenty minutes. Witnesses can confirm seeing Ryan on the road soon after 12:35 p.m. and noted nothing unusual about his appearance. This left ten unaccounted minutes.

Reporters asked several medical men if it were possible for someone to kill the victim and ransack his property in such a short time. They were evasive, but one man did state, "A man can do considerable in ten minutes."[82]

Some town residents tried to link the robbery attempt of Quong Sing on January 23 with the murder. But police dismissed this theory, and stated the persons responsible on that day had alibis for their whereabouts on the day in question.

Family and friends also refuted the police claim that the revolver they had found in Ryan's possession was Quong Sing's. They asserted the gun was very common and there were thousands similar to the model seized by police.

As for the watch, Ryan, upon his arrest, insisted he had bought it from a crew member on the *Olivette* steamer during his trip to Boston

RUM, A TAILOR'S GOOSE AND A SOAP BOX

in 1903. His half-brother, Fred Pierce, knew him to own a silver watch.[83]

Other friends of Ryan claimed another man committed the murder on January 28 and that Ryan was simply a victim of circumstances. The friends alleged that this other suspect had been in Quong's laundry shop just before the murder. They said witnesses overheard the man and Quong Sing arguing over laundry the man had left at the shop. The witnesses insisted that the voice they had overheard was not the voice of Ryan. They also claimed the man was considerably taller than Ryan and that he wore a cap and dark clothes.

Henry Snell and Joseph Tripp heard the description of the man on the day of the murder and believed they had seen him walking west toward Rockland. The two men secured a horse and sleigh and tried to locate him. A number of people in houses along the Rockland road told Snell and Tripp they had seen a man fitting the description walking by. The two men continued for two miles, but could not find him.

Ryan's friends also thought that a statement made by Chester C. Hobart, the salesman who drove a boot and shoe cart in Hanover, clearly showed that there was no possible way that Ryan could be at Mrs. Josselyn's house at 12:40 p.m., where Hobart was able to settle his financial affairs with Ryan, and have the time to have killed Quong Sing. [84]

≈

On January 31, Katie Murray, with the permission of Sheriff Henry S. Porter, visited her fiancé at the jail in Plymouth. Reporters questioned her about the case and her conversation with Ryan. She refused to provide details of her talk. She did tell reporters she and Ryan were not on their way to be married when he was arrested. She also said the silveroid watch and revolver seized by the police belonged to Ryan and he was innocent of the charges against him.[85]

On that same day, Quong Sing's family buried his remains at Mount Hope Cemetery, Boston, in a small section reserved for Chinese interments. Soo Hoo Wing, a cousin of Quong Sing and the owner of a restaurant on Harrison Avenue, Boston, was in charge of the funeral ceremonies and the burial. A small cortege that included a hearse

169

and two carriages occupied by the deceased, his brother and cousin and a few friends, entered the cemetery at about 3:00 p.m. A simple Chinese ceremony took place at the graveside and Quong Sing was laid to rest.[86]

Eight years later, on September 21, 1912, Lewis Jones & Sons, undertakers, at the request of the family, and in accordance with Chinese ritual, exhumed Quong Sing's body. His family shipped his remains to China for reburial.[87]

≈

On Thursday, February 4, a Plymouth County Grand Jury indicted Ryan, charging him with murder. "It is alleged that Ryan assaulted and robbed a Chinese laundryman at Hanover Four Corners and then caused the man's death by forcing his head into a tub of water."[88] County sheriffs removed Ryan from his cell on the same day and brought him before Judge Hardy at Plymouth Superior Court for arraignment on the indictment. Ryan told Judge Hardy he was without counsel, apparently unaware that Frederick Pierce had already retained Attorneys Callanan and Bixby to defend him. The judge told Ryan the court would appoint representation for him and ordered him returned to Plymouth Jail.[89]

≈

On February 6, Plymouth County sheriffs transported Ryan from the jail to the Plymouth County Second District Court at Abington for his scheduled appearance. He pleaded not guilty to a charge of murder. The state prosecutor informed Judge George W. Kelley that Ryan had been indicted for murder and had been arraigned in Plymouth Superior Court on the charge. He requested that Judge Kelley dismiss the charge pending against him in the lower court. Judge Kelley dismissed the murder charge and ordered Ryan held on the murder indictment without bail pending his appearance for trial in Plymouth Superior Court on June 6, 1904.[90]

≈

On Monday, June 6, Cyrus Ryan appeared at Plymouth Superior Court for trial with his counsel, Attorneys John F. Callanan and Fred M. Bixby of Brockton. Justices Stevens and Hardy presided. (When the jurisdiction of capital cases was transferred to the Superior Court in 1891, the statute authorizing the change also provided that three justices of that court should preside at trial, but this was later reduced to two).[91]

Judge William Burnham Stevens was born in Stoneham, Massachusetts in 1843. He was an 1865 graduate of Dartmouth College and studied at Harvard Law School. He was admitted to the Suffolk County bar in 1867 and was District Attorney for the Northern District of Massachusetts from 1880 to 1890. He was appointed to the bench of the Superior Court in 1898.[92] Judge John Henry Hardy was born in Hollis, New Hampshire in 1847 and was a Civil War veteran. He graduated from Dartmouth College in 1870 and studied law at Harvard Law School. He was admitted to the Massachusetts bar in 1872 and was appointed as an associate justice of the Superior Court in 1896 by Governor Wolcott.[93]

Asa Palmer French, Jonathan Wales French and Asa French, ca. 1901
(Courtesy of Braintree Historical Society)

The court crier, Deputy Sheriff George A. Wheeler, opened court with a reading of the declaration, "Hear ye, hear ye, all persons having anything to do before the Honorable, the Justices of the Superior Court in the first session thereof now sitting in Plymouth within and for the County of Plymouth, draw near and give your attendance and you shall be heard: God save the Commonwealth of Massachusetts!"[94]

Rev. John Cuckson, pastor of the First Church in Town Square, Plymouth, offered a prayer and trial proceedings began at 10:40 a.m.[95, 96] District Attorney Asa Palmer French, whose father, the late Asa French, prosecuted James Costley for the murder of Julia Hawkes in 1874, addressed Judges Stevens and Hardy and related the steps leading up to Ryan's arrest and appearance before the court. He then moved for trial. The court proceeded with the empanelling of jurors.

The jury pool consisted of ninety potential jurors. The court drew sixty-nine of these ninety and after attorneys for both sides examined each individually, twelve were selected. The Commonwealth challenged twenty-four and the defense, twelve. The court excused the remainder due to prejudicial opinions, age or infirmities.

The prosecution and defense selected the following jurors: Andrew Gale, building mover, Brockton; Otis L. Barden, barber, Middleborough; Ezra R. Bumpus, farmer, Wareham; John D. Ferguson, undertaker, Scituate; George B. Gardner, farmer, Hingham; Calvin H. Hall, peddler, Brockton; Samuel W. Hammond, farmer, Mattapoisett; George E. Leavitt, shoe operative, Whitman; Henry J. LeLacheur, real estate dealer, West Bridgewater; Austin E. Pratt, shoemaker, Bridgewater; James F. Roberts, janitor, Middleborough; Francis T. Sheldon, milk dealer, Rockland; and Bradford C. Wilder, unemployed, Hingham.[97]

After empanelment, the court recessed until the afternoon. At about 1:00 p.m., the court reopened and DA French requested that the court transport jurors to the crime scene in Hanover. Plymouth County Deputy Sheriffs Blake and Collingwood conveyed the jurors to Quong Sing's laundry shop at Four Corners. There, DA French summarized the events of the tragedy in the presence of defense counsel and the defendant, who was under guard. After viewing the scene and hearing French's account, the jurors returned to the court house at 6:15 p.m.

Justices Stevens and Hardy acknowledged their presence, dismissed them, and adjourned until the next morning.

≈

Court proceedings began at 9:00 a.m. on the second day of trial.[98] Deputy Sheriffs Lincoln and Simmons had escorted Cyrus Ryan to the prisoner's dock in the court room. Ryan smiled and appeared confident.[99] After the jury was seated, DA French addressed the court with his opening remarks. French outlined what the Commonwealth intended to prove, defined the degrees of murder and gave the prosecution's version of Ryan's movements on the day of the murder.[100]

The prosecutor told jurors Ryan earned $9.00 a week at the rubber mill. He paid $4.25 a week to his half-brother, Frederick Pierce, for board, and an additional $1.75 per week for the living expenses of his fiancée, Katie Murray, who also boarded at Pierce's home. French also pointed out that the rubber mill docked a portion of Ryan's pay to settle a debt with a clothing credit company. This, he told the jury, left very little money for Ryan's every day expenses and savings.[101] He also pointed out that Ryan, shortly before he left Hanover on the day of the murder, settled a number of debts with creditors.

DA French went on. He told the jury of the watch and revolver missing from Quong Sing's shop and how investigators found a box of ammunition there with three rounds missing. A revolver seized from Ryan upon his arrest was loaded with three new .44 caliber cartridges, similar to the ammunition missing from the box in Quong's shop.

DA French called John L. Sturtevant, a photographer, as his first witness. Sturtevant identified pictures he had taken of the Masonic Building where Quong Sing's laundry shop was located. Harrison L. House, a thirty-seven year-old civil engineer, described the Four Corners area and identified plans of the Masonic Building. The court admitted the photographs and plans as evidence.

Dr. Henry Dudley, the physician who performed the autopsy, testified as to the condition of Quong Sing's body on January 28. He related that the victim's lungs had been full of water and swollen and the air passages had reddened.[102] The autopsy, which was undertaken the following day, revealed that the tissue of Quong's heart had been very thin and the right auricle had ruptured. The doctor asserted that in his medical opinion the cause of death was drowning. He explained that the soap box placed on the body, the attempts at resuscitation, or attempts to breathe while asphyxiating, might have caused the rupture.

Dr. William Grovestein of Hanover Four Corners, also testified as to his observations in the laundry on the day in question and described his attempts to revive Quong Sing. He was present during Quong Sing's autopsy and corroborated Dr. Dudley's testimony, informing the court he agreed that the cause of death was drowning.

Drs. Andrew MacMillan and Frank Wheatley added testimony consistent with the details provided by Drs. Dudley and Grovestein. Dr. MacMillan also added he had seen Quong Sing alive at 10:00 a.m. on January 28. Newspaper accounts made no mention of cross-examination by defense attorneys. When the defense later presented their case before the court, they called several physicians to the stand to refute the testimony of Drs. Grovestein, Dudley, MacMillan and Wheatley.

DA French called Frederick Pierce to the witness stand. Pierce provided some background information about his half-brother's arrival in Hanover and his situation as a boarder in his home. Pierce testified he hadn't seen Ryan since Ryan was six years old. He told the court Ryan had obtained work at E. H. Clapp Rubber Company three weeks after his arrival.[103]

Pierce said Ryan stayed with him from August until October, when he left to board with a cousin, Richard Smith. Pierce didn't explain the reason for this move. Ryan returned to Pierce's home in December. In that same month, Ryan's fiancée, Katie Murray, arrived from Prince Edward Island and boarded at Pierce's home. She obtained employment at R. C. Waterman's tack factory. Pierce testified he never knew Ryan to own a revolver while he lived in his house. Pierce testified he knew Ryan had a watch, but had never looked closely at it. The prosecutor showed Pierce a watch and Pierce identified it as once having been owned by his half-sister, Annie Ryan. DA French called Pierce's wife, Mary, as his next witness and she corroborated her husband's testimony. She testified she had heard about the murder at the laundry about a half hour before she boarded a 2:15 p.m. Boston-bound train with Ryan and Katie Murray at Curtis Crossing. She said Ryan bought the train tickets for all three.

The prosecution's next witness, Henry Snell, described the events of January 28 as he knew them. He testified he had never seen Ryan in the laundry shop before, never knew Quong had owned a pistol and did not know where he had kept his money. He told the court Quong had owned an open-faced watch. On cross-examination, defense attorney Callanan tried to draw suspicion away from Ryan by questioning Snell about another suspect seen near the laundry shop on the day of the murder. Snell testified again he had never seen Ryan in the laundry shop before the day of the murder. He said he could easily see inside Quong's shop as the curtains were always up. He denied telling Joseph Tripp he had seen a man with a cap on outside the shop, but admitted he did follow a man of that description at Tripp's suggestion. He said he and Tripp had tried to follow the man for about two miles along the road that leads to Rockland, but never found him.

Witnesses William Handy and William Paxton corroborated Snell's account of the events leading up to and following the murder. Paxton knew Quong had owned a revolver and described it as a .44 caliber five shot "Bull Dog" with a black handle. DA French showed him a revolver and Paxton stated he believed it to be the one owned by Quong Sing. Upon cross-examination, Paxton stated he believed all .44 caliber revolvers to be the same. He also admitted he had not seen Quong's revolver in a box.

Snell, Handy and Paxton all testified they had identified Ryan at the State House on the afternoon of his arrest. Upon completion of Paxton's testimony, the court adjourned for the day.[104]

≈

DA French opened the third day of trial with the testimony of witnesses who confirmed Ryan's movements during the day of the murder. He called his first witness of the day, Stanley F. Baker, clerk at Phillips, Bates and Company, who recounted he had dropped off his laundry at Quong Sing's shop at 11:10 a.m. and saw Ryan there with Quong.

DA French called several witnesses who each described what they saw the day of the murder. Barber Domingo Perry stated Ryan had called at his barber shop for a shave on the morning of the murder. He said shortly after his arrival, Ryan had changed his mind and left for Four Corners. John C. Levings, Sarah Christy, Margaret Barry and Catherine Ridgeway all testified they had seen Ryan hurrying along the road between Four Corners and Curtis Crossing. William Appleton testified he had seen Ryan in the laundry shop at 11:45 a.m., not 12:15 p.m., as asserted by Ryan's family and friends. Frank Chamberlain and David Tower, both employees at Howland's stable, stated Ryan had come to the stable at about 12:35 p.m. looking for a team. Charles E. Hunt testified he had seen Ryan at Pierce's home and had helped Ryan carry his trunk from the house to the Curtis Crossing station. Alonzo Whiting substantiated the previous testimony of Paxton and Snell. He also testified he had seen Ryan at the depot on the day of the murder. William Bates stated he had seen Ryan and two women board the 2:15 p.m. train at Curtis Crossing and that Ryan had appeared nervous. John R. Smith, an employee at E. H. Clapp's, stated he had never known Ryan to own a watch or gun. Herbert Cook, another employee, said he had seen Ryan with a gold watch. The prosecutor presented the gold watch that had been seized from Ryan on the day of his arrest and Cook identified it as similar to the one he had seen in Ryan's possession. He could not identify the silver watch and stated he had never seen Ryan with a revolver.

Annie Ryan, Cyrus' sister, identified the gold watch as once being hers. She stated she had given the watch to Cyrus and he had it with him when he arrived in Hanover from Canada in 1903. This corroborated the previous testimony of her half-brother, Frederick Pierce.

As to the revolver, Tom Sing of Pittsburgh, Pennsylvania, a nephew of Quong Sing's, testified he had given the gun to his uncle in 1902. He identified the box and gun given in evidence as similar to the items given to his uncle. Sing stated his uncle had kept the gun on a shelf over his bed.

Then the DA called Quong Sing's brother, Yee Sing, to the witness stand. He showed Yee Sing the revolver in evidence and asked him if he could identify it. Yee Sing told the court the revolver was the same he had seen in his brother's shop.[105]

Eben Waterman, Hanover Selectman, testified about his observations of the laundry shop when the body was found. He identified the revolver box and cartridges in evidence that he, Detective Hodges and Captain Proctor had found in the bedroom. He also identified a cigar box containing cash under a pillow in the bedroom and more money in Quong's clothing and in his cash drawer in the front room. Detective Hodges testified as to his examination of the laundry shop. He corroborated the prior testimony of Eben Waterman.[106] If robbery was the motive, the perpetrator was slipshod in his search.

Loring Phillips, superintendent of the Clapp Rubber Company testified Ryan had quit work in the mill a week before the murder because of difficulty repaying a debt to an installment clothing company. To set a time frame, DA French called Alexander Christy, an employee at the company, who testified he had blown the mill whistle at 12:45 p.m. on January 28. Chester Hobart testified Ryan had paid him a debt of $5.25 at about 1:00 p.m. on January 28. Hobart stated Ryan's hand had trembled as he gave him the money. After completing his testimony, Hobart was excused from the witness stand and court adjourned for the day.

≈

Court opened at 9:00 a.m. on June 9, day four of the trial, and DA French continued to call witnesses for the prosecution. Martin Mullen, an employee of Clapp Rubber, and Daniel F. Kelley of Boston, testified that on January 28 Ryan had repaid them money he had owed them.

Captain William Proctor testified about the events leading up to Ryan's arrest, his capture, and his interrogation at the State House. Proctor also told how he secured the gun and gold watch from Ryan and the silver watch and money from Katie Murray. He stated Ryan had told him he had bought the silver watch from a waiter on the steamer *Olivette*, and that he had brought the gold watch with him when he left Canada for Boston.

The prosecutor showed Proctor a shirt, sized fourteen and one-half. Proctor identified it as the shirt he, Eben Waterman, Yee Sing and Yee's interpreter had found in Quong Sing's laundry shop on January 29. Yee Sing and his interpreter found a reference to the shirt in Quong Sing's account book. The book revealed the shirt had belonged to Cyrus Ryan and that he had checked it for cleaning nearly a year before January 28.

Proctor, Robert Smith of Dorchester, and William H. Rose of Boston provided expert ballistics and firearm testimony about the pistol seized from Ryan. Proctor testified three cartridges he had found in the weapon matched the brand name and caliber of the ammunition found in Quong Sing's bedroom at the laundry shop.[107] All of the witnesses believed the weapon had not been fired more than once or twice. (Proctor would later testify in the famous murder trial of Sacco and Vanzetti in 1921. His testimony on forensic evidence at the trial has become the subject of much controversy. Many historians have asserted that Proctor did not possess the experience, nor the scientific means to competently testify about a bullet allegedly fired from a gun connected to Sacco and have suggested that Proctor's testimony was misleading.)

William R. Atkins of Bridgeport, CT, an employee of Union Metallic Cartridge Company and an expert on ammunition, testified about the company's .44 caliber ammunition found in Quong's bedroom and the company's procedure of boxing the ammunition in quantities of fifty.

The last witness for the prosecution, Ms. Harriet Stalling, a stenographer at Massachusetts District Police headquarters, read her notes made during the interrogation of Cyrus Ryan by Deputy Shaw and Captain Proctor at the State House. DA French then rested his case.

Junior defense counsel John F. Callanan rose from his seat to make his opening remarks to the jury. Callanan startled everyone in attendance when he said his client intended to admit killing Quong Sing. He told jurors he would prove the murder was not intentional, but that Ryan acted in self-defense. It's unclear when Ryan and his attorneys decided to mount a self-defense argument. It is likely that Ryan, after having listened to overwhelming eyewitness testimony placing him at the scene of the crime, decided he couldn't refute it. His only possible chance for an acquittal was to claim he was defending himself from an attack by Quong Sing.

Callanan said, "We will introduce evidence to show Ryan's good character and life from a child up to the present time. On the day of January 28, Ryan went into the laundry to get a shirt before he left town. The Chinaman could not find it, however, so Ryan went out. He returned at about noon and again asked for his shirt. The Chinaman looked again and could not find it. He then went out to the back room and immediately came out with a revolver in his hand, which he pointed at Ryan. Ryan grappled with him and both fell to the floor. Ryan took the revolver away and then noticed for the first time the Chinaman was dead. Ryan admits the whole affair, but contends the Chinaman died from heart failure, and that he attacked him in self-defense. We will show that Ryan was justified in what he did, and that he then left the laundry and later took the train for Boston."[108] Upon completion of his address, the court recessed until 1:00 p.m.[109]

The afternoon session found the courthouse packed with witnesses, spectators and journalists, all anxiously awaiting the testimony of Ryan. Apparently, word of Ryan's self-defense claim had spread quickly. Callanan called Ryan's fiancée, Katie Murray to the witness stand. Katie was born in Clyde's River, Prince Edward Island in 1886. Upon questioning, she said that she had known Ryan for years and they had intended to marry. She said they had made arrangements to leave Hanover on the Sunday before the murder (January 24). "I was to get work in Cambridge and Cyrus in Brookline. Cyrus was not well, so we decided to postpone the trip until Thursday." Murray went on to state that she and Cyrus got up early and had breakfast. She said that Cyrus took money from his trunk and went to Four Corners. Before he left, "He told me to be ready for the 2:15 p.m. train and we left Hanover at that time."[110]

It seemed that Murray was willing to do or say anything to prevent Ryan's conviction. A comment she made to a *Boston Post* reporter the day after the murder that "My Cyrus is a good, upright man and I will stand by him to the last," left little doubt as to her devotion and loyalty. Her testimony for the defense was an obvious attempt by her to show that Ryan's plans to leave Hanover were planned well in advance and not a sudden flight. She wanted the jury to believe that Ryan had a future ahead of him; that the reason he had money on the day of the murder was because he had taken it from his trunk before leaving for Four Corners; and that he had planned in advance to leave on the 2:15 p.m. train. If Ryan had robbery and murder in his mind, wouldn't he have wanted to leave on the next available train?

Upon cross-examination, she testified she had first heard of Quong Sing's death when she was at the State House after Ryan's arrest. It was then that she had heard Ryan was suspected in the crime, but she did not know if Ryan had been in the laundry at the time the killing occurred. She stated she had never heard that Ryan was "hard up for money."[111] DA French never challenged her on her testimony about the plans she and Cyrus had, nor about Cyrus' actions on the morning of the murder. More than likely, French sensed the jury saw through her statements and gave little weight to them.

Upon completion of Murray's questioning, Attorney Callanan called several character witnesses to the stand. Charlottetown natives Rev. Father Johnson, Donald Nicholson, Mayor Frederick Kelly and Charlottetown Police Chief Charles Cameron, who had been incorrectly identified as Tamerson in the newspapers, testified to Ryan's good moral character. Father Johnson told the court he knew Ryan well and he had always been a "straightforward, inoffensive young man." He also said Ryan had belonged to a total abstinence society.[112]

At about 2:55 p.m., defense counsel called Cyrus Ryan. Deputy Sheriff Simmons removed the prisoner from his dock inside the courtroom. The court clerk swore Ryan in and Simmons escorted him to the witness stand.

Sitting erect and perfectly composed, he answered all of Callanan's questions in a clear voice. He told of his upbringing and his trip to Boston on the steamer *Olivette* in 1903 and how he went to the home of his half-brother, Frederick Pierce, in Hanover. He recounted how he had bought some clothes and an overcoat on credit in Boston and had signed an agreement to pay $1.00 per week until the balance was paid in full.

Ryan admitted he had been negligent in making regular payments to the credit company. The credit company called E. H. Clapp Rubber Company and informed them of the debt. Ryan said that on Friday,

January 22, Clapp Superintendent Phillips told him he would have to deduct all of the money Ryan owed the credit company from his pay. Ryan told Phillips he couldn't work if he wasn't going to get paid and quit his job.

Ryan disclosed he had begun to save money the first week he was in Hanover. On January 28, he had about $30. It was in denominations of $5, $2 and $1 bills. He kept the money in a trunk in his room at Pierce's house.

Ryan testified he had intended to leave Hanover the next Saturday, January 23, with Katie Murray, but his sister had arrived on that day and had persuaded him to stay a while longer. Ryan said that on Wednesday, January 27, he told Frederick Pierce he was going to take the 9:15 a.m. train to Boston the next day. Ryan had claimed immediately after his arrest and during his interrogation by Deputy Shaw at the State House that he intended to leave Hanover to marry Katie Murray and move into his sister's house in Brookline.

The defendant recounted how he went to the Hanover Depot to pick up a baggage check for his trunk on Thursday morning, January 28. He was unable to do so and left the station. He went to the post office and then to the laundry to pick up a shirt he had left there ten days before. This statement markedly contradicted previous testimony from several witnesses that Quong Sing's account book showed an entry for Ryan's shirt nearly a year before the murder. Investigators did not find any other entry for Ryan. Continuing his testimony, Ryan said Quong Sing asked him for a check for the shirt and Ryan informed him he had lost it. Ryan said Quong had promised him he'd give him his shirt as soon as he had time to look for it.

Ryan told the court he then went to the barber shop at about 10:00 a.m., but had found no one there. He went back to the railroad station to find the agent and was told that he could find him at Dr. Baker's dental office. Ryan said he went there and met the agent who informed him he could not check his trunk there. The agent told him he needed to check the trunk at the station.

Ryan stated he went back to the laundry shop. Quong Sing told him he hadn't found time to look for his shirt. Ryan told the jury he left the shop and went to the drug store for his mail, then back to the depot for his trunk check. At the depot, the agent told him he needed to have the trunk with him in order to check it.

Ryan said he then went to Perry's barber shop for a shave at about 11:30 a.m. He said he returned to the laundry at about noon and saw Quong Sing in the rear of the shop stirring something in a pot. Ryan stated Paxton came into the laundry shop then. Paxton went to the back room and returned with a pail of water. He said Paxton left the outer door open as he exited the shop.

After Paxton left, Quong Sing came out of the back room with an iron in his hand. He started to iron a shirt and noticed Paxton had left the door open. Quong shut the door and then asked Ryan what he was waiting for. Ryan demanded his shirt. According to Ryan, "He (Quong) took down a parcel and looked at it and said, 'You have no shirt here; get out.'" The defendant then stated Quong Sing went into a little room on the right and came out with a revolver and pointed it at him saying, "Me shoot you dead."

Ryan dramatically disclosed what happened next. "I jumped at him, and as I did so, he clicked the revolver. I got hold of it and took the Chinaman by the throat. We had a struggle into the back room and there the Chinaman put his arms out and fell back on the floor. His face looked queer, and I found he was dead. I did not know what to do. I pulled a tub of water over to where he lay and threw him into it, then put a box of soap on his shoulders. I put the revolver in my pocket, picked up the watch and left the laundry. I went home and afterward, went to Boston, where I was arrested. I know I lied to the Boston police, but I was afraid to tell the truth, as I thought I would be put in jail."

DA French cross-examined Ryan about his movements and the events inside the laundry shop. Ryan told French when Quong Sing had ordered him out of his shop, he had refused. He said Quong "spoke loud and rather cross." Ryan said he "was calm as I am now." The court then adjourned for the day.

≈

At 9:00 a.m. on Friday, June 10, the fifth day of trial, jurors filed into the courtroom and DA French resumed his cross-examination of Ryan. During the one and one-half hours of testimony, Ryan, overwrought by his situation, broke down on the witness stand and wept for some minutes before he could control himself. DA French's questioning did not modify the direct testimony given by the defendant.

The defense then called several witnesses on Ryan's behalf. Attorney Callanan recalled Ryan's sister, Annie, to clarify her brother's plans for leaving Hanover. She testified she left Hanover on January 27 and Ryan's plans to leave on January 28 were made before she left. He then called Domingo Perry, Ryan's barber. Perry stated he had seen Ryan in possession of a good sized roll of bills on several occasions. Benjamin Franklin White, another defense witness, testified he was in the laundry on January 28 and helped remove Quong's body from the tub. He said he saw no water come from the victim's mouth.

Attorneys Callanan and Bixby called four doctors to rebut the cause of death declared by Dr. Dudley. Dr. Henry F. Borden of Brockton, Dr. Wilfred G. Brown, Dr. Horace E. Arnold of Boston and Dr. Timothy Leary of Boston, assistant professor of pathology at Tufts Medical School, gave expert testimony Quong Sing had died from a rupture of the heart and not by drowning.[113] The doctors asserted that when the heart ruptured, fluid, and not the water from the wash tub, entered Quong Sing's lungs.[114]

DA French recalled Ryan to the stand and asked him about the shirt found by Captain Proctor and others in Quong Sing's shop on January 29. Ryan denied that the shirt belonged to him.[115]

The court adjourned at 4:30 p.m. Justice Stevens announced that proceedings would continue at 9:00 a.m. the next day, June 11, which was Saturday. A six-day work week was still the norm and courts generally remained in session, especially during a capital trial.

≈

Trial proceedings on the final day began at 9:00 a.m. The defense did not call any further witnesses and rested its case. The prosecution and defense then made their closing arguments to the jury. Attorney Bixby, senior counsel for Ryan, stressed in his argument that the testimony of

Drs. Borden and Leary refuted Dr. Dudley's claim that Quong's death was caused by drowning. In Bixby's opinion, Quong Sing's defective heart caused his death. He also emphasized the threatening demeanor of Quong Sing and insisted Ryan had acted in self-defense when he had clutched Sing by the throat.

Upon completion of arguments, Judge Stevens charged the jury. The jury retired at 3:00 p.m. and deliberated for three and one-half hours. At 6:30 p.m., the court notified DA French and defense counsel that the jury had reached a verdict. Deputy Sheriffs escorted Ryan into the court room. The *Old Colony Memorial* reported that when Ryan was brought in he was "seemingly the least concerned of any in the courtroom." Judges Stevens and Hardy, DA French, Attorneys Bixby and Callanan and the jury reassembled in the courtroom. According to a reporter present at the reading of the verdict, "when called, he (Ryan) stood without a tremor, held up his head, and gazed steadily at the jury. When foreman Andrew Gale reported the verdict, Ryan never moved a muscle." The jury found Ryan guilty of second degree murder, which carries a punishment of life in prison with the possibility of parole in fifteen years.

Judge Stevens asked the defendant if he had anything to say to the court. Ryan told the court he was not guilty of the murder and denied he had robbed Quong Sing's laundry shop. Ryan then shook hands with his defense team and thanked them. Sheriffs immediately removed Ryan from the courtroom.[116] Judge Stevens thanked the jurors for their service and dismissed them.

≈

On Wednesday, June 15, 1904, Cyrus Ryan appeared before Justice Stevens at Plymouth County Superior Court for sentencing. The judge sentenced Ryan to life in the state prison, the maximum penalty allowable for second degree murder. He was to serve his first three days in solitary confinement. County sheriffs then led Ryan from the courtroom for his transfer to Charlestown.[117]

Later that day, prison guards received Ryan and assigned him Convict #13408. After completing his punishment in solitary confinement, prison officials assigned him to work as a laborer in the prison shoe factory.[118] During an entry interview with authorities, Ryan insisted he had been unfairly punished and told his examiner that he should have been convicted of manslaughter, not second degree murder. When asked for his version of events, Ryan said that he had entered Quong Sing's laundry at about noon on January 28, 1904, to pick up his laundry. He had been there twice the day before asking for it. The last time he went to get the laundry, the Chinaman told him to "go to hell." Ryan said he reached over and pulled Quong Sing's queue. Quong Sing then ran into a bedroom and retrieved a gun. A struggle ensued and Quong let go of the gun. As he did so, he fell across a tub full of water. (Ryan never mentioned, as he had in his trial testimony, that Quong "clicked" the revolver.) Ryan said that he picked up a box of soap that weighed about sixty-two pounds and threw it on Quong's back and ran out. He also said that he took Quong's revolver and a dollar watch from the floor that he thought was his own.[119]

Ryan remained at the prison until October 24, 1912, when prison officials transferred him to Bridgewater State Hospital at Bridgewater, Massachusetts.[120] For many years called the State Asylum for Insane Criminals, it was renamed Bridgewater State Hospital in 1909. Hospital officials discharged him on September 8, 1913 and he returned to prison.

Cyrus Lawrence Ryan, 1912 (Courtesy of Massachusetts Archives)

Three years later, Ryan filed a petition for pardon with the office of Governor Samuel McCall. The governor's office scheduled a hearing for October 26, 1916. On that date, Attorney Peter S. Maher, on behalf of Ryan, asserted that Ryan had been denied effective assistance of counsel during his trial. Maher alleged that several days after the trial had begun, Ryan's attorneys had advised Ryan to plead guilty to the lesser crime of manslaughter. Apparently the two lawyers were convinced that evidence presented thus far by the prosecution would ensure a murder conviction and possible execution. Ryan refused to accept their advice, insisting that he was not guilty of any crime. He firmly believed that the Chinese laundryman had assaulted him and he had only used force to defend himself. Maher stated Ryan told him that because he insisted on continuing with the trial, his lawyers believed the only way he could avoid conviction was to testify as they instructed. Ryan alleged that his defense team concocted a story for him to convey on the witness stand. Ryan followed their advice and was convicted of murder. According to Maher, if Ryan had been allowed to tell his own story and not the tale fabricated by his attorneys, he wouldn't have been convicted. Maher told the hearing officers that Ryan's attorneys, Bixby and Callahan, were unavailable for questioning, as Bixby had died and Callahan's whereabouts were unknown.

Maher gave the hearing officer Ryan's account of what actually happened on the day of Quong Sing's death. He related the same version Ryan had given when he first entered prison, but added a critical fact Ryan had failed to mention to prison officials – that while he was trying to wrest the gun from Quong Sing's grasp, he heard the trigger of the gun "snap." There was no discharge. The gun had either misfired or the hammer had struck an empty cylinder. Maher hoped to convince the hearing officer that Quong Sing tried to kill Ryan and that Ryan was only trying to defend himself during the struggle.

Maher told the board that Quong Sing did not die from drowning. He incorrectly stated that no evidence had been introduced during trial to indicate that water was found in Quong Sing's lungs. According to Maher, "It is said he died of heart disease."

The hearing officer questioned Ryan about Quong Sing's watch, curious as to why he took it. Ryan told him that he saw the watch on the floor after the scuffle and thought it was his own, as it was an "Ingersoll."* Ryan said he got the watch at a picnic in Prince Edward Island. When he got on the train for Boston, he realized he had two watches, his own and Quong Sing's. He also had Quong's revolver in his pocket. Knowing police would implicate him in Quong Sing's death if they found him in possession of the watch and revolver, he threw them away. Unfortunately, he threw the wrong watch away – his own – and was found with Quong Sing's watch in his possession during his arrest. Ryan wasn't aware that the hearing officer had a case file that included a report from Captain Proctor outlining the details of Ryan's arrest in 1904 and the recovery of Quong's gun from Ryan's coat pocket and Quong's silver watch from his sweetheart, Katie Murray.

Ryan's elderly mother testified on behalf of her son and vouched for his reputation. She told the hearing officer that her son was a good boy, that he had worked since he was nine or ten years old and that he always gave her his pay.[121] The hearing was then adjourned and Ryan was returned to prison to await the governor's decision.

≈

On May 12, 1918, Ryan wrote his mother on Mother's Day. His highly emotional, agitated state leapt from the pages. He wanted out, and would do anything to gain his release.

"It is good to be able to write to you today, but you will not expect a cheerful letter as you know I have nothing to say that would bring cheer to you at this time. You have nothing to make you happy on this Mother's Day but do not let the gloomy outlook discourage you."

---

*The Ingersoll Company, established in 1896, produced a pocket watch called the "Dollar" watch, also known as the "Yankee" watch, popular during the late nineteenth and early twentieth century. The watch sold for $1.00 around 1900 – about an average day's wage.

Ryan assured her that he'd "prove his right to be out of prison" if he is just given a chance to try. He knows how much his mother needs his care and tells her that he is the only one left who can provide a home for her. He begs his mother and the rest of his family to support him in his effort to gain a pardon from his sentence. He pleads with her to get him out of prison and "if you have stumbling blocks thrown in your way you can get the best of them by getting up that petition. Do not let anything stand in your way or you will be fooled into believing that I will have to stay here another year. It is up to you all outside to call the bluff and I will expect you to brush everything aside and fight for my life and soul."

Ryan informed his mother that he had requested a commutation hearing before the parole board the week before. He wasn't sure if they'd approve his release. He planned to petition the governor for a pardon. If the governor approved it, "I will want to see him go to Washington in Mr. Weeks' (John Wingate Weeks, U. S. Senator from Massachusetts) place, but if he refuses to take a hand in this matter I will not want to see him hold a public office of any kind."

Ryan continued, "If anything serious should happen to me do not except (sic) a gold brick as a compensation, but forget nothing and make everything public. I am warning you that I am going to make known the truth and I will not be afraid to tell anyone he is a liar or worse when I know I am right. I will let it be known that Bessie (his sister) is forced to pay your board out of her small earnings and that Frank (Ambrose F. Ryan, his brother) is almost too blind to earn his own living. This will be open to investigation and the brute who would oppose my release from here should be sent to Hell."

He closed his letter by saying, "Let us hope that I will be granted a commutation of sentence and when Mother's Day comes around again you will have something worth living for. Your affectionate son, C. L. Ryan."[122]

≈

Ryan's efforts to obtain a pardon or release on parole failed. On October 21, 1919, prison officials transferred Ryan back to Bridgewater.

Hospital officials returned him to the State Prison on December 17, 1920.[123]

In 1931, Ryan wrote a letter from prison to his sister, Annie (Ryan) Brennan. He told her that he didn't want anyone to visit him and that he didn't want money sent to him unless he asked for it. Ryan conveyed a sense of paranoia and persecution as he continued, "Ed (his brother Michael Edward Ryan) should be careful not to let the gang frame him as they did me and if they find out he is trying to help me they sure will get him. Be careful about what you eat because if they don't get you one way they will another; when you see people vomiting and not able to walk you know someone is putting something over. They do these things to get you to talk and then they frame you up and send you to prison or a crazy house."

Ryan wrote that he, "doesn't sleep and can't walk sometimes and the heart stops." He then changed his mind about visitors and told his sister, "Perhaps I will have you visit me anyway." He concluded by writing, "Tell Ed and the rest at home to be careful and I will tell you all about it later. Love to all from Cyrus."[124]

In 1932, prison officials conducted a social case history on Ryan that included comments on his personality and institutional behavior. Ryan, who was then about forty-eight years old, was regarded as "quite lively in physical mannerisms as well as speech. He appears pleasant and agreeable in conversation and although somewhat nervous, does not appear to be very much upset. He is completely convinced of his innocence and has suffered tremendously since his incarceration, but he bears no grudge against society in general nor anyone in particular."[125]

Ryan was illiterate when he entered the prison, but took advantage of the institution's educational opportunities and became "...capable of writing a fairly good letter and is interested in good reading..."[126] Ryan worked in the prison's shoe shop, mostly as a shoe cutter, and became proficient in the trade.

Although he had taken great strides to improve himself, Ryan was not a model prisoner. During the length of his term at Charlestown, prison officials reprimanded him on twenty-four occasions for rule infractions. He was placed in solitary confinement eleven times for more serious violations. During his first few years at the prison, he was reported once a year, on average, for being troublesome, quarrelsome or swearing at an officer. Between 1915 and 1919 his conduct improved, but deteriorated during the following three years, when he was cited seven times and was punished for "gambling, issuing worthless transfers and writing letters to other inmates inducing them to claim insanity in order to go to Bridgewater."[127]

The prison warden had an unfavorable opinion of Ryan and thought him "unreliable temperamentally, dishonest, untrustworthy and profits very little from punishment." The warden did commend Ryan for his work qualities and believed that over the past few years, except in a recent episode of gambling, his conduct had improved.[128]

Prison officials transferred Ryan back to Bridgewater on April 24, 1935. He stayed at the institution for about one month and was returned to the prison on May 31, 1935. Fifteen months later, prison officials transferred Ryan to Bridgewater for the last time.[129]

≈

Clinical psychologists Scott O. Lilienfeld and Hal Arkowitz, in a December 2007 *Scientific American Mind* article, described a psychopath as one who is incapable of feeling guilt, remorse or empathy and is self-centered, dishonest and undependable. The psychopath displays a superficial charm and employs deceit and manipulation to attain his ends. He won't accept responsibility for his actions and blames others instead.

As a youngster, Ryan had been arrested by police for throwing stones at a dog. Ryan insisted during a 1932 interview with prison officials that he was later acquitted of the charge. Cruelty to animals is a known warning sign of psychopathic behavior and a trait commonly found in rapists and murderers.

During his incarceration at Bridgewater State Hospital, Ryan was evaluated by psychiatrists who determined that his behavior was consistent with the features of psychosis and psychopathic personality disorder. His conduct in prison – his deception, dishonesty and unreliability – supported this diagnosis. In the letters he sent from prison to his mother and sister, Ryan never expressed any remorse or guilt over the murder of Quong Sing. He denied responsibility for the killing. Instead, he blamed Quong Sing and insisted that he was only defending himself from Quong's attack. He placed the blame for his conviction on his attorneys and believed they had denied him proper counsel.

Ryan's home life and upbringing may have amplified the effects of his disorder. Ryan grew up in poverty. His alcoholic father likely spent the meager wages he earned as a stevedore on his addiction. This left little for family expenses. His mother and father removed Cyrus and his siblings from school at an early age and sent them to work fourteen hours a day, seven days a week, in the factories and mills of Charlottetown,

It is not known whether Cyrus suffered any specific abuse in the Ryan household or at the workplace, or if any other circumstances existed that may have influenced his adult behavior. But the long hours he spent at work and away from home likely prevented him from receiving the parental supervision and nurturing he desperately needed during his formative years.[130]

Ryan died on December 4, 1962. He was seventy-nine years old and had been incarcerated for fifty-eight years. Dr. Samuel Allen, a clinical psychiatrist at Bridgewater, reported Ryan's cause of death as atherosclerotic heart disease and generalized arteriosclerosis.

When Ryan died he was a broken, forgotten and penniless man. Since he could not afford to pay his burial costs after death, he chose to donate his body to Harvard Medical School for scientific study. Harvard, in accepting his remains, agreed to assume the costs of removal and transportation of the corpse. Funeral director Albert Sullivan of Rockland, Massachusetts retrieved Ryan's body at Bridgewater State Hospital and delivered it to Harvard Medical School.

The school also agreed to pay associated expenses for final disposition of his remains. After Harvard completed its study, school administrators transported Ryan's cadaver for interment at Pine Hill Cemetery in Tewksbury, Massachusetts, a private facility maintained by several medical schools in the Boston area.[131]

So ended the tragic story of Quong Sing and Cyrus Lawrence Ryan. Ryan's sweetheart, Katie Murray, returned to her hometown at Clyde's River, Prince Edward Island, where she married a local man in 1906. The couple had eight children. Katie died in 1970 in Cornwall, Prince Edward Island.[132]

Frederick Pierce and his wife, Mary, adopted a child and remained in Hanover until about 1930, then moved to Rockland, Massachusetts. Mary died in 1933, Frederick in 1949. Both are buried in Rockland.[133]

Cyrus' mother, Elizabeth, died in Boston on Christmas Day, 1935, and is buried with one of her sons and a daughter in New Calvary Cemetery, Boston.[134] All of her children, with the exception of her son, John, eventually settled in the Boston area where several married and had children.

Conclusion

Three violent men, one seized by hatred and rage; another gripped by greed, lust and ambition; and a third, a naïve and impulsive young man bent on robbery, cast a pall of gloom over a community built on a foundation of benevolence and fellowship. Hanoverians knew that Seth Perry's rum selling would some day lead to bloodshed. Every effort to curtail his illicit activities failed. They were perplexed and dismayed at the cruelty he had wreaked upon three hapless victims on St. Patrick's Day in 1845 and condemned him for his actions.

A community still in grief over the carnage imposed by a bloody civil war and the assassination of a beloved president was ill-prepared for the selfish act of violence inflicted upon an unsuspecting and innocent woman less than nine years after the war ended. Although Julia Hawkes had only been a resident of the town for a very short period, townspeople mourned for her. They vilified the actions of a man they had come to befriend, aghast at his deceit and his violation of trust.

Four years into a century promising prosperity and a new way of life, the dreams and aspirations of an innocent Chinese immigrant were shattered. The murder of Quong Sing left residents angered and appalled. They mobilized quickly to apprehend Quong Sing's killer and steadfastly supported the memory of their friend by offering their testimony in the case against Cyrus Ryan.

Although their deaths were separated by nearly three decades over a ninety-year period, a common thread connected the victims of these crimes. All were recent immigrants, escaping poverty and hardship and seeking the promise of a new life and riches in a land of opportunity. The Irish trackmen, in search of a decent wage and a life free of poverty as laborers on America's railways; the widowed Julia Hawkes, struggling to support her only child, seeking work wherever she could find it, performing menial jobs as a domestic in affluent homes and then in a hotel, where she met the man who would seal her fate; and a hard-working laundry man, far from his native China, hoping to return to his family with his earnings and free them from the miserable conditions in which they lived.

As time has passed, faces have changed and memories have faded, the deaths of James and Patrick Stapleton, Julia Hawkes and Quong Sing remain no less tragic. May they, and those who mourned them, rest in peace.

Notes:

Rum

[1] stillness of the chilly March air: S. N. Dickinson, *Boston Almanac for the year 1846* (Boston: Thomas Groom and Company, 1846), 10. The 1846 *Boston Almanac* recorded variable weather conditions with temperatures of 28 degrees at 7:00 AM and 40 degrees at 2:00 PM on March 17, 1845. Microfiche held at Boston Public Library, Fiche 1, *Boston Almanac 1846*, Brookbauer Press, LaCross, WI.

[2] "…his yard stained with blood…": "Shocking Outrages," *Quincy Aurora*, March 20, 1845

[3] "…constituted as a separate township": Jedediah Dwelley and John F. Simmons, *History of the Town of Hanover, Massachusetts: with Family Genealogies*, (Hanover: Town of Hanover, MA, 1910), 9.

[4] adapt their skills to other trades: Massachusetts Historical Commission Reconaissance Survey Town Report: Hanover: 1981, pages 7-8. http://www.sec.state.ma.us/mhc/mhcpdf/townreports/SE-Mass/hnv.pdf

[5] a living as shoemakers: 1850 United States Census, Hanover, Plymouth, Massachusetts, Roll M432, page 332. http://www.ancestry.com.

[6] First Baptist Church in North Hanover in 1812: Dwelley and Simmons, *History of the Town of Hanover, Massachusetts,* 54-76.

[7] "higher mathematics," navigation and surveying: John Stetson Barry, *A Historical Sketch of the Town of Hanover, Massachusetts: with family genealogies* (Boston: S. G. Drake, 1853), 93-94.

[8] homes also appeared: Massachusetts Historical Commission Reconaissance Survey Town Report: Hanover: 1981, pages 6-8. http://www.sec.state.ma.us/mhc/mhcpdf/townreports/SE-Mass/hnv.pdf

[9] "…which threatened to overwhelm": Barry, *A Historical Sketch of the Town of Hanover, Massachusetts,* 168.

[10] "…which ally us to the angels": Ibid., 169.

[11] "…to be drank in like manner": Ibid., 174.

[12] twenty dollars for each offense: *Revised Statutes of the Commonwealth of Massachusetts*, passed November 4, 1835, Printed and Published by Virtue of a Resolve of November 3, 1835; under the direction of Theron Metcalf and Horace Mann – Chapter 47 of the Regulation of Licensed Houses, (Boston: Dutton & Wentworth, State Printers, Nos. 10 & 12 Exchange Street, 1836), Sections 1-3, 375-376. http://books.google.com.

[13] a descendant of early Hanover settlers: Barry, *A Historical Sketch of the Town of Hanover, Massachusetts*, 357.

[14] married in Pembroke…1786: Barry, *A Historical Sketch of the Town of Hanover, Massachusetts,* 357.

[15] where the house still stands: Hanover Historical Preservation Plan, Hanover, MA, September 2007 by Town of Hanover Historical Commission and Hanover Planning Department; Appendix A, page 2: The home of Samuel Perry, built in 1786, remains at 1170 Broadway. http://www.hanover-ma.gov/pdf/forms/planning/preservation-plans/Hanover-Historical-Preservation-Plan.pdf.

[16] Cox of Hanson in 1828: Ibid.

[17] Haveland, born in 1831: Ibid.

[18] Howard, born in 1832: Ibid.

[19] Ann, born in 1836: Ibid.

[20] "…balance of his losses by selling rum": "The Murder of the Stapletons at Hanover," *Boston Post*, June 19, 1845.

[21] common jail in Plymouth: *Plymouth Court Records, 1686-1859,* Boston, MA, Volume 15, page 233, #47 and #48: New England Historical and Genealogical Society, Boston: 2002. http://www.newenglandancestors.org.

[22] who found him incorrigible: Ibid.

[23] "…guns loaded in a back apartment": "Shocking Outrages," *Quincy Aurora*, March 20, 1845.

[24] struck him in the lower jaw: "Shocking Outrages," *Quincy Aurora*, March 20, 1845.

[25] "…demoralizing traffic of…..spirits": "Deadly Affray at Hanover – Two Men Killed, and Another Dangerously Wounded," *Old Colony Memorial*, March 22, 1845.

[26] "…shattering his jaw bone…manner": "Rum and Murder," *Quincy Patriot*, March 22, 1845.

[27] "…sober men, pledged teetotalers": *Old Colony Memorial*, March 29, 1845.

[28] that he had been badly beaten: The Murder of the Stapletons At Hanover, *Boston Post*, June 19, 1845.

[29] poured it into the ground: "Deadly Affray at Hanover – Two Men Killed, and Another Dangerously Wounded," *Old Colony Memorial*, March 22, 1845.

[30] "…as fast as they came in reach": "Murder of Three Men at Hanover!" *Massachusetts Temperance Standard*, March 17, 1845.

[31] "…selling strong drinks, to….business": "The Murder of Three Men," *Boston Courier*, March 22, 1845.

[32] 1845 as a trial date: "Indictment for Murder" *Barre* (MA) *Patriot*, May 9, 1845.

[33] "…and second of my heirs and assigns…": Plymouth County Registry of Deeds, Land Records, Perry to Perry, Power of Attorney, Volume 267, page 261, 1855.

[34] in the church graveyard: "Rum and Murder," *Quincy Patriot*, March 22, 1845.

[35] inherit their goods…Commonwealth: Plymouth County Probate Court, Plymouth, MA, Probate Case 19200 and 19201, Petition for Administration, Appointment, Bond Letter, May 6, 1845, Volume 11, pages 327 and 328.

[36] On April 5: "Commonwealth of Massachusetts," *Old Colony Memorial,* April 5, 1845.

[37] April 12: "Commonwealth of Massachusetts," *Old Colony Memorial,* April 12, 1845.

[38] April 19, 1845: "Commonwealth of Massachusetts," *Old Colony Memorial*, April 19, 1845.

[39] within one year: Plymouth County Probate Court, Plymouth, MA, Probate Case 19200 and 19201, Petition for Administration, Appointment, Bond Letter, May 6, 1845, Volume 11, pages 327 and 328.

[40] property, real or personal: Plymouth County Probate Court, Plymouth MA, Volume 87, pages 302 and 303, Inventory, August 11,1845.

[41] in present day figures: L. Officer and S. Williamson, *Purchasing Power of Money in the United States from 1774 to 2008.* Measuring Worth, 2009. http://www,measuringworth.com/ppowerus.

[42] after sworn testimony by Beal: Plymouth County Probate Court, Plymouth, MA, Volume 89, page 66, Administration Account, February 15, 1847.

[43] price of wheat and oats from 1816-1823: *The Tithe Applotment Books, 1823-1836*,http://www.genealogy.com/ifa/co_cd262.html.

[44] begging was very common: The History Place, copyright 2000, Irish Potato Famine-Before the Famine: http://www.historyplace.com/worldhistory/famine/before.htm.

[45] exclusively in these two areas: Family Tree Maker's Family Archives, "Index to Griffith's Valuation of Ireland, 1848-1864," from Heritage World & the Genealogical Publishing Co., Inc., CD #188.

[46] "civilized domestic cattle": Thomas H. O'Connor, *The Boston Irish: A Political History* (Canada: Little, Brown and Co., 1995), 64.

[47] "...nature of papal authority": Ibid., 43-44.

[48] Pope in Rome was the real enemy: William V. Shannon, *The American Irish: A Political and Social Portrait* (Amherst: The University of Massachusetts Press, 1966), 41.

[49] "...twelve dollars a month for wages": Edward Wakin, *Enter the Irish-American* (New York: Thomas Y. Crowell Co., 1976), 50. http://www.books.google.com.

[50] in the rapidly expanding country: The History Place, copyright 2000, http://www.historyplace.com/worldhistory/famine/before.htm.

[51] "...work of the nineteenth century": Barbara A. Driscoll, *The Tracks North: The Railroad Bracero Program of World War II* (Austin: University of Texas Press, Center for Mexican American Studies, 1999), 13-14. http://books.google.com.

[52] "...under every railroad tie": *Exploring Diversity in Pennsylvania History - Working on the Rails: Irish and Italian Laborers on*

Pennsylvania's Railroads, page 2, by the Historical Society of Pennsylvania, with the Balch Institute for Ethnic Studies. http://http://www.hsp.org/.../studentreadingimmigrantlaborontherailroads_revised.pdf.

[53] "...horror of liberal-minded Concordians": William Barksdale Maynard, *Walden Pond: a history* (New York: Oxford University Press, Inc., 2004) 52. http://books.google.com.

[54] has never been identified: Robert Hedin, *The Great Machines: Poems and Songs of the American Railroad* (Iowa City: University of Iowa Press, 1996), 14-15. http://books.google.com.

[55] a right to a trial by jury: Alan Rogers, *Murder and the Death Penalty in Massachusetts* (Amherst and Boston: University of Massachusetts Press, 2008), 41.

[56] challenges aimed at potential jurors: Ibid., 77.

[57] challenges for cause: Ibid., 118.

[58] Doctor of Laws from Harvard in 1831 and Brown University in 1850: William Thomas Davis, *History of the Judiciary of Massachusetts* (Boston: Boston Book Company, 1900) 181.

[59] appointed to the Supreme Judicial Court: Ibid., 189.

[60] bench of the Supreme Judicial Court in 1842: Ibid., 189-190.

[61] "...an unerring judicial mind": Ibid., v.

[62] for his wit and anecdotes: "Editor's Drawer," *Harper's New Monthly Magazine* (New York: Harper and Brothers, 1870), Volume XL, December 1869-May 1870, 631. http://books.google.com.

[63] "...was almost an impossibility": Leonard Bolles Ellis, *The History of New Bedford and vicinity, 1602-1892* (Syracuse, NY: 1892), 646; http://www.ancestry.com.

[64] "...a faithful counselor and trustworthy lawyer": Dwelley and Simmons, *History of the Town of Hanover, Massachusetts,* 99-100.

[65] Bristol County bar in 1830: D. Hamilton Hurd, *History of Bristol County Massachusetts with Biographical Sketches of many of its Pioneers and Prominent Men,* Illustrated, (Philadelphia: J.W. Lewis & Co., 1883), 12. http://books.google.com.

[66] served a one year term: Ibid., 13-15.

[67] "...guilt of the accused, is fearful": Ibid., 13.

[68] did not recall shooting anybody: "The Murder of the Stapletons at Hanover," *Boston Post*, June 19, 1845.

[69] "…produced a temporary insanity": Ibid., 13.

[70] "…patients once considered incurable": William Richard Cutter, A. M., *New England Families – Genealogical and Memorial: A Record of the Achievements of Her People in the Making of Commonwealths and the Founding of a Nation* - Volume II (New York: Lewis Historical Publishing Company, 1914), 1055. http://www.ancestry.com.

[71] "…either expressed or implied": Sir William Blackstone, Knight, *Commentaries on the Laws of England in Four Books, Book Four: of Public Wrongs* (Philadelphia: Rees Welsh & Co., 1902) 1591. http://books.google.com.

[72] "…sufficiently violent provocation": Ibid., 1599.

[73] "…commission of some unlawful act": Ibid., 1587.

[74] with another gun, shot Dowlan: "Capital Trial at Plymouth," *Boston Courier*, June 20, 1845.

[75] "and his face bloody": Ibid.

[76] "…report of the trial in the *Post* from day to day": "The Murder of the Stapletons at Hanover," *Boston Post*, June 19, 1845.

[77] "…upon their contracted accomodations": Ibid.

[78] "…passions which war against the soul": Ibid.

[79] indictment against Perry for the murder of Patrick Stapleton: Ibid.

[80] "…the deceased making a disturbance at his place": Ibid.

[81] "…always very bustling and business-like": Dwelley and Simmons, *History of the Town of Hanover, Massachusetts,* 108.

[82] graduated from Harvard College in 1839: Hurd, *History of Plymouth County Massachusetts with Biographical Sketches of many of its Pioneers and Prominent Men,* 825.

[83] "…he had repeated it over and over again": "The Murder of the Stapletons at Hanover, *Boston Post*, June 19, 1845.

[84] and Lydia Tilden: Barry, John Stetson, *A Historical Sketch of the Town of Hanover, Massachusetts,* 253.

[85] from Hertfordshire, England in 1635: Ibid., 245.

[86] were brother and sister: Ibid., 249-253.

[87] "...I don't know that I was much mad": Ibid.

[88] he could, "handle any man, Irish or Yankee": Ibid.

[89] "...given them their breakfast that morning": Ibid.

[90] "...and was still ready to treat him so": Ibid.

[91] on the facts as presented in court: Lemuel Shaw Papers, 1648-1923, Microfilm Call Number P-206, Part III-B, Minutes of the Supreme Judicial Court, 1830-1860, Reel 23B, File 4, Frame 921-1377, Massachusetts Historical Society, Boston.

[92] "...what he was doing was wrong": Rogers, *Murder and the Death Penalty in Massachusetts,* 209.

[93] because of his mental state: Ibid. 209.

[94] could not lead to the truth: Ibid. 209.

[95] not guilty by reason of insanity: Ibid. 209-210

[96] "...and reduces it to manslaughter": "The Murder of the Stapletons at Hanover," *Boston Post*, June 21, 1845.

[97] the clerk entered his plea into the record: Ibid.

[98] "...will not be called up by the District Attorney": "Trial for Murder," *Quincy Patriot*, June 28, 1845.

[99] "...and says thereof he is guilty (of manslaughter): Plymouth County, Supreme Judicial Court – *Commonwealth v Seth Perry* (1845), Record Box 2196338, January 1, 1813 – December 31, 1853, Massachusetts State Archives, Boston, MA.

[100] "no direct proof of the fact": "Trial of Perry," *Boston Courier*, June 21, 1845.

[101] "...a severe and desperate struggle": "Trial for Murder,"*Quincy Patriot*, June 28, 1845.

[102] "...in cases of this kind": "Trial of Perry," *Boston Courier*, June 21, 1845.

[103] convicted of the lesser crime of manslaughter: Ibid., 94.

[104] committed by the defendant: Rogers, *Murder and the Death Penalty in Massachusetts*, 112-113.

[105] but the bill never passed: Ibid., 80.

[106] precept of "Thou shalt not kill.": Ibid., 81-82.

[107] arguments proposed by Rantoul: Ibid., 83.

[108] proponent for the abolition of capital punishment: Louis P. Masur, *Capital Punishment and the Transformation of American Culture, 1776-1865* (New York: Oxford University Press, 1989), page 124.

[109] could, and should, be reformed: Rogers, *Murder and the Death Penalty in Massachusetts*, 83.

[110] asking for commutation of punishment: Ibid., 83.

[111] "…justice is defined and administered": Ibid., x-xi.

[112] three year sentence in solitary confinement: "Trial of Perry," *Boston Courier*, June 21, 1845.

[113] large scar on his left knee:, Charlestown State Prison, Commitment Registers, 1805-1930, HS 9.01, Sec. 289X, Roll 2, Commitment register of October 1840-December 1856, Massachusetts State Archives, Boston, MA.

[114] "…as well as the punishment of convicts": O. F. Lewis, PhD., *The Development of American Prisons and Prison Customs, 1776-1845* (Albany: Prison Association of New York, 1922), 67, 68. http://. books.google.com.

[115] (or $47 million in today's economy): Officer, L., and Williamson, S., *Purchasing Power of Money in the United States from 1774 to 2008.* Measuring Worth, 2009. http://www.measuringworth.com/ ppowerus.

[116] by 260 feet prison yard: Lewis, *The Development of American Prisons and Prison Customs, 1776-1845*, 67, 68. http://.books.google. com.

[117] whitesmiths and tin workers: Prison Discipline Society, *Reports of the Prison Discipline Society – 1846-1847, Volume 3*, Boston: Press of T. R. Marvin, 1855, 22. Original from the University of Michigan. Digitized April 27, 2006. http://books.google.com

[118] "…resembles a great manual-labor school": Francis Calley Gray, *Prison Discipline in America* (Boston: Charles T. Little and James Brown, 1847), 47. http://books.google.com.

[119] set aside as a day of rest and reflection: Ibid., 39-40.

[120] received intermittently by one prisoner: Ibid., 49.

[121] died in prison before his execution: Gideon Haynes, *Pictures From Prison Life: An Historical Sketch of the Massachusetts State Prison* (Boston: Lee and Shepard, 1869), 59-73.

[122] "...regulated by the physician": Gray, *Prison Discipline in America*, 48.

[123] "...vegetables for their own use": Ibid., 51.

[124] with $100.00 of prison earnings: Ibid., 53.

[125] help in securing employment: Prison Discipline Society, *Reports of the Prison Discipline Society – 1846-1847*. (Boston: Press of T. R. Marvin, 1855), 38. http://www.books.google.com.

[126] Perry's description and demeanor: John Ross Dix, "A Visit to the State Prison – A Prison Poet" in *Local Loiterings, and Visits in the Vicinity of Boston, by a Looker On* (Boston: Redding and Company, 8 State Street, 1846), 89-92. http://www.books.google.com.

[127] attacking him or the prison guards: Ibid., 89.

[128] "...almost massacred another": Ibid., 90-91.

[129] "...the very incarnation of evil": Ibid., 91.

[130] "...with a cry of vengeance": Ibid., 91.

[131] "...that hardened-looking old man": Ibid., 92.

[132] at the age of 81: Plymouth County Registry of Deeds, Plymouth, MA: Land Records, Volume 294, page 206, 1859, Cephas Perry to Seth Perry.

[133] cause of death as "old age": Vital Records and Statistics, Deaths, Hanover, 1874, Volume 266, page 302, Item 29, Massachusetts State Archives, Boston, MA.

[134] lodged at his sister's house next door: "The Murder of the Stapletons at Hanover," *Boston Post*, June 20, 1845.

[135] brother-in-law and sister, Albert and Wealthy Stetson: 1850 United States Federal Census [database on-line]. Provo, UT, USA: Ancestry.com Operations, Inc., 2009. Images reproduced by FamilySearch. Original data: Seventh Census of the United States, 1850; (National Archives Microfilm Publication M432, 1009 rolls); Records of the Bureau of the Census, Record Group 29; National Archives, Washington, D.C. Hanover, Plymouth, Massachusetts; Roll M432_332; Page: 108B; Image: 220. http://www.ancestry.com

[136] a shoemaker from Hanson, Massachusetts: Vital Records of Hanover 1727-1857, (Online database: NewEnglandAncestors.org, New England Historic Genealogical Society, 2007), (*A Copy of the Records of Births, Marriages and Deaths and of Intentions of Marriage of the Town of Hanover, Mass. 1727-1857. As Recorded by the several town clerks for the said town of Hanover. Prepared under the direction of ... a committee appointed by said town for that purpose.* Rockland, MA, Press of the Rockland Standard, 1898). 182-183, #1. http://www.newenglandancestors.org. The couple married on May 15, 1853.

[137] also a shoemaker: Ibid. 184-185, #11. The couple married on November 24, 1853.

[138] when the Civil War broke out: Ancestry.com. 1860 United States Federal Census [database on-line]. Provo, UT, USA: Ancestry.com Operations, Inc., 2009. Images reproduced by FamilySearch. Original data: 1860 U.S. census, population schedule. NARA microfilm publication M653, 1,438 rolls. Washington, D.C.: National Archives and Records Administration. Hanson, Plymouth, Massachusetts; Roll M653_518; Page: 577; Image: 575; Family History Library Film: 803518. http://ancestry.com.

[139] died of disease...in Hampton, Virginia: National Park Service. U.S. Civil War Soldiers, 1861-1865 [database on-line]. Provo, UT, USA: Ancestry.com Operations Inc, 2007. Original data: National Park Service, Civil War Soldiers and Sailors System, online http://www.itd.nps.gov/cwss, acquired 2007. Microfilm Publication M544, Roll 31. http://ancestry.com.

[140] the balance of Seth Perry's estate: Plymouth County Probate Records, Plymouth, MA: Docket 15727, Volume 129, page 353; Volume 146, page 13; Volume 137, page 361; and Volume 130, page 140.

[141] until her death in 1852: Massachusetts Vital Records and Statistics, Births, Hanover, 1852, Volume 67, Page 249, Item 4, Massachusetts State Archives, Boston, MA.

[142] and their four children: 1860 United States Census, Hanover, Plymouth, Massachusetts, Roll M653_519; Page: 166; Image: 168. http://ancestry.com.

[143] buried at Arlington National Cemetery: Massachusetts Soldiers, Sailors and Marines in the Civil War, Volume II, 338. http://ancestry.com.

[144] Minnie Leland Larkum: Massachusetts Vital Records and Statistics, Births, Hanover, 1863, Volume 160, Page 280, Item 10, Massachusetts State Archives, Boston, MA.

[145] for 54 year-old Enos: Massachusetts Vital Records and Statistics, Marriages, Hanover, 1864, Volume 172, Page 258, Item 26, Massachusetts State Archives, Boston, MA.

[146] a year after her birth: Massachusetts Vital Records and Statistics, Deaths, Hanover, 1870, Volume 233, Page 311, Item 4, Massachusetts State Archives, Boston, MA.

[147] his personal estate at $1,800.00: 1870 United States Census, Hanover, Plymouth, Massachusetts, Roll M593_638, Page 256, Image 514. http://www.ancestry.com.

[148] real and personal property worth: 1870 United States Census, Hanover, Massachusetts, Roll M593_638; Page: 255; Image: 511. http://www.ancestry.com.

[149] was certified as "old age": Massachusetts Vital Records and Statistics, Deaths, Hanover, 1886, Volume 374, Page 328, Item 9, Massachusetts State Archives, Boston, MA.

[150] on February 16, 1899 of "hepatitis": Massachusetts Vital Records and Statistics, Deaths, Hanover, 1899, Volume 494, Page 177, Item 10, Massachusetts State Archives, Boston, MA.

[151] a horse, hay and stones: Plymouth County Probate Records, Plymouth, MA: Docket #2605, Volume 167, Page 597.

[152] "...by any legal course": "Dreadful Affray at Hanover – Two Men Killed, and Another Dangerously Wounded," *Old Colony Memorial*, March 22, 1845.

A Tailor's Goose

[1] travelers passing over the span: Charles Devens Notebook, call number mss. N-1114, box number 8, folder F61-V58, Norfolk County Special Term for Trial of J. H. Costley, December 1874, Massachusetts Historical Society, Boston, MA.

[2] the river's natural confluence: *Climatological Record of the Weather Bureau, 1819-1892*, Microfilm Publication T907A, Roll 228, Fort Independence Station, Boston, MA, National Archives, Northeast Region, Waltham, MA.

[3] slowly rowed back to shore: "Murder Near Braintree – The Dead Body of a Woman With a Weight About Her Neck Found in the River – The Woman Shot Before Being Put Into the River – No Clew (sic) To Her Name," *Boston Daily Advertiser*, May 26, 1874.

[4] red lining on the reverse: "Braintree – Mysterious Tragedy – The Body of a Murdered Woman Found in River," *Boston Journal*, May 26, 1874, Morning Edition.

[5] decomposing corpse more closely: "The Gallows! – Execution of Costley for the Murder of Julia Hawkes – History of the Crime – An Attempt to Escape Frustrated! – Details of the Execution – Picture of the Murderer and His Victim – Scenes and Incidents at the Execution," *Norfolk County Gazette*, June 26, 1875.

[6] and a broad forehead: "Murder Near Braintree – The Dead Body of a Woman With a Weight About Her Neck Found in the River – The Woman Shot Before Being Put Into the River – No Clew (sic) To Her Name," *Boston Daily Advertiser*, May 26, 1874.

[7] star on her right ear: Ibid.

[8] extremities floated to the surface: David Owen, *Hidden Evidence, 40 True Crimes and How Forensic Science Helped Solve Them* (London: Copyright 2000, Quintet Publishing Limited, 2000), 100-105.

[9] seen the woman before: "Braintree – Mysterious Tragedy – The Body of a Murdered Woman Found in River," *Boston Journal,* May 26, 1874, Evening Edition.

[10] further evidence of the crime: Ibid.

[11] before she entered the water: "Criminal – Opening of the Costley Murder Trial," *Boston Daily Globe*, December 29, 1874.

[12] on one side of her jaw: "An Awful Murder," *Quincy Patriot*, May 30, 1874.

[13] in Hanover's Four Corners village: Ibid.

[14] in or near Saint John, New Brunswick: Massachusetts Vital Records, Deaths, Braintree, 1874, Volume 266, Page 228, Line 32, Massachusetts State Archives, Boston, MA.

[15] considered her industrious and frugal: "The Monatiquot River Mystery – Body Fully Identified – Robbery the Motive of the Crime – Rumored Arrest of the Murderer," *Boston Journal*, May 27, 1874, Morning Edition.

[16] hotel cook at Hanover's Howard House: "The Murder of Julia Hawkes – Trial of J. H. Costley at Dedham – Second Day," *Boston Journal*, December 30, 1874.

[17] as a member of their family: Ibid.

[18] on Bedford Street in Boston: Union Institution for Savings Bank Records, Account #16757, manuscript collection of John J. Burns Library, Boston College, Chestnut Hill, MA. http://www.bc.edu/bc_org/avp/ulib/Burns/bankbusms.htmll.

[19] dissuaded her from pursuing it: "The Monatiquot River Mystery – Body Fully Identified – Robbery the Motive of the Crime – Rumored Arrest of the Murderer," *Boston Journal*, May 27, 1874, Morning Edition.

[20] to the State constabulary force in 1872: *Biographical Review, Volume XXV, Containing Life Sketches of Leading Citizens of Norfolk County* (Boston: Biographical Review Publishing Co., 1898) 48. http://www.archive.org/stream/biographicalrevinc1898biog#page/48/mode/2up.

[21] where Costley could be found: "The Hawkes Murder – Additional Evidence for the Government – Third Day's Proceedings in the Supreme Court at Dedham – How the Prisoner Appears – Further Evidence Connecting Him with the Tragedy – Testimony of Chief Constable Boynton, Etc.," *Boston Daily Globe*, December 31, 1874.

[22] an annual rent of $475.00: "The Murder of Julia Hawkes – Trial of J. H. Costley at Dedham – Third Day," *Boston Journal*, December 31, 1874.

[23] shipped by train to Boston: "The Hawkes Tragedy – Fourth Day of the Trial of James H. Costley," *Boston Daily Globe,* January 1, 1875.

[24] shot at the hotel: "The Weymouth Tragedy – Additional Disclosures – The Guilt of Costley Apparently Proven – The Money of the Murdered Woman in His Possession, Et cetera," *Boston Daily Globe*, May 29, 1874.

[25] of having recently been cut: "Suburban Notes – The Hanover Murder," *Boston Daily Globe*, May 30, 1874, page 8.

[26] "…got away on the 4 o'clock train": "The Murder of Julia Hawkes – Trial of J. H. Costley at Dedham," *Boston Journal*, January 1, 1875.

[27] marked "Union Institution for Savings": "The Murder of Julia Hawkes – Startling Disclosures – The Victim's Money Found in the Possession of Costley – A Bloody Room in the Hanover House," *Boston Journal*, May 29, 1874, Morning Edition.

[28] brought them home from the service after the war: "The Murder of Julia Hawkes – Trial of J. H. Costley at Dedham," *Boston Journal*, January 1, 1875.

[29] no improper use…of them: "The Hawkes Tragedy – Fourth Day of the Trial of James H. Costley," *Boston Daily Globe,* January 1, 1875.

[30] appear at 11:00 a.m. on that date: "An Awful Murder," *Quincy Patriot*, May 30, 1874.

[31] a matching imprint behind: "The Murder of Julia Hawkes – Trial of J. H. Costley at Dedham," *Boston Journal*, January 1, 1875.

[32] imbedded in Mrs. Hawkes' brain: "The Hanover Murder," *Boston Daily Globe*, June 1, 1874.

[33] "…the stripes are different": "The Hawkes Tragedy – Fourth Day of the Trial of James H. Costley," *Boston Daily Globe,* January 1, 1875.

[34] returned to Hanover…May 19: "The Murder of Julia Hawkes – Trial of J. H. Costley at Dedham," *Boston Journal*, January 1, 1875.

[35] leased it from Howard in 1872: "The Murder of Julia Hawkes – Trial of J. H. Costley at Dedham – Third Day," *Boston Journal*, December 31, 1874.

[36] "…otherwise acted very strangely": "The End! Execution of Costley," *Dedham Transcript*, June 26, 1875.

[37] cause of death as "colic": Massachusetts Vital Records, Deaths, Hanover, 1873, Volume 257, Page 363, Line 48, Massachusetts State Archives, Boston, MA.

[38] her two sisters, Belinda and Maria: 1850 United States Federal Census [database on-line] Provo, UT, USA: Census Place: Barnstable, Barnstable, Massachusetts; Roll M432_304; Page: 317A; Image: 213. http://www.ancestry.com.

[39] native and fisherman: Massachusetts Vital Records, Marriages, Barnstable, 1855, Volume 87, Page 1, Massachusetts State Archives, Boston, MA.

[40] without disturbing the beans: "The Murder of Julia Hawkes – Additional Evidence Against Costley – Discovery of Her Missing Shoe – New Cartridges Found in the Chimney of the Hanover House," *Boston Journal*, June 1, 1874.

[41] board the 4:00 p.m. train: "The Murder of Julia Hawkes – Trial of J. H. Costley at Dedham – Second Day," *Boston Journal*, December 30, 1874.

[42] Bedford Street in Boston…1874: "The Murder of Julia Hawkes – Startling Disclosures – The Victim's Money Found in the Possession of Costley – A Bloody Room in the Hanover House," *Boston Journal*, Morning Edition, May 29, 1874.

[43] "a friend's house at the South End": "Criminal – Opening of the Costley Murder Trial," *Boston Daily Globe*, Tuesday, December 29, 1874.

[44] her usual and buoyant happy self: "The Weymouth Tragedy – Additional Disclosures – The Guilt of Costley Apparently Proven – The Money of the Murdered Woman in His Possession, Etc.," *Boston Daily Globe*, Friday, May 29, 1874.

[45] along with his brother: "The Murder of Julia Hawkes – Additional Particulars," *Boston Journal*, May 30, 1874.

[46] to them, at least temporarily: "The Weymouth Tragedy – Additional Disclosures – The Guilt of Costley Apparently Proven – The Money of the Murdered Woman in His Possession, Etc.," *Boston Daily Globe*, Friday, May 29, 1874.

[47] never saw her again…date: "The Murder of Julia Hawkes – Trial of J. H. Costley at Dedham – Second Day," *Boston Journal*, December 30, 1874.

[48] that evening for several months: Ibid.

[49] last time she saw Julia: Ibid.

[50] "J. H. Costello and wife, Duxbury, MA": Ibid.

[51] take the team…Landing: "The Murder of Julia Hawkes – Additional Evidence Against Costley – Discovery of Her Missing Shoe – New Cartridges Found in the Chimney of the Hanover House," *Boston Journal*, June 1, 1874.

[52] found one to be unusually heavy: "The Hanover Murder," *Boston Daily Globe*, June 1, 1874.

[53] square box buggy for Costley: "The Murder of Julia Hawkes – Trial of J. H. Costley at Dedham – Second Day," *Boston Journal*, December 30, 1874.

[54] "I wish it was": Charles Devens Notebook, call number mss. N-1114, box number 8, folder F61-V58, Norfolk County Special Term for Trial of J. H. Costley, December 1874, page 17, Massachusetts Historical Society, Boston, MA.

[55] sold a .22 caliber pistol…April 27: "The Murder of Julia Hawkes – Trial of J. H. Costley at Dedham," *Boston Journal*, January 1, 1875.

[56] "Well, if you insist on it, put it in": "The Murder of Julia Hawkes – Trial of J. H. Costley at Dedham – Second Day," *Boston Journal*, December 30, 1874.

[57] missing ring on her left hand: "Costley," *Weymouth Weekly Gazette and Reporter*, May 29, 1874.

[58] June 13 at 11:00 a.m.: *Lowell Daily Citizen and News*, June 8, 1874, Column F.

[59] "…murder of the said Julia Hawkes": "The Hawkes Murder," *Quincy Patriot*, June 6, 1874.

[60] "…his face showed mental discomposure": "Costley," *Weymouth Weekly Gazette and Reporter*, June 19, 1874.

[61] the Commonwealth at the arraignment: Ibid. Also, "Saturday," *Quincy Patriot*, June 20, 1874.

[62] for trial on a capital crime: "Costley Indicted," *Boston Daily Globe*, Friday, September 11, 1874.

[63] on the date in question: "The Murder of Julia Hawkes – Trial of J. H. Costley at Dedham," *Boston Journal*, December 29, 1874.

[64] boarding a train to New York the same night: "The Murder of Julia Hawkes – Trial of J. H. Costley at Dedham – Second Day," *Boston Journal*, December 30, 1874.

[65] "…and Queen Anne's Corner": "Blondin's Case – Grand Jury Will Consider It at Cambridge Today – Special Session of the Middlesex County Body Called – Costley Murder Decision by Judge Gray Determined the Action of Attorney General Parker to Have the Case Tried in Middlesex," *Boston Globe*, March 10, 1902.

[66] appointed to the Massachusetts Supreme Judicial Court in 1866: William Thomas Davis, *History of the Judiciary of Massachusetts* (Boston: Boston Book Company, 1900) 194.

[67] under President Rutherford B. Hayes: Ibid. 195-196.

[68] became Attorney General of Massachusetts in 1872: Ibid. 289.

[69] District Attorney for Norfolk and Plymouth Counties: Duane Hamilton Hurd, *History of Norfolk County, Massachusetts with Biographical Sketches of Many of Its Pioneers and Prominent Men* (Philadelphia: J. W. Lewis and Company, 1884), 25.

[70] were required to preside over capital trials: *Report of the Attorney General for the year ending January 15, 1902* (Boston: Wright and Potter Printing Company, 1902) xvii. http://www.books.google.com.

[71] carried a penalty of life imprisonment: Alan Rogers, *Murder and the Death Penalty in Massachusetts* (Amherst and Boston, University of Massachusetts Press, 2008), 112-113.

[72] as to his or her guilt: Ibid. 116.

[73] "…looks and gestures of another": Ibid. 297.

[74] capital punishment opponents had been purged: Ibid. 297.

[75] real or supposed predisposition: Ibid. 118.

[76] "…finding a defendant guilty": Ibid. 299.

[77] until his return to Massachusetts in 1869: The Trustees of Amherst College, *Amherst College Biographical Record: Biographical Record of the Graduates and Non-Graduates of the Classes of 1822-1962 Inclusive* (Amherst, MA, The Trustees of Amherst College, 1963), 52. http://www.books.google.com.

[78] assistant district attorney in Suffolk County: Jeremiah Wadleigh Dearborn, ed., A History of the First Century of the Town of Parsonsfield, Maine (Portland, ME, Brown, Thurston and Company, 1888), 292. http://www.books.google.com.

[79] until 9:00 a.m. the next day: "The Murder of Julia Hawkes – Trial of J. H. Costley at Dedham," *Boston Journal*, December 29, 1874.

[80] proved damaging to Costley: "The Murder of Julia Hawkes – Trial of J. H. Costley at Dedham – Second Day," *Boston Journal*, December 30, 1874.

[81] "…I don't know where Camden Street is": Ibid.

[82] at the Jefferson House on May 14: Ibid.

[83] an attempt to discredit his testimony: "The Murder of Julia Hawkes – Trial of J. H. Costley at Dedham – Third Day," *Boston Journal*, December 31, 1874.

[84] examined by them…human blood: Charles G. Davis, *Report of the Trial of Samuel M. Andrews, Indicted for the Murder of Cornelius Holmes, Before the Supreme Judicial Court of Massachusetts, December 11, 1868, Including the Rulings of the Court Upon Many Questions of Law, and a Full Statement of Authorities Upon the Subject of Transitory Insanity* (New York: Hurd and Houghton, 1869) 66-67.

[85] originating from a human source: George F. Shrady, Editor, *Medical Record – A Weekly Journal of Medicine and Surgery* (New York: William Wood and Co., 1895) 685. http://books.google.com.

[86] is equivalent to $1.3 million: L. Officer and S. Williamson, *Purchasing Power of Money in the United States from 1774 to 2008.* Measuring Worth, 2009. http://www,measuringworth.com/ppowerus.

[87] adjourned until the next day: "The Murder of Julia Hawkes – Trial of J. H. Costley at Dedham," *Boston Journal*, January 1, 1875.

[88] "…proof beyond reasonable doubt": Ibid.

[89] "…indicate speedy death there from…": *Cases Argued and Determined in the Supreme Judicial Court of Massachusetts –* Commonwealth vs. James H. Costley – Norfolk – February 1-16, 1875, Volume 118, Page 10, Boston: Houghton, Mifflin and Co., 1876, http://books.google.com.

[90] alleged in the indictment: Ibid, pages 17, 18.

[91] unconscious by the wound: Ibid, page 10.

[92] "…and the time of his return": Ibid, pages 16, 17.

[93] file an exception to the ruling: Ibid, pages 8, 9.

[94] until the following day: "The Murder of Julia Hawkes – Trial of J. H. Costley at Dedham – Fifth Day," *Boston Journal*, January 2, 1875.

[95] "…ordinarily falls to any human being": "The Murder of Julia Hawkes – Costley Found Guilty of Murder – Arguments of Counsel and Charge of the Court," *Boston Journal*, January 4, 1875.

[96] the court recessed until 7:15 p.m.: Ibid.

[97] "…prosecuted in the county of Norfolk": Ibid.

[98] "…punished in either county'": Ibid. Also, Cases Argued and Determined in the Supreme Judicial Court of Massachusetts – Commonwealth vs. James H. Costley – Norfolk – February 1-16, 1875, Volume 118, page 19, Boston: Houghton, Mifflin and Co., 1876, http://books.google.com.

[99] "…committed in another county": "The Murder of Julia Hawkes – Costley Found Guilty of Murder – Arguments of Counsel and Charge of the Court," *Boston Journal*, January 4, 1875.

[100] "ragged edge of anxiety and despair": "Costley's Doom – He is Found Guilty of Murder in the First Degree," *Boston Daily Globe,* January 4, 1875.

[101] Dedham Jail to await sentencing: "The Murder of Julia Hawkes – Costley Found Guilty of Murder – Arguments of Counsel and Charge of the Court," *Boston Journal*, January 4, 1875.

[102] smiling slightly as he passed by: "The End! Execution of Costley," *Dedham Transcript*, June 26, 1875.

[103] tell his parents of Costley's fate: Ibid.

[104] …Ever grateful, J. Henry Costley": Ibid.

[105] sympathetic to Costley's cause: "Murdered Julia Hawkes Was Possibly Not Henry Costley's Only Victim. An Old Hanover Tragedy and a Dedham Hanging Vividly Recalled, Doubts About the Man's Guilt and the Doubts About His Burial," *Boston Daily Globe*, August 13, 1887.

[106] his plot to escape had failed: "The End! Execution of Costley," *Dedham Transcript*, June 26, 1875.

[107] overruled the exceptions…Cheney: "Costley - The Condemned Murderer, Who Hangs, Friday - Exceptions in His Case Heard by the Full Bench, Yesterday - No Probability of a Stay of Proceedings – History of the Man and His Crime," *Boston Daily Globe*, June 22, 1875.

[108] already assigned to the jail: "The End! Execution of Costley," *Dedham Transcript*, June 26, 1875.

[109] The rope was…thick: Ibid.

[110] "…happier than any whom I leave behind": "The Execution of Costley – His Last Hours – He Denies the Commission of Murder – The Final Act of the Tragedy – Death Calmly Met," *Boston Daily Globe*, June 26, 1875.

[111] "…Truly gratefully, J. H. Costley": "The End! Execution of Costley," *Dedham Transcript*, June 26, 1875.

[112] "…Very respectfully, J. H. Costley": "The Execution of Costley – His Last Hours – He Denies the Commission of Murder – The Final Act of the Tragedy – Death Calmly Met," *Boston Daily Globe*, June 26, 1875.

[113] "…Gratefully, J. H. Costley – Dedham, June 25th 1875": "The End! Execution of Costley," *Dedham Transcript*, June 26, 1875.

[114] broadcloth and silver mountings: Ibid.

[115] Police Chief George W. Boynton: "The Execution of Costley – His Last Hours – He Denies the Commission of Murder – The Final

Act of the Tragedy – Death Calmly Met," *Boston Daily Globe*, June 26, 1875.

[116] "…the chair having been removed": Ibid.

[117] "…the murderer hung without motion": Ibid.

[118] pronounced him dead: Ibid.

[119] beneath a large maple tree at Hanover Center Cemetery: Hanover Center Cemetery, Hanover, MA, Cemetery Records.

[120] find another burial plot: "The Execution of Costley – His Last Hours – He Denies the Commission of Murder – The Final Act of the Tragedy – Death Calmly Met," *Boston Daily Globe*, June 26, 1875.

[121] a cabinet maker from South Abington: Massachusetts Vital Records, Marriages, Boston, 1879, Volume 308, Page 303, Line 24, Massachusetts State Archives, Boston, MA.

[122] died in Boston on February 24, 1882: Massachusetts Vital Records, Deaths, Boston, 1882, Volume 339, Page 48, Line 1083, Massachusetts State Archives, Boston, MA.

[123] family plot at Hanover Center Cemetery: Hanover Center Cemetery, Hanover, MA, Cemetery Records.

[124] murder conviction in the United States in 1911: David E. Newton, *DNA Evidence and Forensic Science* (New York: Facts on File, Inc., 2008), 10-11.

[125] form the DNA chain differs: Jon Zonderman, *Beyond the Crime Lab – the New Science of Investigation* (New York: John Wiley & Sons, Inc., New York, 1990) 80-81.

A Soap Box

[1] "Kushion Kumfort" shoes for ladies: Massachusetts City Directories – *Rockland, 1902, Hanover Directory,* 140.

[2] now a community of 2152 people: Ibid., 189. 1900 US Census.

[3] his plan to return home: Frankie Hutton and Barbara Strauss Reed, eds., *Outsiders in 19ᵗʰ Century Press History: Multicultural Perspectives* (Bowling Green, OH: Bowling Green State University Popular Press, 1995), 72. http://books.google.com.

[4] profoundly ignorant and naturally violent: Alan Rogers, *Murder and the Death Penalty in Massachusetts* (Amherst and Boston: University of Massachusetts Press, 2008), 140.

[5] entered the country under that alias: Tom Chin, e-mail message to author, August 15, 2008. Chinese Historical Society New England, Boston, MA: http://www.chsne.org.

[6] Southern China as his place of origin: Tom Chin, e-mail message to author, "Re: Help with Name," August 15, 2008.

[7] hoped some day to reunite with them: "Hanover," *Rockland Standard*, February 5, 1904, Vol. L, #25, page 8, column 1 (original newspaper at Dyer Memorial Library, Abington, MA).

[8] his brother at Hon Gong…Province: Chinese Exclusion File for Tom Sing, #2500-1488C, U. S. Department of Labor, Immigration Service, National Archives and Records Center, Northeast Region, Waltham, MA.

[9] laundry service in Hanover at the time: Massachusetts City Directories – *Rockland 1902, Hanover Directory, Laundry,* 178.

[10] laundry shop at 79 Cabot…in 1903: Massachusetts City Directories - *The Salem and Beverly Directory 1904 (*Salem Massachusetts: Henry M. Meek Publishing Co., 1904), 663, listing of Quong Sing, Laundry, 79 Cabot Street, Beverly. http://www.ancestry.com.

[11] typically working ten….day: Judy Yung, Gordan H. Chang amd Him Mark Lai, eds., *Chinese American Voices, From the Gold Rush to the Present* (Berkeley, CA: Regents of the University of California, 2006), 183. http://books.google.com.

[12] between $8 and $20 a week in 1903: Shehong Chen, *Reconstructing the Chinese American Experience in Lowell, Massachusetts, 1870s – 1970's, Making a Living as Laundry Men, 1876-1920* (Boston: Institute for Asian American Studies, University of Massachusetts, 2003). http://books.google.com.

[13] also two cents each; and so on: Renqiu Yu, *To Save China, To Save Ourselves: The Chinese Hand Laundry Alliance of New York* (Philadelphia: Temple University Press, 1992), 11. http://books.google.com.

[14] as soon as he had earned a competence: "Hanover," *Rockland Standard*, February 5, 1904.

[15] "…with their feet in the ovens": "Hanover," *Rockland Standard*, January 8, 1904.

[16] "…it was the coldest since 1856": "West Hanover," *Rockland Standard*, January 15, 1904.

[17] to a high of about eighteen degrees: Blue Hill Observatory Collection, RG27, January 1900-December 1912, Reel 6, National Archives and Records Center, Northeast Region, Waltham, MA.

[18] twelve more inches of snow fell: "Heat and Cold," *Boston Daily Globe*, January 1, 1905.

[19] in a family of eleven:, HS9.01/Series 305, Charlestown State Prison, Inmate Case Files, #13408 – Social Summary, Massachusetts State Archives, Boston, MA.

[20] by Rev. John Corbett: Prince Edward Island Baptismal Index, St. Dunstan's Basilica Baptismal Records, Book 4, page 211. http://www.gov.pe.ca/cca/baptismal/detail.php?id=82172.

[21] work to support the family: HS9.01/Series 305, Charlestown State Prison, Inmate Case Files, #13408 – Social Summary, Massachusetts State Archives, Boston, MA.

[22] Hickey & Nickerson and T. B. Riley: "Ryan's Dramatic Murder Defense," *Boston Daily Globe*, June 10, 1904.

[23] Hickey & Nickerson and T. B. Riley: HS9.01/Series 305, Charlestown State Prison, Inmate Case Files, #13408 – State Prison – Inmate's History and Record, Massachusetts State Archives, Boston, MA.

[24] reach the counter to do his work: HS9.01/Series 305, Charlestown State Prison, Inmate Case Files, #13408 – Social Case History, page 3, Massachusetts State Archives, Boston, MA.

[25] steamer of the Plant Line Steamship Company: "A Dead Chinaman; A Strange Crime," *Boston Herald*, January 29, 1904.

[26] steamer of the Plant Line Steamship Company: HS9.01/Series 305, Charlestown State Prison, Inmate Case Files, #13408 – State Prison – Inmate's History and Record., Massachusetts State Archives, Boston, MA.

[27] Washington Credit Company at 503 Washington Street: HS9.01/Series 305, Charlestown State Prison, Inmate Case Files, #13408 – Additional Report in the Case of Cyrus L. Ryan, S. P. 13408, July 13, 1918 by F. C. Palmer, Agent, page 2, Massachusetts State Archives, Boston, MA.

[28] until his debt was paid in full: "Ryan's Dramatic Murder Defense," *Boston Daily Globe*, June 10, 1904.

[29] at the home of…Pierce, his half-brother: "Ryan's Dramatic Murder Defense," *Boston Daily Globe*, June 10, 1904.

[30] settled in Hanover shortly thereafter: Naturalization Records, United States District Court, Boston, Certificate of Naturalization 1594487, November 7, 1921, National Archives and Records Center, Northeast Region, Waltham, MA.

[31] as a flagman at Curtis Crossing: 1900 US Census, Hanover, Plymouth, MA, Roll T623-674, Page 18B, ED 1124. http://www.ancestry.com.

[32] $4.25 a week for room and board: "Seen Running," *Boston Daily Globe*, June 9, 1904.

[33] temperatures reaching fifty degrees: J. W. Smith, U. S. Department of Agriculture, Climate and Crop Service of the Weather Bureau: Central Office: Washington, D. C. New England Section: Boston, MA, Volume XVI, Number 1, page 8: Boston Public Library, Government Documents, Climatological Data – New England, Microfiche 16.

[34] weighed a mere ninety pounds: HS9.01/Series 305, Charlestown State Prison, Inmate Case Files, #13408 – Social Case History, Massachusetts State Archives, Boston, MA.

[35] "…he is able to defend himself": "Hanover," *Rockland Standard*, January 29, 1904.

[36] the 8:15 a.m. train to Boston the next day: "Quong Sing Killed at Laundry in Hanover," *Boston Daily Globe*, January 29, 1904.

[37] walked with her from her home to the depot: "His Property," *Boston Daily Globe*, February 1, 1904.

[38] the man responsible for the burglary: "Quong Sing Killed at Laundry in Hanover," *Boston Daily Globe*, January 29, 1904.

[39] small articles of value from the house: "Chinaman Foully Slain," *Rockland Standard*, January 29, 1904.

[40] The thermometer read four degrees: Smith, J.W., U. S. Department of Agriculture, Climate and Crop Service of the Weather Bureau: Central Office: Washington, D. C. New England Section: Boston, MA, Volume XVI, Number 1, page 8: Boston Public Library, Government Documents, Climatological Data – New England, Microfiche 16.

[41] in the shop when he was there: "C. L. Ryan's Trial," *Old Colony Memorial*, June 11, 1904.

[42] a few minutes later and left: Ibid.

[43] a few minutes later and left: "Ryan's Dramatic Murder Defense," *Boston Daily Globe*, June 10, 1904.

[44] Clapp Rubber Works whistle blew: "C. L. Ryan's Trial," *Old Colony Memorial*, June 11, 1904.

[45] left the market for lunch: Ibid.

[46] left the market for lunch: "Robbery the Motive; C. L. Ryan Followed to Boston and Arrested," *Boston Post*, January 29, 1904.

[47] Quong Sing was ironing a shirt: "C. L. Ryan's Trial," *Old Colony Memorial*, June 11, 1904.

[48] became impatient and soon left: Ibid.

[49] then left the house: "His Property," *Boston Daily Globe*, February 1, 1904.

[50] walking at a brisk pace: "C. L. Ryan's Trial," *Old Colony Memorial*, June 11, 1904.

[51] the drying room to the right: Ibid.

[52] hole in a shirt on the ironing board: "Quong Sing Killed in Laundry in Hanover," *Boston Daily Globe*, January 29, 1904.

[53] the body was still warm, but lifeless: "C. L. Ryan's Trial," *Old Colony Memorial*, June 11, 1904.

[54] point him out to police if seen: Ibid.

[55] Waterman saw and removed the soap box: "Seen Running," *Boston Daily Globe*, June 9, 1904.

[56] weighed about 75 pounds: "Found Dead in His Tub," *Bryantville News*, Bryantville, MA, February 3, 1904.

[57] hand had grasped it from behind: "C. L. Ryan's Trial," *Old Colony Memorial*, June 11, 1904.

[58] but could not find it: "A Dead Chinaman; A Strange Crime," *Boston Herald*, January 29, 1904.

[59] a small trunk and a satchel: Ibid.

[60] go to another part of the car: "Seen Running," *Boston Daily Globe*, June 9, 1904.

[61] the captain placed Ryan under arrest: "Robbery the Motive; C. L. Ryan Followed to Boston and Arrested," *Boston Post*, January 29, 1904.

[62] watch Ryan had in another pocket: "Ryan Confesses He Killed Quong," *Boston Herald*, June 10, 1904.

[63] inflicted by a left-handed person: "Probe Murder of Chinaman," *Boston Post*, January 31, 1904.

[64] drawer in the shop had been left secure: "A Dead Chinaman; A Strange Crime," *Boston Herald*, January 29, 1904.

[65] her sister-in-law's house in Cambridge: Ibid.

[66] an inexpensive silveroid open-faced timepiece: "Claims Ryan Not Murderer," *Boston Herald*, January 30, 1904.

[67] was a gift from his sister: "A Dead Chinaman; A Strange Crime," *Boston Herald*, January 29, 1904.

[68] could not identify the watch: "A Dead Chinaman; A Strange Crime," *Boston Herald*, January 29, 1904.

[69] in Abington for forty years: Henry Harrison Metcalf and John Norris Clintock, eds., *The Granite Monthly: A New Hampshire Magazine devoted to History, Biography, Literature and State Progress*, Volume XLI (Concord: Granite Monthly Publishing Company, 1909), 261-263. http://books.google.com.

[70] give testimony before a grand jury: "Ryan Is Held Without Bail," *Boston Daily Globe*, January 30, 1904.

[71] marry Ryan upon his acquittal: "Probing Murder of Drowned Chinaman; Ryan's Sweetheart Says Cyrus Accused Unjustly," *Boston Post*, January 30, 1904.

[72] death caused by drowning: "C. L. Ryan's Trial," *Old Colony Memorial*, June 11, 1904.

[73] forty-eight years old at the time of his death: Massachusetts Vital Records, Deaths, Hanover, 1904, Volume 47, Page 83, Certificate # 4, Massachusetts Archives, Boston, MA.

[74] Sparrell Funeral Home in Norwell: Ibid.

[75] handled funeral and burial arrangements: Mount Hope Cemetery records, Boston, MA: Soo Hoo Yee Yoke, burial, 1904, Section E, Grave 56. Exhumation, 1912.

[76] "…very bitter against Ryan": "Ryan Is Held Without Bail," *Boston Daily Globe*, January 30, 1904.

[77] settlement of his estate in probate court: Ibid.

[78] claim finished and unfinished laundry: "Hanover," *Rockland Standard*, February 12, 1904.

[79] left the shirt…before January 28: "C. L. Ryan's Trial," *Old Colony Memorial*, June 11, 1904.

[80] an additional $1.00 in Quong's clothing: "Seen Running," *Boston Daily Globe*, June 9, 1904.

[81] found $9.00 inside: "A Dead Chinaman; A Strange Crime*," Boston Herald*, January 29, 1904.

[82] "A man can do considerable in ten minutes": "To Clear Ryan," *Boston Daily Globe*, January 31, 1904.

[83] knew him to own a silver watch: Ibid.

[84] time to have killed Quong Sing: "His Property," *Boston Daily Globe*, February 1, 1904.

[85] innocent of the charges against him: Ibid.

[86] Quong Sing was laid to rest: "Slain Chinaman Rests in Grave," *Boston Herald*, February 1, 1904.

[87] shipped his remains…for reburial: Mount Hope Cemetery records, Boston, MA: Soo Hoo Yee Yoke, burial, 1904, Section E, Grave 56. Exhumation, 1912.

[88] "…into a tub of water": "Indicted for Murder," *Fitchburg Sentinel*, February 4, 1904, http://www.ancestry.com.

[89] returned to Plymouth Jail: "For Murder," *Boston Daily Globe*, February 5, 1904.

[90] for trial in Plymouth…1904: "C. L. Ryan's Trial," *Old Colony Memorial*, June 11, 1904.

[91] this was later reduced to two): *Report of the Attorney General for the year ending January 15, 1902* (Boston: Wright and Potter Printing Company, 1902) xviii. http://www.books.google.com.

[92] appointed to the bench of the Superior Court in 1898: William Thomas Davis, *History of the Judiciary of Massachusetts* (Boston: Boston Book Company, 1900) 266-267.

[93] Superior Court in 1896 by Governor Wolcott: William Richard Cutter, ed., *Historic Homes and Places and Genealogical and Personal Memoirs Relating to the Families of Middlesex County, Massachusetts,* Volume IV (New York: Lewis Historical Publishing Company, 1908), 1563. http://books.google.com.

[94] "…God save the Commonwealth of Massachusetts": Ibid.

[95] trial proceedings began at 10:40 a.m.: Ibid.

[96] trial proceedings began at 10:40 a.m.: Massachusetts City Directories, *Plymouth, 1905*, page 199. http://www.ancestry.com .

[97] Wilder, unemployed, Hingham: "Ryan Faces Murder Charge," *Boston Herald*, June 7, 1904.

[98] the second day of trial: "In Laundry," *Boston Daily Globe*, June 8, 1904.

[99] smiled and appeared confident: "Murder of Quong Sing the Charge," *Boston Herald*, June 8, 1904.

[100] movements on the day of the murder: "C. L. Ryan's Trial," *Old Colony Memorial*, June 11, 1904.

[101] every day expenses and savings: "Murder of Quong Sing the Charge," *Boston Herald*, June 8, 1904.

[102] air passages had reddened: "In Laundry," *Boston Daily Globe*, June 8, 1904.

[103] three weeks after his arrival: Ibid.

[104] the court adjourned for the day: "C. L. Ryan's Trial," *Old Colony Memorial*, June 11, 1904.

[105] he had seen in his brother's shop: "Murder of Quong Sing," *Boston Herald*, June 9, 1904.

[106] testimony of Eben Waterman: Ibid.

[107] bedroom at the laundry shop: "Ryan Confesses He Killed Quong," *Boston Herald*, June 10, 1904.

[108] "…took the train for Boston": "On Trial For His Life," *Rockland Standard*, June 10, 1904.

[109] recessed until 1:00 p.m.: "Ryan's Dramatic Murder Defense," *Boston Daily Globe*, June 10, 1904.

[110] "…we left Hanover at that time": "Ryan's Sweetheart Says Cyrus Accused Unjustly," *Boston Herald*, June 10, 1904.

[111] "hard up for money": "On Trial For His Life," *Rockland Standard*, June 10, 1904.

[112] belonged to a …society: "Ryan Confesses He Killed Quong," *Boston Herald*, June 10, 1904.

[113] not by drowning: "Say Quong Sing Was Not Drowned," *Boston Herald*, June 11, 1904.

[114] entered Quong Sing's lungs: HS9.01/Series 305, Charlestown State Prison, Inmate Case Files, #13408 – Additional Report in the Case of Cyrus L. Ryan, S. P. 13408, July 13, 1918 by F. C. Palmer, Agent, page 3, Massachusetts State Archives, Boston, MA.

[115] shirt belonged to him: "Say Quong Sing Was Not Drowned," *Boston Herald*, June 11, 1904.

[116] removed Ryan from the courtroom: "Second Degree," *Boston Daily Globe*, June 12, 1904.

[117] his transfer to Charlestown: "Given Life Sentence," *Boston Daily Globe*, June 16, 1904.

[118] in the prison shoe factory: 1910 United States Census, Boston Ward 5, Suffolk, Massachusetts, Roll T624-615; page 7A, ED 1322, line 50. http://www.ancestry.com.

[119] he thought was his own: HS9.01/Series 305, Charlestown State Prison, Inmate Case Files, #13408 – Social Case History, page 2, Massachusetts State Archives, Boston, MA.

[120] at Bridgewater, Massachusetts: Commitment Registers, Charlestown State Prison, September 1882-December 1930, roll #2, Massachusetts Archives, Boston, MA.

[121] he always gave her his pay: HS9.01/Series 305, Charlestown State Prison, Inmate Case Files, #13408 – Hearing on the Petition for Pardon of Cyrus L. Ryan, October 26, 1916, Massachusetts State Archives, Boston, MA.

[122] "…Your affectionate son, C. L. Ryan": HS9.01/Series 305, Charlestown State Prison, Inmate Case Files, #13408 – Letter of Cyrus L. Ryan to Mrs. E. E. Ryan, May 12, 1918, Massachusetts State Archives, Boston, MA.

[123] returned him to the State Prison on December 17, 1920: Commitment Registers, Charlestown State Prison, September 1882-December 1930, roll #2, Massachusetts Archives, Boston, MA.

[124] "…Love to all from Cyrus": HS9.01/Series 305, Charlestown State Prison, Inmate Case Files, #13408 – Letter of Cyrus L. Ryan to Mrs. A. D. Brennan, September 9, 1931, Massachusetts State Archives, Boston, MA.

[125] "…nor anyone in particular": HS9.01/Series 305, Charlestown State Prison, Inmate Case Files, #13408 – Social Case History, Part VIII, Personality Characteristics, Massachusetts State Archives, Boston, MA.

[126] "…is interested in good reading…": HS9.01/Series 305, Charlestown State Prison, Inmate Case Files, #13408 – Social Case History, Part IX, Education, Massachusetts State Archives, Boston, MA.

[127] "…in order to go to Bridgewater": HS9.01/Series 305, Charlestown State Prison, Inmate Case Files, #13408 – Social Case History, Part IX, Work; Punishment, Massachusetts State Archives, Boston, MA.

[128] his conduct had improved: HS9.01/Series 305, Charlestown State Prison, Inmate Case Files, #13408 – Social Case History, Part IX, Warden's Report, Massachusetts State Archives, Boston, MA.

[129] to Bridgewater for the last time: Commitment Registers, Charlestown State Prison, September 1882-December 1930, roll #2, Massachusetts Archives, Boston, MA.

[130] needed during his formative years: Interview with Margaret Johnson, PhD., Professor of Psychology, Bridgewater State University, Bridgewater, MA.

[131] medical schools in the Boston area: Town of Bridgewater, Certificate of Death, Registered Number 143, Cyrus L. Ryan, December 4, 1962.

[132] in Cornwall, Prince Edward Island: Ancestry.com, http://trees.ancestry.com/tree/12813024/person/-176868126/media/2

[133] buried in Rockland: Massachusetts Vital Records, Deaths, Rockland, 1949, Volume 81, Page 34, Certificate #28, Massachusetts Bureau of Vital Records and Statistics, Boston, MA.

[134] in New Calvary Cemetery, Boston: Massachusetts Vital Records, Deaths, Boston, 1935, Volume 26, Page 279, Certificate #11098, Massachusetts Bureau of Vital Records and Statistics, Boston, MA.

Bibliography

Rum

Barker, Barbara, and Molyneux, Leslie J. *Images of America: Hanover.* Charleston, SC: Arcadia Publishing, 2004.

Barry, John Stetson. *A Historical Sketch of the Town of Hanover, Massachusetts: with Family Genealogies.* Boston: S. G. Drake, 1853.

Blackstone, Sir William. *Commentaries on the Laws of England in Four Books.* Philadelphia: George T. Bisel Company, 1922.

Clark, W. L., Marshall, W. L., and Lazell, H. B. *A Treatise on the Law of Crimes.* Chicago: Callaghan, 1952.

Cutter, William Richard, A. M. *New England Families – Genealogical and Memorial: A Record of the Achievements of Her People in the Making of Commonwealths and the Founding of a Nation - Volume II.* New York: Lewis Historical Publishing Company, 1914.

Dix, John Ross. *Local Loiterings, and Visits in the Vicinity of Boston, by Looker On.* Boston: Redding and Company, 1846.

Driscoll, Barbara A. *The Tracks North: The Railroad Bracero Program of World War II.*

Austin: University of Texas Press, Center for American Studies, 1999.

Dwelley, Jedediah, and Simmons, John F. *History of the Town of Hanover, Massachusetts: with Family Genealogies.* Hanover, MA: Town of Hanover, 1910.

Eliot, Samuel Atkins. *Biographical History of Massachusetts, Volume II.* Boston:

Gray, Francis Calley. *Prison Discipline in America.* Boston: Charles T. Little and James Brown, 1847.

Haynes, Gideon. *Pictures From Prison Life: An Historical Sketch of the Massachusetts State Prison.* Boston: Lee and Shepard, 1869.

Hedin, Robert. *The Great Machines: Poems and Songs of the American Railroad.* Iowa City: University of Iowa Press, 1966.

Hurd, D. Hamilton. *History of Bristol County Massachusetts with Biographical Sketches of many of its Pioneers and Prominent Men, Illustrated.* Philadelphia: J. W. Lewis & Co., 1883.

Lewis, O. F., PhD. *The Development of American Prisons and Prison Customs, 1776-1845.* Albany: Prison Association of New York, 1922.

Masur, Louis P. *Capital Punishment and the Transformation of American Culture, 1776-1865.* New York: Oxford University Press, 1989.

Maynard, William Barksdale. *Walden Pond: A History.* New York: Oxford University Press, Inc., 2004.

O'Connor, Thomas H. *The Boston Irish: A Political History.* Canada: Little, Brown and Co., 1995.

Officer, L., and Williamson, S. *Purchasing Power of Money in the United States from 1774 to 2008.*

Rogers, Alan. *Murder and the Death Penalty in Massachusetts.* Amherst and Boston: University of Massachusetts Press, 2008.

Shannon, William V. *The American Irish: A Political and Social Portrait.* Amherst, MA: The University of Massachusetts Press, 1966.

A Tailor's Goose

Rogers, Alan. *Murder and the Death Penalty in Massachusetts*. Amherst and Boston, University of Massachusetts Press, 2008.

Davis, Charles G. *Report of the Trial of Samuel M. Andrews, Indicted for the Murder of Cornelius Holmes, Before the Supreme Judicial Court of Massachusetts, December 11, 1868, Including the Rulings of the Court Upon Many Questions of Law, and a Full Statement of Authorities Upon the Subject of Transitory Insanity*. New York: Hurd and Houghton, 1869.

Davis, William Thomas. *History of the Judiciary of Massachusetts*. Boston: Boston Book Company, 1900.

Norris, Curt. "The Case of the Scarlet Slipper." *True Police Cases,* June 1975 Edition.

Norris, Lowell Ames. "Evidence from a Low-Studded Attic." *Yankee Magazine*, September 1966 Edition.

Officer, L., and Williamson, S. *Purchasing Power of Money in the United States from 1774 to 2008.* Measuring Worth, 2009: http://www.measuringworth.com/ppowerus

Owen, David. *Hidden Evidence, 40 True Crimes and How Forensic Science Helped Solve Them.* London: Quintet Publishing Limited, 2000.

Newton, David E. *DNA Evidence and Forensic Science.* New York: Facts on File, Inc.,
2008.

Witthaus, R. A., and Becker, Tracy C. *Medical Jurisprudence: Forensic Medicine and Toxicology, Volume 1.* New York: William Wood & Company, 1894.

Zonderman, Jon. *Beyond the Crime Lab: the New Science of Investigation.* New York: John Wiley & Sons, Inc., New York, 1990.

A Soap Box

Cutter, William Richard, ed., *Historic Homes and Places and Genealogical and Personal Memoirs Relating to the Families of Middlesex County, Massachusetts,* Volume IV. New York: Lewis Historical Publishing Company, 1908.

Davis, William Thomas, *History of the Judiciary of Massachusetts.* Boston: Boston Book Company, 1900.

Hutton, Frankie, and Reed, Barbara Strauss, eds. *Outsiders in 19th Century Press History: Multicultural Perspectives.* Bowling Green, OH: Bowling Green State University Popular Press, 1995.

Yung, Judy, Chang, Gordon H., and Lai, Him Mark, eds. *Chinese American Voices, From the Gold Rush to the Present.* Berkeley, CA: Regents of the University of California, 2006.

Chen, Shehong. *Reconstructing the Chinese American Experience in Lowell, Massachusetts, 1870s – 1970's, Making a Living as Laundry Men, 1876-1920.* Boston: Institute for Asian American Studies, University of Massachusetts, 2003.

Yu, Renqiu. *To Save China, To Save Ourselves: The Chinese Hand Laundry Alliance of New York.* Philadelphia: Temple University Press, 1992.

Metcalf, Henry Harrison, and Clintock, John Norris, eds. *The Granite Monthly: A New Hampshire Magazine devoted to History, Biography, Literature and State Progress, Volume XLI.* Concord: Granite Monthly Publishing Company, 1909.

Manufactured By: RR Donnelley
Momence, IL USA
January, 2011